JAMES VELLA-BARDON is the author of several books to date, including *The Cream of Chivalry*, *Mad King Robin* and *A Rebel North*. His debut, *The Sheriff's Catch*, was the winner in the 'best novel' and 'best historical fiction' categories at the International Royal Dragonfly Book Awards 2019.

"The new king of historical fiction"
– *The Scotsman*

"Remember the name of rising author James Vella-Bardon"
– *Reader's Digest*

"Reminds me of works by today's masters such as Bernard Cornwell, Conn Iggulden and Wilbur Smith"
– *Yorkshire Evening Post*

"Has what it takes to become a literary giant"
– *The Star*

"Sheer quality, historical integrity and emotional resonance"
– *The London Economic*

"A master storyteller, moving Abel through
a land of wonder and danger"
– *The US Review Of Books*

"The pacing is superb; non-stop all the way until the end"
– *The Wishing Shelf Book Awards*

"Gripping, vivid historical fiction told from an unfamiliar perspective, the book is packed with characters with complicated relationships, and filled with difficult human emotions"
– *Manchester World*

"Impressive level of historical exactitude"
– *Lancashire Post*

"Vella-Bardon's style is wonderful, his language is era-appropriate"
– *The Pigeonhole Book Club*

"If you liked Outlander you'll love this"
– ***Goodreads reviewer***

www.jamesvellabardon.com

Hero of Rosclogher

PART THREE

of

THE SASSANA STONE

Pentalogy

JAMES VELLA-BARDON

TEARAWAY PRESS

Copyright
Published by Tearaway Press 2024
PO Box 477, Belrose West, Sydney NSW2085

Copyright © James Vella-Bardon 2023
James Vella-Bardon asserts the moral right to be identified as the author of this work.

ISBN: 978-0-6451230-5-0

This novel is a work of fiction.
The names, characters and incidents portrayed in it are the work of the author's imagination. Any resemblance to actual persons, living or dead, events or localities is entirely coincidental.
All rights reserved under International Copyright Conventions. By payment of the required fees, you have been granted the non-exclusive, non-transferable right to read the text of this book. No part of this text may be reproduced, transmitted, downloaded, decompiled, reverse engineered or stored in or introduced into any information storage and retrieval system, in any form or by any means, whether electronic or mechanical, now known or hereinafter invented, without the express written permission of the author.

Cover design and typesetting by Rafael Andres
Editing by Hatch Editorial Services

To my parents, Frank & Josanne.

Cast of Characters

The MacGlannagh Tribe

Tadhg *Óg* MacGlannagh, Gaelic chieftain of the MacGlannagh tribe.

Dervila Bourke, Anglo-Norman wife of Tadhg *Óg*.

Muireann Mac an Bhaird, widow of Tadhg *Óg*'s late son Aengus *Cliste*.

Lochlain, only son of Aengus and Muireann.

Cathal *Dubh,* Tadhg *Óg*'s marshal (cavalry commander) and nephew.

Donal *Garbh* MacCabe, Scottish constable of the tribe's gallowglass troop.

Redmond O'Ronayne, a Jesuit and a qualified physician.

Nial *Dhá Chlaíomh* Ne Dourough, a bondsman in the service of Tadhg *Óg*.

Spaniards

Francisco de Cuéllar, a sea captain shipwrecked in Ireland.
Abelardo de Santiago, a widowed marksman shipwrecked in Ireland.

Sassenachs

George Bingham, English sheriff of Sligo.
John Gilson, an Irish renegade lieutenant in the service of Bingham.
Treasach Burke, an Irish renegade sergeant in the service of Bingham.

The dead

Aengus *Cliste*, only son of Tadhg *Óg* and Dervila, husband of Muireann, father of Lochlain.

Cathal *Óg*, previous chieftain of the MacGlannagh tribe and called *An Faolchù* (The Wolf), also the elder brother of Tadhg *Óg* and the father of Cathal *Dubh*.

Elsien van der Molen, late wife of Abeldardo de Santiago.

Maerten van der Molen, late brother of Elsien.

Reynier van der Molen, late father of Elsien, Maerten and Pieter.

Other

Sir Brian *na Múrtha* O'Rourke, lord of Breifne O'Rourke and overlord of the MacGlannaghs.

Thomas Geraldine, also known as 'Old Tom', an Anglo-Norman rebel.

The story so far...

In 1585, the war between the Spanish crown and Protestant Netherlands is still raging. During this clash, Abelardo 'Santi' de Santiago, a veteran soldier in the Spanish Army of Flanders, finds himself barracked in the Brabantian village of Willebroek. After taking part in a surprise raid on a band of Protestant mercenaries in the surrounding woods, Santi returns to Willebroek to discover that his pregnant, native wife, Elsien van der Molen, was killed by a fellowship of his own comrades. In his rage, Santi deserts the army and, along with his brother-in-law, Maerten, rides away from the village to find and get revenge on the departed killers.

Santi and Maerten chase Elsien's murderers all the way to Seville. Yet upon reaching the great city, they are captured by Ramos, who sells them to a cruel overseer of the Spanish Armada. The wretched pair find themselves turned into galley slaves rowing a hospital ship. Following the Armada's defeat by the English fleet at the famous sea battle of Gravelines, the hospital ship is shipwrecked off the west coast of Ireland during a terrible storm. Santi's brother-in-law, Maerten, is tragically lost at sea, while Santi somehow reaches the shore and journeys inland. He soon discovers a country oppressed by heartless English troopers that the natives call Sassenachs, which to Santi's Spanish ear sounds like 'Sassanas.'

Santi is himself hunted down by these Sassanas, who have orders from their queen's viceroy in Dublin to capture and kill all Spanish Armada castaways. He is eventually captured by the brutal English sheriff of Sligo Town, who imprisons Santi and has him tortured. Through an unlikely twist of fate, Santi flees Sligo with an invaluable emerald ring which belongs to a Spanish nobleman who also sailed with the Spanish Armada. As he flees his pursuers through the wilds, Santi also rescues a revered Irish bard, Muireann Mac an Bhaird, from a Sassana night raid in which Muireann loses her husband: the Irish prince, Aengus MacGlannagh.

Santi and Muireann form an unlikely pairing as they travel north while seeking to elude their enemies. Muireann leads Santi deep into her tribe's rebel kingdom of Dartry, ruled by the feared chieftain, Tadhg Óg MacGlannagh (the MacGlannagh). Upon reaching it, Muireann and Santi are rescued from pursuing Sassanas by a force of natives led by the MacGlannagh's nephew, Cathal the Black. Santi is taken to an infirmary near the tower house of Rosclogher, where he recovers from his wounds.

Santi is treated by the Jesuit Redmond O'Ronayne, also a qualified physician in the service of the MacGlannagh tribe. He also befriends the MacGlannagh's nephew, Cathal the Black. Following his recovery, Santi is escorted to the chieftain's hall in the tower house of Rosclogher, where he meets the MacGlannagh. The chieftain asks Santi to tell him the story of the Armada's journey and its defeat to the English at Calais.

The MacGlannagh also rewards Santi for rescuing his daughter-in-law, Muireann, by offering the Spaniard his protection. During his audience with the chieftain, Santi is also mocked by a powerful Scottish mercenary, Donal MacCabe. Donal leads a troop of terrifying Scottish mercenaries called 'the gallowglasses', who are in the employ of the MacGlannagh, and who feel threatened by Santi's more modern fighting skills.

Donal's hatred of Santi only grows in the following days, when the tribe hold games to celebrate the election of Cathal the Black to the position of tanist (second-in-command) in the tribe. During these contests, the tribesmen are also excited to discover Santi's exceptional sharpshooting skills. Following Santi's fine display of marksmanship, the MacGlannagh orders him to train the Dartrymen in marksmanship.

More Spanish castaways eventually reach Rosclogher, while Santi is invited by Dartry's queen Dervila to join her and Muireann on a hunting expedition. During the hunt, Santi's previous experience as a bodyguard helps him to thwart an attempt on the queen of Dartry's life. Dervila repays the favour to Santi by providing him with men and a guide in Muireann, to rescue a shipwrecked Spanish sea captain, Francisco de Cuéllar, from captivity. Santi and Muireann lead a band of Dartrymen on this highly dangerous mission through lands crawling with Sassanas.

Thanks to their combined skills, Santi and Muireann succeed in rescuing the Spanish Captain de Cuéllar and returning him to Rosclogher. The celebrations among the tribe are however short lived, when they learn that the English viceroy has left Dublin and is travelling to the west of Ireland at the head of an army which is two thousand strong. The MacGlannagh's attentions are soon drawn elsewhere, when word reaches him that a Spanish sea captain, Francisco de Cuéllar, is being held captive by a blacksmith in his lands. O'Ronayne convinces the reluctant MacGlannagh to assign him a force of Dartrymen, who include Muireann. Muireann leads the men towards the blacksmith's location during the night, yet the travelling Dartrymen are attacked by Burke and his hunting party during the night. Santi and O'Ronayne manage to foil the attack, and Burke and his men flee into the night. The following morning Santi's band of Dartrymen find the Spanish captain de Cuéllar and return him to Rosclogher. There follow terrible tidings when the tribe learn that the English viceroy has left Dublin and is travelling west at the head of an army which is two thousand strong.

'...For the people in one village becoming aware that in another there are cattle, or other effects, they immediately come armed in the night, and 'go Santiago' (attack), and kill one another, and the English from the garrisons, getting to know who had taken, and robbed, most cattle, then come down upon them, and carry away the plunder. They have, therefore, no other remedy but to withdraw themselves to the mountains, with their women and cattle...'

- Captain Francisco de Cuéllar,
City of Antwerp, 4th October 1589

XXVII

Rosclogher, Dartry, County Leitrim

2 – 13 November 1588

With each passing day, word of the enemy's movements grew like a large ocean wave about to collapse on us. As the viceroy marched westwards and war approached our borders, O'Ronayne's preachings at the altar became more fervent and filled with references to battle. Tidings abounded of how the Viceroy FitzWilliam had been warned against leaving Dublin during the winter, only for him to ignore this counsel. As had happened since feudal times, the English governor had called the old rising-out, proclaiming a great gathering of levies and money compositions. This had contributed to a baggage train which was composed of many carts, filled with goods which were forcibly taken from the inhabitants of Dublin by the Crown, in order to maintain the troops.

This practice infuriated many of the Irish gentry residing in Dublin, some of whom still sympathised with the rebel chieftains of Connacht and provided their agents with every scrap of information obtained from the detested colonists. Word spread freely of the viceroy's declared intention to hasten towards the west of Ireland, so as to root out all Spaniards and prevent them from teaching their fighting ways to the Irish.

When they were gathered in Rosclogher, the assembly of freemen expressed much surprise at this advance, since it had long been believed that the Sassenachs did not have the funds to mount an offensive against the rebels. The highborn Dartrymen's amazement was also coupled with a great dismay, for the approach of such a great army would mean that the fields to the east and north would no longer be safe.

This, in turn, meant that oaten bread could only be obtained through paltry trade with the north, or through the grey merchants who deviated from their course to engage in clandestine trade with the Dartrymen. It was not only the freemen of Rosclogher that were severely rattled by this development.

Nial grimaced and whispered to me that Manglana could not return from Duncarbury soon enough. 'I hear tell that the *tuatha* grow restless. They have suffered long and hard since our lord allied himself to O'Rourke's rebel cause. Their loyalty shall never be more sorely tested than by this large force which approaches from the east.'

The Viceroy's approach did not falter. One day news reached us that he had crossed the Shannon, before tarrying briefly in Athlone and then advancing upon Sligo. I could not help but shudder at the mention of the dreaded coastal town, which reminded me of the mark of the Spanish spider upon my breast. This terror was further compounded by the new voices that reached us from the chieftain in Duncarbury whose agents informed him of the new bands of men from the south and east of Ireland who had joined the viceroy's army. FitzWilliam's provisions were also replenished through the shipping that arrived from Dublin, which bore his men all manner of supplies.

The English troops resided in Sligo just long enough to recover from their inland march, and the townsfolk of Sligo must have breathed a collective sigh of relief when these men finally departed along a northward track. The sheriff George Bingham was also ordered to also accompany FitzWilliam, who now embarked upon the most violent part of his journey. All Spaniards and rebels in his path were smoked out, with all those falling into his power being put to the sword.

Rumour of these happenings sparked great debates in the hall of the Rosclogher tower-house, where Donal MacCabe resumed his outbursts against the sheltering of Spaniards along the banks of Lough Melvin. This earned him a stiff rebuke from Manglana's wife Dervila, who surprised everyone when she ordered him to respect the assembly's decision to take in the Spaniards, and not to engage in any further cowardly tirades.

Of course the queen of Dartry had more cause than most to defend us poor castaways, for while Manglana resided at his chief seat of Duncarbery, she had once more resumed her dalliances with Captain de Cuéllar, who was also lodging in the keep during the chieftain's absence. Far from feeling intimidated by the eventual repercussions of this hospitality, de Cuéllar saw fit to attend all meetings of the freemen and often requested Nial to serve as his interpreter. Upon returning to the outhouse the bondsman would often describe what had passed in the tower-house.

'Lady Dervila does little to bridle her alien guest,' he said to me one afternoon, 'and chuckles openly whenever he contradicts or dismisses the words of the senior Dartrymen. They've come to behold him with unmasked disgust and reddening expressions of rage.'

'It's all we need,' I sighed, 'it won't end well for us Spaniards.'

'You should see how the plucky Andalusian seaman carries himself through the corridors of the tower house,' continued Nial, 'with four of his Spanish cronies forming a protective ring about him. He acts as if he fancies himself to be above the chieftain, for he does not acknowledge a single soul apart from the lady Dervila Bourke, and some of his men bare their teeth at any natives who do not steer clear of their path.'

If the Feast of Martinmas was subdued, the days which followed possessed a greater solemnity when news reached us that the English Viceroy's army had stormed the castle of a rebel chieftain on its way north. The following morning Donal MacCabe led his troop of gallowglasses towards Duncarbery to answer the summons of Manglana, who feared for his seat of power which lay in the path of the approaching army. Many highborn cavalrymen rode ahead of these detested redshanks, leaving only a score of bluejackets in the ringfort to defend Rosclogher.

Yet our relief at the departure of the savage Scots quickly turned to consternation when word reached us that the viceroy's force had stormed the castles of another four Irish chieftains along the western coast, taking many of their subjects and all Spanish castaways as prisoners. These unfortunates were promptly sentenced to death at FitzWilliam's order, leaving a trail of men swinging from tree branches as the Sassanas pursued their journey of death and destruction along the western coast.

Many rebels had already fled to the mountains and the deep woods with their cattle, while tidings of the viceroy's advance were received at Rosclogher from runners despatched by Manglana from Duncarbery. Their news greatly distressed the townsfolk, who were further alarmed when Dervila received a despatch from her husband, ordering her to commence preparations to repair to the mountains. This order was met with much dismay, for the herdsmen had only just descended from the mountains to spend the winter along the banks of Lough Melvin. Yet they were forced to undo all of their backbreaking preparations and make ready to return to the surrounding heights once more. Many long faces were to be seen as the village was swept up by sounds heard before a fray, with bowyers and fletchers labouring amid the shriek of sharpened blades to prepare for the dangers which lay ahead.

The great hustle and bustle briefly subsided when word reached us that FitzWilliam's army had ridden past Manglana's seat of power, having avoided Duncarbery altogether. Without tarrying any further, the enemy marched on the garrison town of Ballyshannon, which left the natives in Rosclogher visibly relieved. All clung to the hope that Dartry's fierce reputation might have reached the ears of the viceroy, which might also spare them the brunt of winter in the wilds. Greater relief was felt by the natives in Manglana's town when we learned that upon reaching Ballyshannon, a few bands of horse and footmen turned back to Sligo, which seemed to indicate that the viceroy had abandoned all further plans for battle.

It was therefore distressful in the extreme when tidings reached us but a few days later, that the Sassanas had seized a marshal of the O'Donnell forces from the castle of Belleek, since many feared that this move by the viceroy FitzWilliam was committed to furnish himself with intelligence about the surrounding areas. This concern was well warranted, for Belleek lay only six miles to the north from us, and our fears only worsened when rumours emerged that the army was preparing for a march south. To further compound our misery, the spies of the Irish rebels within FitzWilliam's camp reported that mention of the word 'Rosclogher' had been heard upon the enemy's lips.

Needless to say, the mood of all but the most sympathetic of natives instantly turned sour towards the Spaniards in Manglana's town, for none could understand why the viceroy had steered clear of Duncarbury, the chief seat of power belonging to Manglana which guarded the road between Connacht and Ulster, only to march on the distant tower-house of Rosclogher which was of no strategic value. In turn this only worsened the belligerence openly flaunted by de Cuéllar and his *camarada*, which only served to further divide opinion as to what was to be done with us Spaniards. Meanwhile the villagers once more resumed their preparations for fleeing into the mountains, mobbing every new runner who crossed the marsh to despatch messages to the lady Bourke in the chieftain's hall.

Their fears were somewhat tempered by relief when Manglana himself reappeared in Rosclogher at the head of his army and beneath the flapping red lions upon his banner, as dusk was setting in on Saturday. We beheld the silhouettes of his cavalry with wonder, as the spears of the Irish kerns pricked the air behind them, followed by the ominous figures of the Scottish gallowglasses who shadowed their footsteps. The following morning after Mass I found myself summoned to the hall with Nial. Manglana glowered at us from his seat in the presence of his bard, Fearghal, and his tanist Cathal the Black.

At his left elbow sat his queen, Dervila on the remaining throne in the hallway, which was slightly lower in height although it still surmounted the flagstones below it by the length of a rifle bore. Before the handful of steps leading up to her seat sat the five women closest in rank to her, which included the ollave Muireann, who no longer turned her head away when she saw me. Closest to these women stood the unlikely duo of Captain de Cuéllar and the returned gallowglass constable, MacCabe, who still railed at the king and queen of Dartry.

'But I must protest my lady!' cut in Captain de Cuéllar with a loud exclamation, the palms of his hands outstretched before him. 'Why request my presence when I cannot understand a word uttered by this brute?'

MacCabe clearly bristled when the slur was translated to him, but averted his hands from his axe handle at the sharp stare of Dervila, and even went as far as to repeat his previous Irish words in Latin.

'Why steer clear of our lord MacGlannagh's seat of power only for the *Sassenachs* to now make for Rosclogher? It is clear that it is the Spaniards that the viceroy wants! We should cast these men out of our lands and haste them on a northward journey! If we spread word of this to the four winds, FitzWilliam and his army may yet reconsider their advance!'

'Nonsense, man!' was de Cuéllar's immediate reply, as the captain stamped his foot defiantly and shook his fist before the glowering eyes of the gallowglass constable. 'Ye should unite at haste with neighbouring tribes, and resist the advance of these heretical servants on the open field! Ye have men of Spain to assist with thy resistance!'

MacCabe tossed his head back and issued a bark of mocking laughter.

'What neighbouring tribes dost thou speak of, first among fools? They all look to their own lands and cattle, holding onto every single soldier they can muster! O'Rourke himself is fled! And has served us with an invitation to join with his forces in the heights of Breifne! I repeat that it is you Spaniards that the viceroy is after, and you should leave these lands forthwith.'

A chill of unease pierced my stomach at the veracity of his words, and in that instant I felt overwhelmed by guilt, so that I almost drew the emerald ring from my bandolier to declare my part in the enemy's movements. In that instant I also noticed that while Dervila's face did not betray a whit of sentiment, the chieftain's appeared the picture of consternation, and his mouth was half open as if he were about to speak.

I had never noticed this look of confusion on his face before, since he had always appeared more stoic than his wife. He was evidently distressed at having to uproot his tribesmen and their herds during the winter, so it was in a faltering voice that he interrupted the gallowglass constable and the Spanish sea captain, who were locked in a heated exchange.

'Could a mere handful of Spaniards be the cause of an entire army's advance? Surely there must be something that we are not seeing.'

My skin crawled at these words, then the chieftain grasped his face in his hands, stunning all present with his public gestures

- XXVII -

of desperation. When at last he raised his face again, his eyes were red and raw, whether from grief or a lack of sleep or both. Once again he reasoned openly before his freemen, in a tone that requested a solution to his quandary.

'Indeed, I feared mischief from Bingham, that he might seek to catch me unawares in the winter, so great is his eagerness to displace me. It is why I retained the services of the Scottish mercenaries during the months ahead. For not for any love of their company do I request my people to host them, so great and so vile a burden do they impose on all of us in the tribe!'

At these words Dervila seemed to stir slightly in her chair, for although she often rebuked and interrupted Constable MacCabe who also bristled before her, the constable and his men had after all been a gift to the chieftain which had formed part of her dowry many years earlier. I had often seen her seize upon the smallest perceived slight by the chieftain to pronounce a remark that was both disparaging and insolent. Yet although her aquiline features quivered for an instant, her lips remained still, perhaps because of the black mood that had descended upon her spouse. As usual Manglana appeared ignorant of his wife's sentiments, and suddenly rose to his feet with his lips pursed and his fists tightly clenched before him.

'Oft I did expect trouble, but who would have foreseen the entire town of Dublin emptying itself upon our lands! And what use do they see in marching on Rosclogher? This land is both barren and mountainous, and only important because of the road along the coast! Yet why seize this concealed tower-house and not my seat of strength!'

'Let him come, my lord!' snarled Cathal the Black. 'We shall hide our goods and families in the mountains and harry the Sassenachs in the woods.'

Manglana glared at his tanist before delivering a reply which left none in doubt as to his sentiments towards repairing to the mountains.

'Readily dost thou speak of flying to the heights at the year's start! Hast thou no memory of the daring of starving wolves that have precious little to feed on? Or of the frost which shall slay our babes and blacken our hands and feet?'

The raw passion of the chieftain's outburst meant that the tanist was next to fall silent, while Manglana continued his lament.

'Yet flee to the mountains I must, with all my people, cattle and families. For I have not the means to withstand so great a force. May God deliver us from the elements, for we will be hard put to it to survive the winter ahead.'

His stare was lifted from the ground, and fixed itself upon de Cuéllar.

'Ye Spaniards must think on what ye desire to do with your lives. The road north has become ever more perilous and is perhaps a more hazardous choice than flying with us to the mountains.'

So saying, he arose and quickly descended the steps from his throne while averting his glance from anyone, as de Cuéllar called after him, pledging that he would soon provide him with an answer. Manglana appeared not to hear him. Nobles stumbled out of his way as the chieftain marched straight towards the doors of his hall. His bard scurried out quickly after

- XXVII -

him, as did his bodyguard of bluejackets who followed him even unto his bedside.

As he disappeared behind the hall's doors I could not help but feel wretched for all that had been inflicted upon a man who had done nothing but strive to protect his Catholic allies. I also could not help but wonder if I was indeed the direct cause for the misery which was to be inflicted upon him and his people. After leaving the keep and returning to the outhouse with Nial, I tossed and turned in my sleep, wrestling with the guilt I felt at still concealing the trinket that I feared had spelt the tribe's doom.

'They would all do the same,' I hissed to myself at dusk. 'Sassanas, chieftains, rebels and even my own fellow Spaniards...not to mention that mouldy old Jesuit! Which is not to mention his church that fattens itself on saints' hipbones and indulgences not worth the vellum they're scrawled on! All that matters is plunder and gain, it is all that has ever mattered to everyone that I ever knew!'

The burning discomfort of guilt had been somewhat eased by my lament when there suddenly appeared in my mind a vision of the aquiline features of Muireann, wearing an expression that was at once severe and prolonged. It caused me to turn on my side and cover my face with my forearm in a futile attempt to dispel the vision.

'She would also do the same' I groaned to myself, although I knew at once that I was a lying wretch, whose shame could only be relieved by slumber.

I was next plunged into a dream that was so real that I could almost feel the warmth of the Mediterranean sun of Malta upon my face. I was once more a child, walking across the courtyard towards a man who stood with his back to the light, swathed in shadow but instantly recognisable as he who had sired and then rejected me: my father Juan de Zanoguerra, a sergeant-at-arms who was both proud and brave, who was slain by the Turk upon the bastions of Fort Saint Michael.

The slight weight on my shoulder alerted me of a hand which had come to rest there, and I knew before turning my head that it was Fra Nicola, the man who had raised me since my first steps were taken. He was known to us foundlings of the Knights of Malta simply as Fra 'Cola, and his expression appeared forbidding to the stranger, yet was one that could instantly become crinkled with warmth and a broad smile. It was the closest thing to paternal affection that we bastards in the foundling home would ever know.

'He has spared no expense, Juanito,' he murmured, and it suddenly occurred to me that I had spent a lifetime being referred to in the diminutive. 'He has spared no expense to keep thee well fed. For gain means little to him, and honour is everything. Honour and the sword.'

Fra 'Cola's prompts went on as he berated me for not having changed my linen and urging me to use my best Latin. Yet already his words had stung me too deeply. I arose from my slumber with a start, and amid loud gasps of breath I placed the palm of my hand against the beads of sweat on my forehead. My jaw hung open as I looked in disbelief from side to side, stunned by memories which seemed to further confirm my sense of hopelessness.

'Honour and the sword are all that count to him,' I hissed, 'that cursed bastard who spoke only once to his son and then only to curse at him.'

- XXVII -

I fell back in a heap upon the straw, with my chest rising and falling like a storm-tossed ocean while I sought to regain my breath. And I knew in that moment that the ring had a great hold on me, one which could not be relinquished even by the fleeting thoughts of my honourable father and the reputable Fra 'Cola, memories which I had always treasured like gold dust.

Other dreaded recollections returned to me then of my strikingly handsome father in full armour, mortally wounded by a Turk as he died with his body caked in an unholy admixture of blood, sweat, dust and piss. Before his eyes glazed over, he cast me a final glance as I collapsed at his side, sprayed by the scarlet that sprouted from his breast, holding his head in my hands.

'Father!' I gasped, while hoping that in his last living moments he might spare me some endearment which might lend some meaning to my years spent living as an abandoned bastard.

Yet all I received was the scornful stare of a man who had seen the worst depravities of war, so that even his last breath was dedicated to the fight.

'Behind you, you dolt.'

It was a warning that would not have saved my life, for in that instant the huge Algerian who had crept up behind me was struck down by my father's comrade before he, too, was despatched to the next world by a hail of gunfire which felled all who stood about me. Recollections of the sun-baked precincts of Fort Saint Michael wafted away, leaving me to regain sight of the wattle ceiling of the outhouse.

'Indeed Santi', I whispered to myself, turning onto my side amid a rasping gasp from Nial, 'how you are still alive the Lord only knows. Yet to what end, I wonder?'

On the following morning the first herdsmen were seen leaving the village and making towards the jagged outline of the distant peaks. They journeyed towards the chieftain's lofty fastnesses in the heights of the mountains of Dartry. It was sad to see families trudging back to the wilds after barely a month spent alongside the lake, facing certain suffering and misery. More heart-rending still were the tidings that Nial later bore me from the chieftain's hall, where the assembly agreed after lengthy discussion to set the keep aflame and collapse its walls. Upon noticing my sadness at these tidings, the bondsman placed his hand on my shoulder and smiled gently.

"'Tis common practice amongst chieftains, to raze every fort in their possession before flying to the woods. Nothing of advantage shall be left to the enemy.'

Daybreak also found Cathal the Black at the head of a score of his finest horsemen, who were despatched to ride throughout Dartry and warn the *tuatha* of FitzWilliam's advance. They would also order the herdsmen across the land to lead their families and livestock into the mountains. After witnessing another day of hurried preparations, I endured yet another night of fitful slumber, in which I was racked by guilt. Early the following morning I decided to take a walk at the first light of dawn, which is when I found de Cuéllar standing along the edge of the lake. He also seemed weighed down by thought as he skimmed pebbles across its surface and seemed not to notice my approach as he hurled yet another stone across the water.

- XXVII -

'Why would the viceroy leave Dublin in winter?' he said, after greeting me. 'It is the worst season for battle.'

I shrugged while observing the boatman on the distant jetty.

'There have been hundreds of us captured. Who knows what stories must have reached Dublin? He must want a share of all the booty from the Armada wrecks.'

The captain slowly nodded.

'That is true. He must keep a few spies among the men of the Binghams.'

His hands were folded behind his back when he spoke, giving him an almost scholarly air while he gazed at the keep of Rosclogher. I also turned my stare towards the stronghold that stood across the water from us, wondering what it was that had struck de Cuéllar's notice as an uncomfortable silence grew between us.

'I thought they might have put up a fight,' I said at last, more to break the growing awkwardness than to make any attempt at conversation.

De Cuéllar started at my words, just as he was about to hurl another pebble at the water.

'How do you mean?'

'A mere handful of men could defend their fortress.'

Wrinkles gathered about the captain's narrowing eyes as they bore into mine, and an ironic smile grew across his lips.

'Tell that to the four chieftains whose keeps the viceroy seized prior to having them beheaded. The walls of that crude pillar would cave in upon being struck by the first cannon shot. Its irrelevance is probably the only reason it has survived for so long.'

I was stung by his sarcasm as I momentarily bit my lip and gestured beyond the town and the green in the direction of the thick ring of bog.

'Granted, it is not the most formidable fortress,' I replied, 'and does not possess features like the trace italienne, which you can find in the meanest castles on the Continent. Yet a team of the stoutest oxen could not drag a single cannon out here. The marsh is waist deep and stretches for over a league. Which is not to mention that the Sassenachs cannot swim to save their lives.'

In the corner of my eye, I could see de Cuéllar's head turning from left to right, and his mouth slightly widened as if at the sight of an unexpected gift. His voice descended into an awed whisper.

'It is indeed the truth, Hospitalarios. The tower house appears impregnable.'

A sudden unease overcame me at his realisation, for I knew him to be as bull-headed as he was erratic. I instantly feared that my argument might have swayed him to persuade the tribe to defend the tower-house and not depart for the mountains.

'It would, of course,' I hastened to add, 'be sheer lunacy to defend it.'

He appeared not to acknowledge my remark while he observed the environs of the lake. After a time he returned his attention to the keep's defences, and his limp form was like that of a lifeless statue until he issued an awed whisper.

'We would not even need heavy guns upon the battlements.'

'Not that there are any' I remarked, feeling somewhat flattered by his acknowledgement of my observation, until I realised to my great unease that he had used the word 'we'.

- XXVII -

I decided not to engage him in any further conversation, so I slowly backed away from him, leaving the captain to mull over his thoughts upon the bank of Lough Melvin.

To my great distress, my fears proved truer than I first realised, and that evening all of the Spaniards within the town were summoned to the chieftain's hall. At first, I feared that one of our number had committed yet another act of depravity, yet I was shocked to find that the cheeks of our protector glistened with tears which slid from his red-rimmed eyes. Our presence had been anticipated by that of Captain de Cuéllar, who stood to attention before the chieftain and his wife, with his back straight as a ramrod and his face as sombre as that of a Roman statue. At our appearance Manglana rose from his seat and descended the steps towards us, embracing each of us heartily before his assembly.

'Ye have my utmost gratitude, worthy Spaniards, for your desire to defend my keep. Your captain has humbly submitted your proposal to me, which brave proposition I wholeheartedly accept.'

It was all I could do to prevent my bunched fists from quivering with indignation, hoping that my face had not turned a scarlet hue. Before any of us could utter a word, de Cuéllar stood forward and made one last appeal to the freemen who were gathered about us, beseeching them to also stand their ground with us. The captain's entreaty was loud and fearless, and his finger wagged in the air before him for emphasis.

'Better to man the fortress than to scurry away like rabbits. Ye cannot flee forever; there comes a time when ye must stand and face the enemy.'

As expected, the gallowglass constable Donal MacCabe was the first to pour scorn upon the captain's haughtiness, speaking the thoughts of many when he jeered de Cuéllar.

'It shall be a massacre! Ye are outnumbered by more than two hundred to one!'

The captain beheld him indignantly as he hissed beneath his teeth.

'Numbers do not always count if a man is ready to die!'

Their argument soon reached an impasse. Both the chieftain and his wife at first proposed that they defend the tower-house but they found opposition from the highborn freemen gathered before them. Most of the assembly backed Donal, who insisted that they retain the course of flight. As always, their arguments were in turn backed by the bard O'Dalaigh, who was quick to seize upon popular opinon, despite his many previous odes about taking up arms against the heretic.

'Those devils are invincible', cried the aged bard, for once resorting to Latin. 'They have destroyed every tribe in their path.'

When the chieftain retired from his hall, Nial walked over and grabbed me by the arm.

'What you Spaniards are proposing is suicide! The viceroy will not grant you a scintilla of mercy!'

I shrugged off the bondsman and made straight for the captain, whom I spotted making for the steps with his band of four cronies. The Canarians and the Milanese adventurer were also furious, and together we swiftly descended the steps after him, seething with rage. One of the country boys grabbed the strutting peacock of a captain by the shoulder, before sending him flying with a hefty fist to the mouth. De Cuéllar tumbled onto the grass as his crony fat Juande turned onto the captain's aggressor with a snarl, felling the Canarian with a blow of his own. Meanwhile the captain rose off the grass holding his jaw. He next separated the other Canarian from Juan and yelled at us to be still, all while serving us with a look of incredulity, as though it were us that were mad.

'What is this? A mutiny? I shall have you all flogged to the bone!'

His assailant climbed onto his knee while pointing an accusing finger at the captain.

'You bound us to an oath of which we knew nothing! We are now honour bound to the chieftain!'

De Cuéllar frowned and shook his head in open disbelief.

'Do not tell me you would rather flee with those barefoot cowherds into the wild!'

His retort left me further incensed.

'You yourself told me that the Sassanas have crushed four castles already! Why would they spare us?'

De Cuéllar snorted aloud.

'You soft, French popinjay, Hospitalarios. Even you doubt my choice?! You said yourself that the tower-house cannot be taken! He shall not tarry through the brunt of the winter frost.'

I bit my tongue, further regretting my talk with him the previous day.

'And what if the winter is not as harsh as you predict it will be?' said Dal Verme, the Milanese adventurer.

The captain laughed.

'Not harsh? Did you not feel those gales when our ships were ravaged? The stoutest chords were snapped and that was mid-autumn! We shall see how long those bastards last when they find themselves buffeted by freezing gales.'

I bit my fist in a mad rage, finding myself furious at his audacity.

'We are nine men, Captain! Nine! What if they decide to wait? They are in their hundreds, yet two score men shall suffice to take us!'

De Cuéllar appeared to regain his composure, before resting a forefinger upon his lips.

'I understand your concerns, Hospitalarios. Yet do not shout, for the tribesmen are scared enough already. Tell me, what choice do we have? Do you really want to run off with those savages? Eat uncooked meat and have your toes bitten off your feet by the frost?'

'That is a far preferable fate to being captured, tortured and put to death!'

He shook his head.

'Nonsense Juan. The enemy shall not take us behind these walls. Here we can live like kings, eat all the food these fools leave us before they roam the hills like vagabonds. We shall have a roof over our heads whilst a fire dances on the hearth. Trust me, it will be as child's play compared to the horrors which shall be endured by the tribe.'

His brazen words angered me more.

'That is easy for you to say. The moment the Sassanas learn that you are an officer you will be kept for ransoming. It is the rest of us that shall swing from the trees!'

The others angrily cried their assent as de Cuéllar growled at me in disgust.

- XXVII -

'Do not confuse matters. Are you afraid? I am ready to remain here alone.'

The open questioning of their men's courage was a last card played by all officers when they found their backs against the wall. It was particularly effective in the imperial army, where every last Spaniard had the embers of a great pride burning deep within his breast at all times, ready to flare up when stoked. We fell silent at his last remarks, and after a while the captain walked up to me with a smug grin and slapped me on the back with a laugh.

'Now now Juanito, you will thank me in the end. You just wait and see.'

I was too distraught to reply, although the captain cared little for my thoughts. He turned away and hobbled off towards the ferry with his foursome of footpads who clung to him like stray mongrels. When I witnessed his awkward gait, I recalled the great injury he had suffered to his leg during his shipwreck upon the western coast of Ireland. I bit my lip more fiercely at the sight, realising the main reason for his gallant offer.

It was for nothing that Dal Verme and the Canarians remonstrated with him during the evening and the following day, for the captain was as stubborn as a mule. When the protests became too heated, he decided to pull rank, reminding the complainants that he was the most senior officer in the town, and that any further questioning of his orders would be reported to the Duke of Parma upon his eventual return to Spain.

The following morning found us lined up along the green at daybreak, where we had been summoned to take our oath. Manglana was present, along with all of his highborn subjects and retainers, with all of the townsfolk gathered to watch the proceedings. The chieftain wordlessly approached us on foot, flanked by his grandson Lochlain who held a bowl out before them. After he had stopped a few paces away from us, the chieftain drew a dagger from his belt, then snatched the bowl from the young prince and held it in the air above his head.

'In the name of the Almighty, I beseech ye, worthy Spaniards, to take an oath before all men gathered here! I shall grant ye command of the keep of Rosclogher in my absence, if ye shall only swear not to abandon it, nor to surrender it to the enemy, even if ye are to perish from starvation. Let he who shall not drink from this bowl depart from *Dartraigh* forthwith, where he may chance upon the mercy of the lands to the north!'

So saying, he returned the bowl to a bewildered Lochlain before clasping his dagger blade and slicing open the palm of his left hand. When this was done, he clenched the sliced hand into a fist, causing blood to trickle freely from it and land into the bowl held by the princeling. When this was finished, he took the bowl and held it out to the Spaniard who stood closest to him. Manglana eyed his guests closely and issued a single command, loud as a thunderbolt.

'Drink!'

Each of us Spaniards drank from the bowl of usquebaugh mixed with Manglana's blood which was passed among us. We next took an oath which was duly translated by O'Ronayne, that we would not abandon the keep or surrender it to the enemy, even if we were to starve. Some swore by the hand of the chieftain, while others swore an oath by the lives of their sons or other kin.

Once this ceremony of sorts was ended, files of women and children could be seen making towards the hills in the distance, behind groups of armed men who returned droves of cattle towards the mountainsides. The sight reminded me of the Exodus of Israel from Egypt, as the Dartrymen travelled towards the distant heights, their belongings borne by their ponies. I squirmed in discomfort upon noticing that some of the women in the train were with child, and I sought to avoid thinking of the suffering which lay ahead of them.

After most of the townsfolk were gone, I noticed that the troop of gallowglasses was next to depart, with the MacCabes marching off towards the heights. I felt relieved by the thought that I would soon be free of their presence, so that I walked over to the green to watch them go with a smug smile growing across my face. Their women and children trudged disconsolately behind the mailed men, who were flanked by their senior officers who rode on horseback. The smile on my face quickly vanished when three of the mounted Scots rode away from the gathering, heading in my direction. My fears only worsened when I made out the rugged features of the gallowglass constable, who reined in his steed and roared at me.

'Wouldst that thou bear the same smile when thou perisheth with thy fellows, grey wolf! The viceroy shall string ye all up by the balls!'

I averted my gaze from him, hoping that nothing worse than angry words would befall me. My great distress was slightly relieved when he wheeled his horse about and charged back towards his troop, with his two riders in tow. His words had not been in vain, for they had found their mark and left me feeling weighed down with unease. Shortly afterwards, I made out the figure of O'Ronayne riding towards me with the returned tanist, Cathal the Black, their faces as grey as the heavens above us. Behind them was gathered a host of over a score of retainers, and I could recognise amongst them the attendants of O'Ronayne from the infirmary, together with a handful of invalids borne on mantles by their fellow tribesmen.

The tanist signalled a halt, then kicked his horse towards me with the Jesuit behind him. When they were both a few paces away from me, they dismounted, and when the tanist approached me he ignored my swift bow and extended hand before grabbing me in a tight embrace which left me flushed with embarrassment. His eyes were red-raw in a face caked with ceruse, and his voice faltered when he bade me farewell.

'Loath am I to lose a soldier of honour and a marksman of thy ability to the Sassenachs. Readily would I spirit thee away with my men. Yet thou art forthwith honour bound to an oath, and there is little left to us but to have faith, that we shall one day meet again.'

I smiled back at him ruefully, since the uncertainty of the following days hung over me like the pronouncement of a death sentence.

'In the next life, perhaps.'

O'Ronayne stood at Cathal's side as he fixed me with a keen stare.

'May the Lord protect you, grey wolf,' said the Jesuit, 'and should the unthinkable happen, you must pledge to me that you shall torch the tomes of Aengus which I have had delivered into the tower-house, rather than let the enemy get their hands upon them.'

Although my prospects looked grim, the Jesuit's words were of some solace to me, for there was nothing that delighted me more than having access to books, especially since sieges were always long and dreary affairs.

'You have my word, reverend father,' I replied, bowing deeply, 'for I am still in your debt for your treatment of my wounds following my arrival in Dartry.'

When they returned to their mounts I watched them lead the tanist's gathering of cavalrymen and kerns across the green in the direction of the ring of bog. They were still disappearing into the trees that skirted it when I heard more whinnies behind me. I started at the sound and turned to find a dozen riders on bare-backed garrans, followed closely by a score of heavily armed kerns on foot. Two great wolfhounds bounded ahead of the foremost horseman, their jaws frothy as they beheld me with auburn eyes, and I instantly recognised them as the ollave's dogs Roe and Bran. Their mistress followed closely behind them, but I barely caught her lingering stare in my direction as my mantle flapped against my cheek.

Muireann's hair fluttered freely in the wind as she reined her mare in alongside me. She appeared sorrowful, for her red-headed son, Lochlain, had ridden away from the keep an hour earlier with his paternal grandmother, the lady Bourke. Manglana's wife had decided to return to the lands of her father's people rather than endure the torrid winter months in the heights of Dartry.

Meanwhile the ollave had instead elected to remain behind and endure the toils of her late husband's retainers, who were every inch as loyal to her as they had been to him. In previous days she had also overseen the movement of a great quantity of goods into the tower house of Rosclogher. These goods had reportedly included at least a dozen beehives, whose value would have been significant, although they were as nothing when compared to the price of the honey which could be produced by their winged tenants.

'Is there anything thou require, that I may provide?' she asked.

I cleared my throat awkwardly at her address before I replied.

'There is one thing I wish for, if indeed this were to be my last request.'

The ollave's eyes narrowed whilst she beheld me warily.

'And what might that be?'

I gently took her wrist and fell onto one knee, staring at her hand of iridescent white. The faintest of kisses glanced it before I returned to my feet with a wry grin as her arm fell back by her side.

'It is something I have meant to do ever since we reached the tribe. But a small gesture of thanks for helping me to flee the enemy, despite having to abandon thy husband.'

A tear instantly appeared upon her eye, then slid down her face. Muireann's cheeks reddened as she masked her emotion with a forearm. I looked away as she fought back the tears, and her voice was almost angry when she spoke again.

'How shalt thou survive?'

'I know not, my lady.'

Her hands were clenched into fists before one of them was held to her mouth, and the row of knuckles quivered as new tears glistened in her eyes.

'What will they do to thee?'

I could only shrug in response. The low of cattle was heard in the distance as other villagers called out to one another. We turned to face the source of the noise which relieved the awkwardness which had grown between us. After a few moments she frowned before more tears appeared. There was a stern resolve in her whisper, which was out of earshot of those who surrounded her.

'Perhaps thou shouldst escape. I know of a safe place where thou may hide.'

Taken aback by her words, I beheld her in disbelief.

'I have taken an oath, my lady.'

Her cheeks were slightly crimsoned by shame, and she toyed pensively with her horse's bridle. When one of the kerns stepped towards her, she raised a hand towards him, causing him to retreat to her band of retainers as she spoke her last words to me.

'For too long have I misjudged thee. Farewell, Abelito, I can only hope that our paths will one day cross again.'

My jaw dropped when she spoke the name used by the dying captain Fernández before his mercy killing in the shadow of Keeloges. I bowed my head deeply.

'Godspeed, my lady Muireann Mac an Bhaird.'

The ollave kicked her horse's flanks, causing it to stand on its hindquarters and wheel about. Then she galloped away ahead of her hounds, leaving me to muse that she might rein in her steed, dismount and return to me. My hope never dimmed until she was a distant figure that vanished over the hill. I stared into nothingness for what seemed an age before returning to the muddy bank of Manglana's town, where I found the chieftain surrounded by a force made up of his highborn cavalrymen and his blue jacketed bodyguards, who had tarried to help execute the final siege preparations.

After I finished helping a band of tribesmen kick down and burn three of the wattle huts in the town, Nial appeared with beads of perspiration on his darkened brow, to tell us that Manglana's scouts had already caught sight of the enemy. His news did little to allay our fears, since we knew that the English troopers were heading in our direction without showing any intention of veering east. The bondsman's expression turned grim when he spoke words which he appeared loathe to utter, causing trepidation amongst his listeners.

'It is an army without count, an endless stream of pennons. We must make haste, for much remains to be done. We must leave nothing for them in the town.'

XXVIII

Rosclogher, Dartry, County Leitrim

14 November 1588

Relics and ornaments were carried from the chapel into the castle, while peat was piled by the hearths. A half-dozen crossbows and muskets clattered onto the ground after servants bore them to our quarters, with the chieftain's steward Malachy swiftly addressing us.

'We have left you all that can be spared. In the kitchen stores are supplies of beef and bread.'

'And to drink?' asked de Cuéllar, as he fumbled with one of the weapons he had picked up off the ground.

'The *dun* bears great cisterns which are full of rainwater. If you ration carefully, there is enough to last you over six months.'

A frown appeared on the captain's face.

'I meant a drink, not a bath.'

We worked hard for the rest of the morning on the final preparations. Offal and the carcasses of slaughtered animals were hurled into the well, along with fish guts and other waste which had been collected from the middens on the edge of the town. Our labours were merely the finishing touches to a huge effort which the whole tribe had immersed itself in over the last few days. All able-bodied women and children had also taken part in these activities, after being divided into squads which had dug deep trenches along the banks of the lake to hinder the enemy's attempts to camp alongside it.

Anything that could serve of use to the Sassanas was taken into the mountains or destroyed, for Manglana had ordered that we 'do not leave those base colonists a single rotten egg'. The chieftain's sawyers quickly went to work on large, wooden structures, so that before long the town was reduced to a flattened stretch of grassland, for even the great stones of the ringfort were taken apart. In their resolve to render their home worthless for the approaching army, the townsfolk had even scoured the earth of Manglana's town itself, ensuring that every stone which could be used as a missile by the enemy was consigned to the bottom of Lough Melvin.

It was with a tinge of sadness that I witnessed the small jetty being set aflame. The natives rightly feared the enemy might use its proximity to send a great heap of brushwood and timber piled upon a raft towards the keep, thereby choking its defenders with smoke and causing us to abandon it. As a further precaution, a palisade of stakes was dug into the bed of the lake to flank the side of the crannog, to protect it from any other rafts of blazing driftwood which the enemy might send in our direction.

During this entire feat of destruction, the Spaniards hosted in the village more than proved their worth. Our great energy

- XXVIII -

could of course be explained by the fact that we were chiefly acting to protect our own hides from a ruthless enemy. Yet we were also veterans of the terrible war in Flanders that had unleashed untold misery on countless civilians, meaning that the razing of the houses belonging to country-folk was second nature to us. We proved so good at destroying the town which had hosted us, that a few natives openly remarked on how fortunate they considered themselves to count upon us as allies and not enemies.

Stables, byres and barns were all burned to useless heaps of smouldering ash, which along with the flattened huts and cabins would hinder the Sassanas from setting up camp. These delays would thwart the besiegers' efforts as winter set in, when it was hoped that their health would suffer in sleet and heavy snow.

I stood atop the roof of the keep, which had long been stripped of its tin slates which were used to pay for the upkeep of Manglana's mercenaries. From the lofty height I could behold the blackened pile, which was all that remained of Nial's outhouse. Behind it the Abbey of Saint Mel appeared a structure both curious and lonely. Its holy significance ensured that it remained the only building to be left untouched, at least until the enemy arrived.

A church surrounded by burned-down houses, I thought to myself. *When was the last time I witnessed it? Didn't end well back then; as for this time...*

The distressing memory of Elsien's corpse returned to me then, so that I almost laughed in desperation at the thought that I somehow wanted to reach her youngest brother. I banished the thought from my mind, nodding my approval at the red-faced bluejackets who had appeared on the roof. On their backs they bore large wicker baskets filled with earth, which would serve as protection against the rifles of enemy snipers. These great gabions would also allow us defenders enough cover that we could pick off any approaching threat from atop the keep.

Towards late afternoon most preparations had already been carried out, and the fort was well furnished with victuals and a good store of arms. A final task was entrusted to Nial, who asked me to join him to measure the depth of the bog. As we rode across the green, the grey skies overhead seemed a portent of the impending doom of Rosclogher. I turned my attention away from it to assist the bondsman - after the relentless showers of rain in previous days, my staff almost vanished when it was dipped into the mud.

'This side is deeper, by a few feet,' I called out to him.

Nial nodded at me.

'It is the same at this end; the level has risen. It is as I expected. With some luck the army might not even make it past the bog, let alone the banks of the lake.'

So great was my trepidation at his mention of the advancing force that I shivered at the sound of a muffled whinny behind us. A handful of strangers approached us across the bog, holding their mounts closely by the bridle. They traversed the mire over the partly concealed passage of great boulders, and despite the gloom I could make out the green cloak of their leader who was a man both tall and thin, with white hair and a beard fluttering over his left shoulder. The most memorable aspect about him was his piercing gaze, which verged on the terrifying in the way it seemed to reach down into your very soul. The bondsman observed this elderly man and muttered darkly beneath his breath.

'The Anglo-Norman, Old Tom. What brings him here?'

When he reached us, the stranger spoke up in a husky voice, and I had learned enough of the Irish tongue to realise that the elder desired to speak with the chieftain. Since our task was already completed, the bondsman reluctantly escorted the band of men to the banks of Lough Melvin, where they were relieved of their weapons before a couple of bluejackets ferried us across the water on a skiff.

Manglana still appeared to be shaken by news of the advancing enemy, and had not smiled since his reappearance after Martinmas. Yet the slightest of grins flickered across his pallid face at the appearance of the strange visitors, whom he received in a hall that was distinctly bare of anything save for us Spaniards and his closest bodyguards. Old Tom bowed low before the king of Dartry. Their exchange in Irish was largely tranquil except for when the chieftain raised his voice twice; on each occasion, his angst was quelled by the insistent and composed tone of the stranger.

'Who is this man?' I whispered to the usually jovial Nial, who still wore a dark scowl across his face.

'A rebel adventurer who ventured west out of the Pale. They say he was amongst the highest born in his youth, and that the enemy dashed his prospects, leaving him to flee Dublin an outlaw. He is an avowed enemy of the Sassenachs.'

'But why is he here?'

'Thomas Geraldine is a trusted agent of our overlord, the O'Rourke, who has sent him with a message of the highest confidence: to relay his whereabouts to our lord MacGlannagh, that they might join forces in the mountains.'

Old Tom looked baffled when he pointed at the munitions which had been stacked up in the hall, and his jaw dropped when the chieftain gestured towards us Spaniards. It took the Anglo-Norman a few moments to regather his composure before he ran up to the captain and fell on his knees, to the surprise of all those present. His hands were clasped together as his voice resounded across the hall.

'Never have I witnessed such valour among our allies! Please admit me into your company, O valorous captain, that I might partake in your holy stand against these vile heretics!'

His Spanish was fluent albeit accented, and the captain regarded him offhandedly.

'Your Spanish will spare me from using anymore Latin, but are you seasoned in battle?'

Geraldine appeared flustered by the question, and his knuckles whitened about the sword pommel at his belt when he finally managed a reply.

'War is all I have ever known, Captain.'

'And yet you are old and grey,' exclaimed the captain with a wicked smile, 'which means that you are either a fearsome warrior or very fortunate. Either of these qualities would be a great asset to us, for ours is hardly an embarrassment of numbers.'

So saying, de Cuéllar looked at the chieftain, who was keenly listening to Nial's translation of the Spanish dialogue. Manglana was quick to understand the inference of the captain's gaze and raised his hand as he spoke up.

'Geraldine is a worthy servant of our holy cause and is not bound by the will of my assembly. He and his men may join

- XXVIII -

your number if they so desire, although they must agree to be bound by your command for the duration of the siege. Yet one of them must also depart forthwith, to relay my acceptance of the O'Rourke's invitation.'

'My thanks O worthy lord!' cried Geraldine, 'for my greatest desire is to perish with a sword in my hand, while serving the will of God.'

'That is all we need,' whispered Valdo behind me, 'another lunatic crusader amongst our number.'

'Yet allow me a moment to confer with my men,' continued Old Tom, 'for I shall not bind them to this siege if they are not willing to join it. They have served me well in years past and I shall not force them into martyrdom without their consent.'

If I was feeling ill at ease before Geraldine's appearance, his talk of martyrdom made my stomach crawl, and I would have felt sick if my belly were not empty. My great distress in recent days had severely reduced my appetite, so that it came as no surprise when Geraldine's men declined the offer to join the impending siege and instead chose to return to their lord the O'Rourke. The bondsman drily referred to this choice as we left Manglana's hall.

'Small wonder that those men chose to save their hide. It is a miracle that one of them has chosen to remain behind on your fool's errand.'

'True,' I said, 'although another pair of hands is better than nowt. Every man counts in a siege.'

The bondman cast me a dark stare.

'Geraldine is an Anglo-Norman, the son of usurpers. Gaelic blood does not course through his veins. You should be wary of him at all times.'

His warning left me feeling uneasy as we descended the last ladder towards the lowest floor and stepped outside the keep. We tucked our hands beneath our armpits due to the chill, as the chieftain gathered his men about him and turned to address us one last time.

'Verily hath word reached us from distant lands, that the men of Spain are the bravest in the world. Do thy part, old rogue. Thou art now under the command of the captain.'

Old Tom's deep bow belied his years.

'That I shall, O worthy lord. There are no soldiers that I would trust more, save thine own.'

Manglana was silent for a few moments as he beheld our ragged gathering. He was possibly amused at the sight of Spanish soldiers, men who stormed forts across three continents and crushed all resistance beneath their heel on the battleground, suddenly finding themselves powerless on the open field. It was a state of affairs rendered more novel by the fact that a fellowship of true believers was about to be besieged by heretics, something which was largely unheard of on the Continent. Yet there was no air of amusement about Manglana when he delivered his final address, and his cheeks were moist with sentiment.

'And now that all is accomplished, I am loath to leave ye. Were that I was not chieftain and that I could do as I please and fight alongside ye. But alas, I must now depart. May ye be blessed a hundred times over and the Lord give ye heart in the face of the heretic. If ye rescue my keep, ye shall not find me ungrateful.'

We bowed our heads low as we knelt before Manglana to avoid any whiff of his dragon breath. His steward, Malachy, issued his last instruction to us after he had despatched his kerns to ready the boats.

'At their approach, our signal fires along the heights will light up the sky. They shall travel faster than any messenger.'

Nial grabbed my arm hard in his gauntleted hand so that I flinched. His usual smile was missing when he spoke, and he seemed to struggle to keep a rein on his emotions.

'Until we meet again, grey wolf. In this world or the next.'

'Indeed, my friend,' I said, grabbing his forearm. 'Thank you for everything.'

He was silent for a few moments, as he stared back at me.

'Speak nothing of it. But tell me, is there anything you need me to do for you? Any message or thing you need me to deliver or keep safe?'

I hesitated for a moment as the thought of the ring exploded in my mind, so that I was almost on the point of asking him to take it. Then something, maybe greed, stopped me from mentioning it to him.

'There is...nothing. Thank you.'

A look of confusion briefly appeared on his face.

'Very well. I wish you the best of fortune.'

He walked over towards Manglana's band who were boarding the boats, while we entered the fort which was to be our prison for we knew not how long. We suddenly felt very much alone, and the steel door was slammed shut with a loud crash which possessed an eerie note of finality. After we had barred it, we climbed the ladder to the second floor, where we saw the ferries of the household kerns making towards the edge of the lake alongside the demolished infirmary.

After stepping onto land, the chieftain's men drove holes in their boats and sank them close to where the jetty once stood. Large rocks were also placed upon these drowned ferries before Manglana's company rode off across the green and vanished into the trees surrounding the bog. None spoke while our gaze lingered after our protector, awed by the moment of his disappearance which the captain swiftly sought to alleviate.

'Let us find ourselves some usquebaugh!'

In the evening I was spared the night watch, so I slunk away from the other Spaniards and slept near the hearth in the chieftain's hall, until the bickering of the country boys roused me the following morning. The Canarians sat cross-legged upon the floor as they argued over their handfuls of dog-eared cards, and I rubbed my eyes and pushed off my black sheepskin blanket.

A distant sough of wind could be heard outside the keep, and a crown of embers still glowed behind me, which was all that remained of the previous night's fire. I tossed a handful of peat upon them and stoked up a flame before following the way of the Dartrymen and baring my backside to its warmth. Once my buttocks had been well warmed, I lowered my mantle again and turned to the youngsters behind me.

'Pedro, Franco, what word of the enemy?'

There came no reply as they stared at the cards in their hands with gritted teeth, as if their lives depended upon their next moves.

'No sign of them yet.'

'This silence is sinister.'

Pedro absently rolled a die in his palm.

'Perhaps they have returned to Dublin.'

I grunted when I walked past them.

- XXVIII -

'Do not be too hopeful.'

'Ah,' remarked Franco, 'that is true, Hospitalarios. Hope is too much to wish for in this land.'

'And safety,' added Pedro.

The apt remark filled me with unease as I staggered wordlessly out of the room, without any wish to further expand on the subject.

At the end of the steps the captain was lying across the flagstones with legs and arms apart. A drained wineskin was rested upon his chest, and at his feet his crony fat Juande played the half-witted game of jabbing the point of a blade betwixt his fingers as fast as he could. This practice was popular amongst idle soldiers to show off speed of hand and daring, but as I stepped over the captain, I heard a cry and turned to find Juande howling in agony, with the point of his blade half-buried in his thumb.

I turned my back on him and quickly stepped away from Koldo the Basque and Enano, who were wrestling with one another in a drunken bout. I kept well away from them as they collapsed to the floor, twisting and turning like a pair of street cats, with each of them trying to stick a drawn blade into the other.

These unfortunate scenes were all too commonly observed during my time in the Army of Flanders. It was a standing force which had in recent decades become forced to grow larger, so that it became swollen with men who would never have been admitted into the soldiery. I bit my lip as I descended the steps, wondering how on earth we were to survive the siege with the quality of the tosspots at our disposal, whose only purpose seemed to be to further besmirch the reputation of

Imperial Spanish troops. Further along, Old Tom was guarding a slit window. The Anglo-Norman sat cross-legged, polishing a musket whose gleam matched that in his eyes, such was his pride to form part of our company. He nodded slightly in my direction when I drew nearer.

'Is there any sign of them yet?' I asked.

The yellowed fronds of Geraldine's white hair shook when he nodded. A youthful twinkle shone in his cavernous eyes when he replied.

'No sign of the bastards yet.'

'We may as well be in a port town's hostel.'

He issued a bark of laughter as I sat down beside him.

'So you are kinsman of the O'Rourke?' I asked, feigning complete ignorance of his origins.

'No, Spaniard!' he exclaimed in shock before his voice softened again. 'You are the first man in these parts to confuse a member of an Anglo-Norman house with a Gael.'

'Then how did you end up on the side of the rebels?'

'The story is a very long one, my friend.'

'Have you much else to attend to?'

He laughed once more, issuing a deep-throated chuckle.

'Very well, but do not say that I did not warn you. In these parts I am called one of the Old English or Anglo-Normans. We are those whose forebears were Norman knights, swords of William the Conqueror who invaded and occupied England. Our great-grand sires were their sons who travelled to Ireland with Strongbow, the rightful Earl of Pembroke, whose famous host included the famous White Knight of Kilmallock. After winning large territories in Ireland my people found themselves lords of a mystical land whose ways seduced them, and before long they had adopted all manners of the Irish themselves, until they became themselves even more Irish than the Gaels.'

An air of nostalgia hung heavily about him when he spoke, and he seemed to stare beyond me right into his own past.

'Those are days long distant now. I would spend most of my time in the library of the Earl of Maynooth, dreaming of becoming a writer. Little did I suspect the many years of fighting which lay ahead of me.'

Old Tom went on to speak of his house of Geraldine, which was a foremost family among the Anglo-Normans. In time they had been deceived by a rival house, who had allowed the English heretics a foothold in Ireland.

'It was my house who made the Parliament in Dublin strong. Then the cursed Butlers betrayed us to Satan's servant Henry Tudor, the eighth of his name, who issued the order from London that he approve of all of our bills. Marriage between heretic and Catholic was forbidden, and our language and dress became outlawed. In one fell swoop he destroyed all that my house had achieved.'

His fist trembled as the memory rankled within him.

'What happened next?' I asked gently.

'We refused to pay his tax! And spurned his Poynings' Law which rendered Dublin a mere slave of the English Crown! Not long thereafter, the head of our family was thrown into the Tower of London, and his son flew into rebellion only to be killed three years later. My father was one of the slain. I was but a lad without whiskers back then, yet so consumed by rage that I partook of another revolt.'

A watery sheen glistened within Geraldine's eyes.

'The Geraldine League led by my kinsman Silken Thomas...I have never known such glorious days. The air crackled with a great spirit of rebellion, and we clawed back most of Leinster before laying siege to Dublin. But then the enemy were reinforced with siege cannon they had brought over from England. When the tide turned we lost Maynooth, and I barely fled north with my life beyond the Pale, never knowing when the agents of our enemy might overtake me.'

Old Tom's story helped explain many things I had witnessed, and for the rest of the morning I listened to the rest of his account, completely enthralled as we proceeded to walk around the keep.

'All hell broke loose when the pope excommunicated Elizabeth. Reprisals against Catholics grew, and my adopted tribe was put to the sword. I wandered a smoking and ravaged land alone, my stomach churning with hunger and my heart bursting with hate as I witnessed the fate befalling our blessed isle of *Erin*. It was in those days of vagrancy that I attained a desire to understand the meaning of my suffering, and I finally came to see our rebellion for the crusade that it is, a holy war against the first kingdom of heretics.'

His eyes bulged when he spat these last words, wildly gesturing at me to remain silent.

'In time it also became clear that our enemy's mission was not the one of conversion which they had always claimed, for their ministers were poorly provided for, and scant effort was made to preach their falsehoods in our tongue.'

'Then what do these Sassanas want?'

'The whole of *Erin*! Only the land, mind, and not its peoples. All that matters to them are the profits they can derive for their great joint stock company. It is the reason why our woodlands are butchered for our timber to be sold to make their ships and casks. They lust for the riches to be gained from this land, where they even drain our bogs to make way for their plantations!'

His face fell into his hands, and he looked so downcast that I could not but pity him when a rasped whisper was issued beneath his breath.

'So grievous are their crimes against the country, that they have broken and destroyed it.'

He lifted his head and stared at me.

'Oh, but for the day when this land will claim its oppressors. It would only be just.'

With a deep sigh, I spoke a phrase bandied about by sailors in Seville who were bound for Spanish holdings in the New World, a distant place where they eyed riches and exploitation.

'Conquest and civilisation.'

Old Tom hissed and shook his fist in my face.

'Civilise us? By having us reduce the yards of linen on our tunics from ten ells to five? By banning the men's glibb and the head-dress worn by our women? No, my dear Spaniard, these heretics do not want civilisation. They are all but profiteers, who are but second sons and outlaws in their own land.'

Flecks of spittle shot from his lips when he said this, hitting me in the face. Yet his animated gestures and expression amused me, so that I was spurred to prolong our discussion.

'But is that not the way of all conquerors?'

He grabbed my arm in shock as his cavernous eyes bored into mine, as if searching for the slightest hint of an insult.

'Are you not listening to what I am saying? Before their arrival Ireland was a country where all were accepted. French,

Flemish, Normans, Welsh and even English became Hibernicised. My people also adopted the ways of the Gael, with our Norman children sent to their chieftains to be fostered. This was a land where none went hungry and trade thrived, where man lived at peace with nature without raping the land. Yet these new English have resisted the land's seductions. They have brought over army after army to crush the natives and have made laws prohibiting our very clothing and houses! Which is not to mention the unjust outrage of their surrender and regrant policy! The chieftains are right to resist it, for they are left with no choice! Our quarrel with the Sassenachs is not one of culture but of greed!'

He paused for breath and shook his head in disgust.

'But we should not marvel at the avarice of these heretics. At their king's decree I was forced to learn their tongue as a boy in Dublin, which allowed me to travel through their kingdom later on in life. And there I learned that what they have inflicted upon us is no different to how they treat their own people. For the woodlands in England are also rapidly shrinking, yet most landlords do not regret this loss, since it provides space for agriculture. This has in turn driven up the price of wood, which explains why they lust for our forests. Many a tenant has been evicted by their landlord to replace good arable land for sheep, while others use the former homeland of these poor peasants to create their deer parks. For theirs is not a happy kingdom, yet one racked by unrest caused by this eviction, and of course the issues of religion. Many a homeless husbandman did I meet in their towns, begging for alms while weeping besides the starved bodies of their dead family members.'

I stepped away from him, taken aback by his fervour.

'Greed has always been the way of the world,' I said dismissively. 'Long have I fought for kings whose only purpose is gain, to acquire more lands for more taxes to create bigger armies.'

Old Tom flashed me a look of disgust.

'I know of what you speak, Spaniard. I have myself ventured past these shores and seen peasants leaving their fields to rot in crowded, stinking towns which are choked with the poor and hungry. You need not enlighten me of the lot of people abroad, ruled by princes whose only mark is their greed and cruelty, and who bend the law without second thought. Many an alien have I encountered who called the Irish 'beggars', yet happily did I return to the tribes of this land, where most have their place in their society both secured and protected. Where women are respected and kin are true to each other, and where few, if any, get left behind. Even the unsound of mind are provided for.'

His righteous gaze was unflinching, and I could not meet it for long since I knew that he spoke truth. When he saw that his words had left their effect on me, his voice became suddenly lower.

'The Sassenachs care nothing for us and have even defiled our centres of learning which once housed many a foreign scholar. At an early age my destiny was clearly laid out to me, to fight for these people whose ways my forefathers had adopted. I was first thrust into battle as a whiskerless boy when my kinsman Silken Thomas rose against Henry Tudor. And I was also one of the four companions of the Earl of Desmond, when he, too, started his rebellion.'

Tears glistened upon Geraldine's cheeks as he told me about the end of Desmond.

'I had to abandon him due to hunger, and when the English found me, they took me for a bounty hunter down on his luck, due to my flawless English. Desmond was not the most formidable of men, yet he steadfastly embraced his duty in the end. I was forced to flee his side, and his cries of rage and desperation still resound in my ears to this day.'

The old Anglo-Norman sighed.

'I have partaken of every fight against the heretics, and I now know every secret pass and hiding place in this land. Yes, both Leinster and Munster have been broken, and now the fight shifts to Connacht while the might of the great Ulster lords remains dormant. It is here in the west that the heretics are closing in, but if the backbone is broken, then God save Ireland! Even these poor Gaels do not fully understand the significance of what they fight for!'

He turned and faced me with a look that seemed to border on terror.

'Make no mistake, friend Spaniard! The tribes of the west are the last hope of Ireland, if not of mankind.'

This last utterance led me to fear that he might be a lunatic, but I nodded slowly and agreeably, trying to find words with which to assure him that I shared his views.

'Theirs is indeed a worthy cause.'

Geraldine sighed.

'They are left with no choice. Peace was attempted with the Bingham devils, but to no avail. Those vermin crossed the Shannon into Connacht years ago and have since even put women and children to the sword, like that butcher of Malby before them. They have inflicted every worldly misfortune upon us, yet they made the mistake of hanging the son of my lord the O'Rourke, who was a priest that had only returned from Rome to visit his father. My lord flew into rebellion with the MacGlannagh, after he swore revenge on the murderers. The Binghams are a law unto themselves; they have broken the spirit of tribes without count. Long have they starved and purged us. I have seen children dead in their mother's arms, and starving fathers brought to heel with their mouths full of grass.'

'So, what hope do you have?'

Old Tom served me with a deadly stare.

'Whatever hope remains to be clung to! All is not lost, Spaniard! This land is now a place where many forces are at work. Besides us and the enemy, there are the Scots and Spain, the Vatican and the Jesuits. It is a holy war taking place, and not all hope is lost. Catholic Spain still sends priests in all manner of vessels, sends gold with which the chieftains buy arms from Scotland. We shall resist for as long as we sport our outlawed glibb fringes, and as long as the bards inflame our peoples with verse and vigour, commemorating brave deeds against the Sassenachs through song in firelit circles and secluded glens! For the tribes spread across the land of Erin are like a bed of glowering embers, constantly stoked up by the English with bursts of flame occurring now and again, where least expected!'

After his passionate outburst, Geraldine paused for breath.

'Here in the west our enemy has been foiled time and again. The Sassenachs want the chieftains to surrender their titles, to render tribute unto the Crown. Yet in Dartry and Breifne the Brehon laws are still upheld. They will not be stamped out!'

'Yet I have heard tell of tribes in the west that freely serve the Sassanas.'

My aged companion frowned, and in that moment of silence we heard the wind howling against the face of the keep.

'Then you have heard tell a horrific truth. There are many that the Sassenachs have won over with their false promises, for that is indeed their greatest weapon. But our enemies have their divisions too. It is common knowledge that the dislike which the Binghams and the English viceroy share for the Irish is only exceeded by their hatred for one another. And in that division lies a glimmer of hope.'

'And yet,' I replied, 'they ride against us together.'

'That they do, Spaniard! But I tell you that there is no love lost between them. When the viceroy is in Dublin, the Binghams write endless letters to their queen in London to undermine him. The Binghams are known to completely ignore the viceroy's orders, a fact which has reportedly also raised concern in London. 'Tis part of the reason why he has ventured so far.'

'So can the tide against them be turned?'

Geraldine's eyes bristled with defiance as he spat his assurances.

'The MacGlannaghs are a small tribe compared to the O'Donnells in Donegal, which is not to mention the O'Neills of Tyrone in Ulster. MacGlannagh's overlord, the O'Rourke, can summon hundreds of men. But these warlords view each other suspiciously; they will only unite behind the one who makes the first move. All we need is a single victory.'

A small breviary was whisked from his tunic before he shook it wildly in my face.

'As the Bible says: it only takes some yeast to raise the whole loaf!'

- XXVIII -

Old Tom had hardly shared this quote, when he gasped and pointed to the window behind me, terror fleetingly revealed in his stare. When I jerked my head backwards, I could see huge beacons blazing upon the heights in the distance, thick streams of smoke rising towards the heavens while announcing the very minions of hell.

XXIX

Rosclogher, Dartry, County Leitrim

16 – 23 November 1588

With a cry Old Tom rushed towards the staircase. I hurried after him holding my unslung rifle, calling out to the other men that the enemy host had at last arrived. When Geraldine reached the roof, he stripped off his tunic, leaving me to marvel at the sight of lean muscles on so old a body. As he punched the air with his drawn swordblade, his face became contorted with hate as he issued a piercing shriek which had the hair stand upon the back of my neck.

'Crom Abù! Crom Abuuuuuuuuuuuuuuuuuù! Crom Abuuuuuuuuuuuuuuuuuù!'

As his war cry was unleashed, I reached his side at the gabions along the edge of the roof. Peering through the wicker defences, I gasped at the snake-like sight beyond the lake. The long file of flags and pennons which slowly crept through the bog and swarmed through the trees upon the green left me speechless.

- XXIX -

Fifers played a brisk air ahead of hundreds of yeomen and mace-bearers while rows of pikemen followed them amid the screech of bagpipes. They sang their own songs on the march as heralds blew on brass trumpets with battle caps shining above their scarlet doublets.

The scrape of soles was heard behind us, accompanied by deep huffs of breath when the other Spaniards reached the edge of the roof. To a man they were transfixed by the terrible sight of hundreds of enemies that had found their way through the ring of marsh, since we had long hoped that it might delay their advance if not hinder them altogether. In that moment there could not have been one man amongst our number who was not tempted to scramble out of the keep in an attempt to cross the lake to the furthermost bank. Yet being proud soldiers of Spain who were used to facing impossible odds and prevailing, we stood rooted to the spot in silence, thereby observing our oath to Manglana. A deep groan was issued by Koldo the Basque once the whole of the army had entered what was left of the town.

'They knew how to cross the bog,' he muttered. 'How did they know?'

De Cuéllar scowled at this revelation.

'They still have to cross the water. And they do not come bearing cannon.'

'We did not expect them to bear any,' was my instant reply.

As the large force drew closer to the lake, its troop of mailed riders drew another exclamation from Juande.

'Jesus wept! We have a fight on our hands.'

Tears of awe streaked the fat Galician's cheeks as the formidable army drew nearer, and we could even make out the officers and trumpeters. We were then further distressed to hear the sound of crashing glass from the Abbey of Saint Mel, as the heretics set about destroying an as yet undefiled church of Rome. There followed the great rumble of kettle drums while tents of hide were pitched and fires started using great faggots of wood which had been borne from the forest. If the beating of the drums had not been enough to unsettle us, the sight of the soldiers unpacking long scaling ladders upon the opposite bank had us crushed by foreboding, so that one of the country boys even began to gibber in fright.

'Spaniards besieged by heretics!' wailed Pedro. 'This cannot be happening! What sort of land is this? What is the world coming to when Spaniards are besieged by heretics!'

The irony of his words was not lost upon us, for our experience in the Low Countries was that of us constantly besieging towns occupied by Protestants and other misbelieving curs. Yet although Pedro's lament was understandable, given that he had suffered some torment at the hands of the enemy before finding his way into Dartry, it was a dishonourable and womanly rant. After a few minutes his moaning riled me so much that the back of my hand began to itch, and I was about to serve him with a smack in the mouth when an almighty burp was heard above our heads, so loud that even the drums across the lake stopped beating for a few instants.

To our surprise we looked up to see the figure of Captain de Cuéllar sitting cross-legged atop one of the large wicker baskets, having just issued a belch which must have rattled every bone in his body. With a broad grin he produced a flute from his doublet, and when the sound of the enemy's drums recommenced, he proceeded to blow upon this instrument, issuing a clarion sound which rose above the rumbling before us, the high notes of a spirited tune playfully and mockingly using the drums as accompaniment. After a couple of songs were played, the captain paused to take a swig from the wineskin which hung from his shoulder, and the drums instantly crashed with renewed vigour in an attempt to drown him out.

When he had drunk his fill, de Cuéllar wiped his mouth with the back of his hand, then snatched up his flute again and issued a tune which skipped and soared through the heavy beats across the water. With the exception of Old Tom, we sang along to the music produced by the captain's pipe, for the tune he played was an old anthem which accompanied fresh faced recruits on the march, as they travelled the well-trodden Spanish road into the living horror of the war in Flanders. At the end of our chant Old Tom once more resumed his war cry, causing us to laugh aloud as the captain proceeded to play other tunes with his seemingly bottomless lungs.

Loud cheers followed once again, and we were hurling a stream of insults at the Sassanas when my sniper's eye caught sight of a half dozen archers along the bank of the lake, aiming their bolts at de Cuéllar who still issued shrill blasts on his flute.

'Get down, Captain!' I cried, and almost instantly Valdo the Catalan threw himself at the gabion with an agility that belied his middle-aged appearance, with a leap which almost toppled the captain over the wall. Yet before de Cuéllar could plunge towards the ground, the back of his jerkin was clasped by his kinsman who hauled him back towards us. It was not a moment too soon, for in that very instant the captain's wickerwork seat was struck by a half dozen arrows, and I cowered fearfully as a shaft fizzed towards me and bounced off the ground between my feet.

'Down!' cried Valdo, still clutching the captain. 'Get down!'

We followed his lead and quickly crawled towards the roof wall. Other shafts whistled over our heads as we watched the Catalan's futile attempts to wake de Cuéllar. The captain appeared to have passed out after his narrow escape, and his mouth was wide open with his empty wineskin still dangling from his shoulder. Valdo eventually resorted to slapping him a couple of times in the mouth, yet this only produced a feeble groan from our leader. After releasing yet another volley, the enemy appeared appeased, so that no more arrows were released amidst the beating of drums. When I peered over the battlements, I could see that the archers had returned to their camp.

With some effort we rolled de Cuéllar onto his brat mantle, lifted him off the ground and hurried towards the stairs which led back down to the chieftain's hall. Once inside the keep, we relieved ourselves of our slumbering load, hurling him upon a bed of rushes. Having thus disposed of the captain, we gathered about in a circle to discuss strategy. We had not yet laid any plans, since the captain had always put off discussing them, with continual assurances and guarantees as to our safety. Old Tom, however, was quick to serve us with advice in the captain's absence, and he regarded us with a deathlike severity.

'We must assign a strict watch and learn the sounds of the keep. You should recognise them with your eyes closed. The slightest scrape or scuttle might mean the difference between life and death. Rosclogher Tower must become known to you

- XXIX -

more intimately than your dearest lover, and we must care for it more dearly than our own mother.'

A couple of Spaniards frowned uneasily at his words, as they traded knowing glances. This did not go unnoticed by Geraldine, who instantly qualified his last instruction.

'As for those motherless whoresons amongst you, you should love this keep as if it were yourselves.'

Although bereft of any practical details, the advice was a clear reminder of our stark predicament. Valdo the Catalan was swift to start dispensing orders, and we duly accepted them, given that he was the eldest in our group, and the only member of de Cuéllar's fellowship to command any respect amongst the rest of us. A watch was devised whereby all the windows in the upper two floors of the keep would be guarded, with the remaining four of our number left to rest until they were summoned to take over. Short straws were drawn, and as the names of the first watchers were announced by Valdo, the country boy Franco, whose eyes had strayed to an oylet, let out a shrill cry.

Upon hearing this we gathered about the slit window, and stared in dismay towards the town. A score of our enemies had gathered along the banks of the lake and proceeded to remove rocks from beneath the water. As piles of them grew upon the grass, the small skiffs which Manglana's knaves had sunk, prior to the chieftain abandoning the village, floated to the surface. Fat Juande cursed as the recovered ferries were dragged onto land.

'Do the bastards know everything?'

Pedro, the other country boy shuddered.

'Let us hope they have learnt nothing of which we are ignorant.'

We stared at the Sassanas with growing unease as they set about repairing the holes in their newly acquired craft. After some time, Dal Verme, who had drifted away from us to sit against a wall and recite his prayers, rose to his feet.

'These concerns are futile,' declared the Milanese nobleman in a haughty voice, 'for a few skiffs shall make no difference to our safety. Yet the air is now rank with your petty fears, and I shall not join in your womanly shivering while there is still life left within me.'

So saying, he headed for the chieftain's hall, although none took any notice of the Milanese adventurer's departure since the activity in the enemy camp was far more engaging. I noticed to my further distress that a few of the tents on the periphery had a tankard or a flag hung outside them, which was immediately recognisable as the mark of a sutler. I should not have been surprised, for no army travelled without a tail made up of a throng of hangers-on selling provisions to the troops.

Yet the sight of victuallers and merchants was enough to further dash any hope I had held onto until then that the force might dwindle after finding the town razed to the ground. It was clear that the Sassenachs intended to remain until our keep was taken and that the enemy did not intend to sit idly by and let us toast our feet by the fire and feast on the chieftain's stocks.

I could not help but worry about whether the viceroy had learned of the emerald ring, but another cry from Franco returned my attentions to the opposite bank where a handful of enemies could be seen knee-deep in the water, dragging one of the ferries in behind them. As it floated alongside them, they seized it by the waist and wobbled it a few times to ensure that it was worthy of being boarded. Having completed this

- XXIX -

exercise, they flung themselves into the vessel and took up their paddles, making towards us with swift intent. When this bold party of rowers was hardly halfway across the water, I snatched my rifle and shoved my way through the other defenders, who were gathered around the slit window.

As the rifle's muzzle was passed through the narrow aperture, my eye was trained upon the hat of the group's leader, who stood with one leg raised upon the prow of the ferry with the air of some great conqueror who had dared to go where others had not. As the boat drew nearer, I could see that the man's hat was possessed of some fine large feathers, possibly belonging to a grouse, and his doublet and hose and the thin rapier upon his hip revealed him to be someone of rank. The usual whisper immediately left my lips as my forefinger caressed the serpentine of the wheel-lock and I crouched slightly forward to take better aim at my mark:

> *'This day will the Lord deliver thee into mine hand;*
> *and I will smite thee,*
> *and take thy head from thee.*
> *The Lord saveth not with sword and spear;*
> *for the battle is the Lord's,*
> *and he will give you into our hands'*

As I squeezed the trigger, the fluttering plumage on the fine sailor's hat was instantly ripped to shreds. The cry from his men brought a grin to my face, followed by a cheer from my party, who had been peering over my shoulders.

'Excellent shot, my son!' shouted Valdo with a heavy slap on my back, which was repeated a dozen times by the other Spaniards.

'What is all this hubbub!' yelled someone behind us, and we grinned like devils as we turned to see Dal Verme descending the steps towards us. He glared at us contemptuously, and his black hair fluttered about his tunic whilst he raised a skin of water towards his lips. We ignored him again and returned our attentions to the boat, our chuckles turning to peals of mocking laughter as the small skiff was seen turning about swiftly and heading back in the direction of the town.

'That will teach them!' crowed Pedro. 'They expected to walk into the keep with only the water to stop them!'

'They will be back,' whispered Geraldine from the shadows, a statement which had Valdo turn towards him with a stern look.

'And what of it old man?' said the Catalan. 'Their every advance shall meet with setback'.

'I trust your valour as much as I value your comrade's aim,' replied Old Tom, with a nod in my direction, 'yet it is clear that they knew that we might be here; otherwise they would have sailed with more boats instead of sending a single one to make their discoveries.'

'And pray do tell us, O worthy Irishman,' retorted Valdo hotly, 'what discovery have our enemies made?'

'They know that a marksman of great skill does indeed defend this keep. Which in turn means that it is not unguarded and that we have not fled, as may have been expected from men of less devotion.'

'And how will they profit from such knowledge?' demanded Valdo.

'For one, they will know that their spies' reports are true,' replied Geraldine, 'and they will plan accordingly. After all, every marksman needs sleep, almost as much as he requires powder.'

His observation quickly wiped the smiles off our faces and a sickening gurgle was heard behind us, instantly followed by rasping breaths.

'Verme!' cried Franco.

We spun about in alarm to find the Milanese nobleman upon his knees, holding his throat as his face turned a hue of the palest white. Old Tom was first to react as he ran over to Dal Verme with a swiftness which belied his years, seizing up the bulging water skin which had fallen from the stricken adventurer's hand.

'Poison,' he growled, before seizing Dal Verme by the hair and pulling his head back. The Anglo-Norman next shoved his fingers down the Milanese's throat, then skipped away as a spurt of vomit burst from the Italian's mouth. There soon followed a rotten stench as the proud mercenary soiled himself in his angst. Dal Verme next collapsed onto the ground in a heap, holding his stomach. Geraldine beckoned to the two country boys to help him drag the adventurer to a corner of the great hall where he was covered with blankets.

Meanwhile the remainder of us beheld one another in horror, for it was obvious to all but the greatest dunce that our haughty companion had slaked his thirst with water from the great cistern on the roof. It was our chief source of drink, so that it was immediately obvious that our supplies were far less than first estimated. Memories of the swollen tongues of thirsting Spanish troops stationed in North Africa quickly sprung to mind, and in that moment I gave myself up to despair. After a few moments of stunned silence, Koldo the Basque asked the question on all of our minds.

'Was it arsenic? Or laudanum?'

'What does it matter?' spat Enano. 'Where we had little hope before, we now have none!'

Fat Juande held his face in his hands.

'How can we hold to an oath when the tribesmen themselves have betrayed us?'

'The tribe never betrayed us,' cut in Valdo, 'yet there is obviously a traitor among their number.'

'And a high-ranking one too,' I said, 'one with access to enough poison to foul a cistern.'

As I said this, I could not help thinking of Lady Dervila and her secret apothecary, although I could not see why she would have done such a thing.

'We must flee while we still can,' rasped Koldo.

'And lose our honour?' protested Valdo.

'Of what use is our oath to us if we do not have water?' replied the Basque, his face twisted in a fierce sneer.

The Catalan was silent until Juande spoke up.

'I saw the water borne into the keep from the lake not a day before Manglana left us. Someone in his party must have fouled it before they rode off.'

'Or afterwards,' hissed Enano, as his eyes widened in shock.

'A-afterwards?' stammered Valdo in horror, clearly overwhelmed by the assertion. 'But w-who would have dared?'

Of course, the innocence of we Spaniards was not doubted, which made for a particularly frosty mood when Old Tom reappeared with Pedro and Franco at his back. Upon noticing

- XXIX -

the scowls in his direction, the Anglo-Norman stood still and rested his hands on his sword belt.

'What is amiss?'

'You!' snarled Koldo, stepping before his peers and pointing an accusatory finger at Geraldine. 'You have been up to much mischief upon joining our number.'

Geraldine's eyes narrowed as he regarded the approaching Basque.

'What in God's name do you speak of, man?'

'The water upon the roof!' cried Enano, as he whipped out his dagger. 'Now we know why you were so desperate to join in our plight! You would have us perish one after the other whilst the enemy waits outside.'

'I see,' replied the Anglo-Norman, and a ring of steel was heard as he drew his sword, then raised it above his head. 'This nonsense has gone far enough.'

'Come now,' I called to the two Spaniards. 'Be reasonable. He has fought the enemy for years.'

'Tell that to our comrade who lies in his own vomit, Hospitalarios!' spat the Basque, who also drew his blade and circled Geraldine.

'Stay your hand, friend Spaniard,' roared Geraldine, 'or I shall have to resort to severe means!'

At the sight of Old Tom's two-handed sword, both of de Cuéllar's cronies hesitated, and the aged Anglo-Norman observed them scornfully.

''Tis indeed a poor pair of fools who see a foe where there stands only a friend! If I wanted you dead, I would have slit your throats after you passed out from drinking too much wine!'

The truth of his words was impossible to ignore, so that the two Spaniards saw reason and grudgingly backed off as Old Tom returned his sword to its sheath.

'And now that that nonsense is sorted,' he said, 'let us hasten to the roof!'

Geraldine's voice was possessed of such authority that our argument was instantly forgotten and we took up his lead. As we hurried up the steps I was suddenly curious about the plight of the Milanese mercenary and called out to Franco.

'What of Dal Verme? Is he still alive?'

'Yes, for the time being,' replied the country boy. 'The Irish madman thinks that the spewing might yet save him, but whether he lives or perishes is in the hands of the Lord.'

'That is all we needed,' muttered Pedro at his brother's side, 'to lose another defender. Now our watches will have to be even longer.'

I felt a twinge of sorrow at the fate of Dal Verme, for although the Milanese defender was haughty, he was also possessed of a great sense of honour. He had never partaken in any of the vileness carried out by de Cuéllar's band. It was for this reason that they had always spurned him, for apart from not being Spanish he had never tolerated their excesses and was quick to denounce them by speaking his mind openly. We had also lost a capable swordsman of great valour, descended from a family with a famous military tradition. I whispered a prayer for him beneath my breath, that he might somehow manage a swift recovery.

When we had climbed the steps, Geraldine pointed to the grey heavens above us.

- XXIX -

'Tonight it shall rain, or I am a stranger to this land,' he growled. 'We must return downstairs to find every single vessel we can find, from the slightest thimble to the largest chest, and bring them up to the roof. If we cannot rely on our main water supply, then we must look to the heavens for refreshment. We must henceforth ration our provisions with the greatest of care, and discard those skins which you filled from the cistern.'

As we rushed back down the steps to follow his instructions, I was hauled backwards by Geraldine who seized me from the shoulder.

'Keep watch up here,' he said, 'for the enemy might yet despatch another skiff, which will be followed by others should its progress not be impeded.'

When he was gone, I was left alone with only the beating of distant kettle drums for company. I unslung the rifle from my shoulder and walked to the southern side of the roof, still amazed by the large number of tents which had been pitched outside the defiled abbey and across the green. Men scurried about their new quarters as if they were ants bustling around the crushed body of a larger insect. I then engaged in the most inexplicable of actions, as almost by instinct I reached for the lowest bandolier upon my belt. The emerald ring dropped out of it into my right palm, and in a quiet act of defiance I held the stone above my head.

'You'll never get your hands on it,' I whispered defiantly, 'whatever you put me through. I will do all in my power to prevent it.'

I dived behind a gabion upon hearing a swishing sound, and as other arrows struck the battlements, I dropped the ring back in the ampoule. It was not long before Geraldine reappeared at the top of the staircase with the other Spaniards behind him, bearing all manner of iron trunks and pails and pans and any other item they could use to capture rainwater. No sooner were these things laid out across the roof, than Geraldine ordered the Canarians to keep watch in turn with me, so that one of us gained rest while his fellows watched all sides of the crannog.

Another three of the Spaniards were tasked with patrolling the slit windows on upper floors, in the unlikely event that the watchers on the roof missed any of the enemy's movements. It was evident from our small number that the days ahead would be gruelling, with each of us sleeping for four hours before being roused to partake of an eight-hour watch. On the first day all went well, with guards being posted at the windows and relieved in timely fashion by those who slumbered while not on duty.

On the first night of my watch, I shuddered from both cold and fear whilst across the water scores of fires were lit, which resembled hundreds of glinting embers in the darkness. The meaning of the sight was not lost upon my companions, so that the following day they were all sticking to Geraldine's proposed course of action.

On the second day Captain de Cuéllar rose from his drunken stupor, making his presence felt during my hours of rest. I awoke with a start and found him shouting at the two Canarian boys on the roof.

'What is this mess up here!' he bawled, kicking over a pail of precious rainwater. 'Clear a path for me or I'll have you strung from the gallows!'

The captain was hardly the picture of authority, for his hair looked like a windswept haystack, and his eyes were as bleary as

- XXIX -

those of a bear roused from its hibernation. It took the protests of all three of us to stop him from helping himself to the cistern, and such a row was kicked up that I dreaded to think what the Sassenachs across the water would have made of it.

Eventually the captain's shouting brought his cronies running to the roof with their blades drawn, but Valdo had enough sense to see what the tussle was all about. At his order his three fellows returned their swords to their sheaths. I drew a huge sigh of relief, for the sight of Juande, Koldo and Enano flashing gritted teeth and drawn steel would have tested the mettle of most. Thereafter the senior Catalan explained to de Cuéllar that the cistern had been fouled before offering him his own skin of water which had been drawn from the lake.

The captain helped himself to a swig and returned downstairs. He was still complaining about the untidy state of the roof, his four fellows following him like hounds. Geraldine later told me that following his descent into the keep, the captain had been less than grateful to the Anglo-Norman for organising the watch, while also being openly disdainful of the preparations which had been made.

'What about morale?' he had yelled at the baffled Anglo-Norman. 'Have you thought of that?!'

'I would have regarded our safety as being crucial to our morale' was Geraldine's terse reply.

'Nonsense, man!' yelled the captain. 'What does having the men move from window to window like lost ghosts have to do with our protection? We have watchers on the roof who will raise the alarm at the first sight of the enemy upon the lake! There are many long and dreary days ahead of us, so what we need is wine and song! Not to mention women!'

'No women were allowed to remain in the keep!' retorted Old Tom.

Yet in vain did he protest, for the captain instantly despatched his four cronies to fetch enough firewood to get Rosclogher's hearth raging, while ordering Geraldine to move the stricken Dal Verme to a lower floor to reduce the sound of the Milanese's moaning. A cask of usquebaugh was broken and a pig set on a spit, before de Cuéllar crowned the festivities by ordering his men to fetch a wooden trunk from the quarters where they had piled their belongings. When the trunk was brought in and opened, the captain shocked Geraldine by helping mad Orla out of it. She shook with laughter as the men sat her down alongside them.

The captain's fellowship next proceeded to indulge in their excess like a handful of pigs, which caused a disgusted Old Tom to swiftly remove himself from their presence and head to the roof to share his unfortunate tidings. We were much dismayed by the Spaniards' behaviour and left with no option but to wake one of the Canarians and send him downstairs to help poor Geraldine keep a watch from the windows and to attend to our poisoned Italian comrade.

In truth de Cuéllar's attempts to boost morale did little to foster any great bond amongst us defenders, for he had clearly mistaken the manning of a besieged fort with being at sea all over again, leaving any alert of the enemy's approach to the lookout in the crow's nest. The lookout duty was shared by me and the country boy Franco. Although I was glad not to depend on the members of de Cuéllar's fellowship for my own protection, I was exhausted by the long periods of guarding the rooftop. Eventually Geraldine had another stern word with the captain, finally prevailing upon him through the intervention of Valdo to dedicate his cronies to the defence of the keep.

The involvement of another four men allowed me longer periods of rest, which would have been still longer had the captain partaken of the collective effort. Yet de Cuéllar held partaking of guard duty to be below him, and he retired to the chieftain's hall like a sea captain tucking himself away in his cabin, leaving us with nothing but the giddy cries and screams of mad Orla. On occasion he would resurface with a sly grin on his face, which was so broad that one would have thought he had just bedded Helen of Troy. He would next proceed to urge men carrying out guard duty to join him in his drinking and gaming.

I pitied the poor, toothless crone whom he kept locked away in the chieftain's hall, who was bereft of her wits as she was forced to meet the captain's every whim. At times I thought of her daughters in the mountains and wondered if they were worried sick, trying to understand what had become of their wretched and beleaguered mother. This was not to mention that the captain's own ruthlessness had left me cold, although he was a naval man and therefore used to cavorting with every port-town creature which passed for a woman.

In truth I felt that being under siege was like being at sea all over again, with the captain and his close circle of cronies being increasingly despised by those who did every task under the sun to maintain the ship. All of which led to a growing rift between the two factions of defenders, with the captain and his fellowship of four doing whatever they pleased about the keep, and the remainder of us missing out on countless hours of slumber to maintain our vigilance, lest the enemy attempt to scale the walls and pass through the windows.

On the sixth day Luigi Dal Verme returned to his feet, and ignoring Geraldine's insistence that he obtain more rest, the Milanese nobleman insisted that he partake in guard duties. Despite his odd nature and eccentricities, it was heartening to see him strutting through the floors of the keep like an indomitable rooster, his chin raised high above a puffed-out chest. The defiant way in which he held his hand on his sword was reminiscent of the proudest knight, although he only wore a stained tunic about his torso instead of armour.

His return raised our spirits no end. Yet as the empty days rolled on, our greatest enemy became laxity. A mutinous sentiment developed among those who held true to the cause, with the sleep deprivation caused by our comrades' idleness only making matters worse. One night, I descended cold and rigid from the rooftops, to find that Koldo the Basque had abandoned his post at the window in the women's quarters. In a blind rage I stormed into the chieftain's hall to find the rascal making merry with the rest of de Cuéllar's fellowship, who regarded me with such contempt that one would have thought I had interrupted them during their prayers.

'Hospitalarios!' boomed the captain cheerily. 'Join us for a drop of fine vintage!'

The sight of him sitting alongside a warm fire with his hand curled about mad Orla's breast nettled me no end, his invitation only adding stinging salt to the wound. I unslung my rifle from my shoulder and aimed it at his head, all the while swearing aloud and letting him know where he could put his fine vintage. His companions instantly drew their steels, yet the captain waved at us as nonchalantly as if we were but summer flies in Madrid, and laughed away my concerns.

'We are beyond harm within these walls Hospitalarios! You must stop fretting for nothing!'

Matters hardly improved in the days which followed, and this nearly cost us dear. When not eating or sleeping, de Cuéllar would draw men away from their posts to play games. On rare occasions he could be found slouching by a loop window as if it were a ship's gunport, taking swigs of drink from a skin and taking wild pot-shots with his rifle at the enemy across the water. Yet for the most part he treated our situation with an approach verging on disdain, which left me to take my guard duty on the roof with the greatest seriousness. At all times I feared that our lookouts on upper floors were not at their posts, which might allow our enemy a quick entry through one of the higher, wider windows.

On Thursday my shift ended at the first glow of dawn and I shuffled wearily down the steps to the chieftain's hall to wake one of the Canarians who was to relieve me. Yet I had hardly crumpled to the ground before I heard a cry issued from the boy Pedro who had risen from his blankets and made his way to the staircase to the roof. With a curse, Old Tom kicked off his mantle and rose to his feet, and we beheld one another fearfully before darting towards the direction of the cry.

To our horror we saw the young Canarian valiantly hacking away at an intruder upon the bloodstained steps as he held his wounded midriff. We had appeared none too soon, for poor Pedro fell to his knees before the heretic who had managed to somehow find his way onto the roof. As the Sassana turned towards us I shot him through the neck, and Geraldine howled behind me as we drew our swords and set upon the other three enemies upon the steps.

'To arms! To arms!'

The Anglo-Norman then turned tail and ran off just as we had cut our way to the rooftop, where I found myself surrounded by over a score of the dripping rats bearing knives and swords. My blade was knocked from my hand as I fell to my knees beneath a flurry of blows to my head and body. When I rolled onto my back the sole of a boot fell upon my throat, and I looked up in terror as I made out the grin of Treasach Burke in the wan sunlight.

His men drew away from me at the sergeant's low whisper, and the renegade rested his forearm upon his raised knee as he leant closer towards me. I shuddered as drops of water fell from his hair onto my face, and he was so close that I could even smell barley when he spoke again amid his heavy pants for breath.

'We meet again, my rabbit. Now hand me the bauble, and I swear I'll end you quick.'

As I hesitated to reply, he whipped out a dagger from his belt and pricked my throat with its point. It was all the convincing I needed, so that I reached for one of the ampoules on my bandolier. No sooner did he notice this than his hand fell onto my shoulder and he attempted to pull the leather belt over my head. A muffled cry was heard from behind him when he did this, which was followed by a loud shot. Burke released his grip as a low groan was heard from one of his men, and he lifted his boot from my throat as he turned to find out what had happened.

It had been an unforeseen slice of fortune on my part which led to this disturbance. For after silently crossing the lake in the dark and scaling the wall of the keep with a light ladder, the English had failed to pull it after them onto the roof. How the enemy had managed to carry it across the water was beyond my reckoning, although more obscure methods had been devised to break into a fortress, as we Spaniards knew only too well.

Yet Geraldine had instantly suspected the method of entry, so that after leaving my side he had swiftly gathered every Spaniard who would follow him. He next led them towards an unguarded window where they clutched at the rungs just outside it. The worthy Anglo-Norman later told me that Franco had been quick up behind him, being keen to avenge the wound suffered by his brother; as was Luigi Dal Verme who was so keen to exact some form of revenge upon an enemy which had almost poisoned him to death.

After climbing over the battlements, the three of them had engaged in a vicious attack on the enemy. Old Tom's advantage of surprise was soon quelled by the enemy, who were at least a score in number, yet another surprise lay in store, since we were soon joined by Captain de Cuéllar and the remaining defenders. After days of idleness, the Spaniards confronted the intrusion with relish, hurling themselves almost joyfully into a fight with men outside of their own number.

The enemy's advantage was quickly addressed the moment Valdo the Catalan hurled himself over the crenellations, followed closely by the deadly duo of Koldo and Enano, with fat Juande bringing up the rear. They were true veterans of Flanders and seasoned in the business of slaughter, so that they proceeded to unleash a typical Spanish fury upon an enemy which wilted like a tree before an unexpected burst of holy flame. For although we were the crudest pigs who served

God and renowned for our arrogance and cruelty, the brazen courage displayed by Spaniards in the face of certain death was matched by none, except perhaps for the infidel Turks.

Which in turn meant that the Sassanas never had a hope of repelling us, given that most of the English who served in Ireland instead of the Continent were wretched material to begin with, being mostly pressed men and gaolbirds who often fell sick or deserted the army. Their resistance was also foiled by a lack of the armour which they had abandoned in order to cross the water; this made our numeric inferiority a formality as we threw ourselves into the fray with a bloodthirsty Anglo-Norman.

Meanwhile, I had flown off the ground and hurled myself upon the surprised Treasach Burke who tried to wound me with a dagger thrust. I jerked my chest away from his swing and struck his crotch with one knee causing him to sag sideways with a loud gasp. Yet just when I thought I had bettered him, he snatched the eighth ampoule on my bandolier and sought to pluck it off. I struggled desperately to wrest it free of his grip as more of his men were slain about him.

He soon desisted from his attempt to take the powder charge, perhaps alarmed by the sight of his remaining men being cut down. Realising that further delay might cost him his life, Burke hurled me away and tore through Geraldine and Enano. Koldo was already hot on the renegade's heels as he ran towards the roof's southern edge. Displaying the agility of a ship's cat, he hurled himself off the battlements towards the highest rung of the ladder, flinging himself over with it towards the ground. When he was halfway towards the grass below, he pounced off

- XXIX -

the higher rungs towards the water and disappeared beneath it, having missed the edge of the crannog by the length of a pike.

Burke's astonishing show of nerve unsettled us in that it seemed almost otherworldly, so that we hesitated to seize up our muskets and bows and attempt to wound him. His wits had not been dulled by his fall, for as soon as he hit the water he pulled the ladder behind him, using it as a float as he kicked his way towards the bank of land. He was still mindful of my marksmanship when he reached the site of the former jetty, so that he scampered off in the direction of the green, as my rifle shots struck the grass about his feet.

'Holy host!' I cursed in my frustration, dismayed to have missed so repulsive a target.

Yet my disappointment was interrupted by heavy panting at my shoulder, and I turned to find Geraldine staring at me in amazement.

'Thank God you are still alive! But how?'

I shrugged.

'Yours was a timely reappearance, Old Tom.'

The Anglo-Norman shook his head in disbelief, as he bent over to wipe his sword blade upon the doublet of a dead Sassana.

'We have drawn first blood,' he said.

The other defenders about us regained their breath, before proceeding to search the bodies of the slain. It did not take long for my old soldier's habits to reveal themselves, and I fell to my knees and rubbed elbows with them.

'Leave something for me, you filchers!'

In my haste to search the dead, I had not noticed that there were enough pickings to serve all our party. By the end of our exertions, we had taken enough clothing to dress us twice over. Our enemies' canvas doublets and breeches were hastily traded for the yellow lice-infested tunics which had been granted to us by the Dartrymen. We gladly also wore the shirts and kersey stockings which were stripped off our foes. It led the blood-spattered Enano to make a wry observation, which drew a pained frown from Geraldine.

'Civilised attire at last! Even the heretics are better dressed than Manglana's savages!'

'Time for some decent apparel!' cried de Cuéllar gleefully as he secured cloth breeches about his waist, hauled woollen stockings up to his knee and slipped on a pair of oxhide shoes.

He was soon wearing a canvas doublet and cassock like the rest of our band, and although the clothes were still damp from the lake water, a certain renewed vigour was felt at wearing clothes which were familiar to us. I particularly delighted in snatching a wide-brimmed hat off the ground and pulled it low over my nose. Somehow the act of donning it felt like a reunion with a long-lost friend and returned to mind the clothing I wore in Seville prior to my capture by Ramos. When we were finished, Geraldine regarded us with open scorn on his face, seemingly bothered that we had taken so quickly to the clothing of the dead heretics while so readily abandoning our Gaelic clothing.

'What shall we do with them?' asked Koldo the Basque, gesturing towards the pale, dead bodies which lay stripped upon the ground.

'Why, we shall dispose of them according to the land's customs!' exclaimed the Anglo-Norman, a purposeful expression

- XXIX -

suddenly appearing upon his torn face as he drew his large sword from its scabbard.

He next proceeded to raise the blade and sever a head from a corpse, then held it up like a trophy. The barbaric sight of the shorn head almost made me retch, but Geraldine proceeded to wordlessly cut off all the corpses' heads, before calling to the country boy to fetch him a few lengths of twine. Old Tom used the cord to splay his score of severed heads upon the crenellations along the rooftop.

It was a sight which could not have gone unnoticed across the water, and Geraldine next asked a few willing Spaniards to help him roll the mauled bodies onto a blanket, to toss them over the battlements towards the lake. A loud cheer of 'for Saint James!' was heard whenever one of the corpses hit the water with a loud splash, and before long the ominous drums were heard rumbling across the water as a warning of what lay in store for us, despite our fleeting moments of triumph.

Our water vessels were turned back upright, our spirits were further raised when our new clothes were smoked over a peat fire which we lit on the roof, which rendered them almost completely free of lice. In the days that followed I spent long hours alone in the company of the low flames, grateful to be spared of constant itching as well as the confusion that reigned in the floors below me. For de Cuéllar continued to disrupt our tactics, so that it was soon obvious that entrusting a naval officer to the guard of a tower house was about as useful as assigning the command of a fleet to a cavalry captain.

It was during times like these that I fell back on my years of experience spent serving a useless highborn officer who led from the back. Yet a mutinous sentiment soon began to develop among the Canarians and Dal Verme, with Old Tom himself unwittingly fanning the flames of their resentment with certain remarks that exposed the captain's ineptitude. I did all I could, whenever possible, to ensure that a certain harmony was somehow maintained between the defenders, yet de Cuéllar's behaviour did little to help my cause, and I also lost my patience at times.

On the following Sunday, loud cries stirred me from my post, and I raised my head to see the captain and fat Juande poking their heads through a window beneath the rotting skulls along the crenellations. Loud cries were heard from below them, and I tiptoed unnoticed to the corner of the roof to see three Sassanas at the door who called out for mercy in high pitched pleas.

'Let us in, we beg of ye! The viceroy wants us dead!'

My rifle was already primed when de Cuéllar could be heard whispering beneath his breath.

'The poor whoresons, perhaps we should let them inside.'

Juande nodded keenly at de Cuéllar as his cheeks shimmered with fat from the chicken leg he still held in his hand.

'But we must make haste, Captain, before that bastard Hospitalarios finds out. You know how seriously he takes our vow to the savages!'

The blood seethed in my veins when I heard his words, and before they could speak again, I aimed my rifle at the men below and jerked back the hair trigger. One of the men shrieked an imprecation in English when the leaden ball struck his foot, while one of his fellows drew a musket from under his cloak and discharged a shot. No sooner did this happen than all three enemies were shielded by a cloud of thick, white smoke, and when it cleared all that was left of them was a trail of blood which led down to the lake. After checking the tower's surrounds, I swiftly ran downstairs to find de Cuéllar upon his back and the fat fool Juande crying out in distress.

'The captain's wounded! Woe is me! The captain's been wounded!'

I shoved the fat Galician aside, yet his cries only brought more of the Spaniards to join our number. When I turned de Cuéllar around, his face was white as he held his shoulder in a bloodied hand.

'Will I live?' he whispered.

I snorted aloud as I rose to my feet.

'It is but a graze.'

'The Lord be praised!' cried fat Juande. 'But can it be true?!'

'You deserve a reward, Hospitalarios,' declared the captain as he rose to his knees, 'for revealing the true allegiance of those treacherous imposters! Tell me what it is that you desire, for I shall accord you anything that I can provide.'

With a sigh I made to return to the battlements, then suddenly decided that it was best not to ignore the captain in front of his men.

'Bear me some wood from the hall below,' I finally replied, 'that I may have some warmth during my watch.'

De Cuéllar regarded me suspiciously.

'Is that all? Are you sure? I can fetch the harlot if it is warmth that you seek.'

I restrained a shiver at the thought of mad Orla while doing my best to appear serious.

'Thank you for the offer, Captain. Yet the wood shall suffice.'

As de Cuéllar disappeared down the steps with his fellowship, I wondered how much longer our defence would hold out. The hours in which to consider this were as long as they were cold, until I was at last relieved by Franco. I made my way down to the great hall, where I obtained the wood which had never appeared. With a weary sigh I carried it up to the roof, for the benefit of a fellow sufferer who was still true to our cause.

XXX

ROSCLOGHER, DARTRY, COUNTY LEITRIM

24 November - 1 December 1588

After our two narrow escapes, the days which followed were bleak and drear. It was not long before the captain and his cronies reverted to the trappings of slovenly indiscipline once more. Yet as galling as the antics of their roguish fellowship were to the rest of us, the keep still had to be defended from a dogged and determined enemy. My close encounter with Treasach Burke had left me in little doubt as to the motives behind the siege, which filled me with a piercing guilt and greater commitment to our cause.

Yet a guard duty that tested ten men was even harder to maintain among five. I often found myself nodding off to sleep, only to wake up minutes later in a state of fear that the enemy might have slipped across the lake unnoticed. To my great fortune this never occurred, although this fact did little to relieve my concern as to the desperate plight in which we found ourselves. At midday, the tireless Geraldine would often appear to provide me with both food and companionship, sometimes also carrying an old chessboard he had found in a trunk downstairs in order to alleviate the hours of boredom.

We spent hours sitting cross-legged alongside the battlements, chewing on strips of cowflesh, with our attentions divided between our surrounds and the pieces we moved along with snatches of conversation. During this time which we spent together, Geraldine proved to be a mine of information about Ireland; he was always keen to answer my questions about the Gaelic tongue, and to instruct me in certain phrases and expressions. In this way I quickly learned to be more conversant in it, to the point that Geraldine was impressed by how many words I could remember from one day to the next.

I often asked myself whether the wily Anglo-Norman suspected my true motives for wanting to learn so much about the land and culture in which I found myself, for beyond a pure academic interest, I had long surmised that if by any miracle we survived the mess in which we found ourselves, I might one day avail myself of all the knowledge I had gleaned about my surrounds, to perhaps make a successful escape back to Spain.

For much as I found myself respected and honoured among the Irish tribesmen, I knew that it could only be a matter of time before the prize which I bore became known to them. It was a distressing thought, for I knew that they would not take kindly to me endangering their livelihood by harbouring so valuable a bauble. It was also not lost upon me that the Sassanas would stop at nothing to recover it, and that the large army camped across the water could not have appeared solely at the order of Treasach Bourke.

- XXX -

Yet Old Tom never once questioned my motives, though he proved as keen of sight as he was masterful at our game. Sometimes I wondered what challenge he found in pitting his wits against mine, although he was probably starved of adequate conversation amongst the other Spaniards who mostly regarded him with suspicion. Geraldine was certainly never dull, and he was also possessed of manners inherited from a noble household, having been educated for a highborn lifestyle that the cruelty of fate had snatched away from him.

I saw in him an elderly mirror of myself, a vagrant equipped with education and knowledge, yet forced to wander all over the world to earn his living through any causes he chose to fight for. I wondered whether such a purpose might direct the latter years of my life as I listened reverently to Geraldine. The Anglo-Norman paused to pick up one of the enemy's arrows which had littered the roof in previous days, using its feathered end to scratch his back as he peered at the chessboard.

'You appear to be under siege again, friend Juan.'

A lean smile grew across my lips as he proceeded to tear off the scroll which was bound about the length of the haft.

'Listen to this one!' he chortled, unfurling the parchment and holding it out before his face, 'Spain and home awaits thee if ye but surrender.'

We laughed aloud at the lie which was promised to us by the heretics across the water, for most of the arrows possessed similar messages and false promises, all intended to weaken our resolve and cause the abandonment of our defence. Some arrows even bore threats and demands for our surrender, accompanied by depictions of the various forms of torture that would be used on us if we did not lay down our arms. With a snort Old Tom got to his feet and made his way to the wooden pail we used as a chamber pot, with the scrap of vellum still clutched tightly in his hand.

'Will they ever give it up?' I sighed, concentrating on my rook, which was trapped betwixt one of Geraldine's knights and bishops; one of my last, fast-dwindling pieces. Old Tom had revealed himself to be a master of the game, for he still had twice the figures with which to assault my remaining three. As he sat but a few feet away from me, I could make out the crafty grin across his face as he squatted over the pail to relieve himself.

'There is no shame in honourable surrender, friend marksman.'

'Never!' I cried, then swiftly proceeded to castle my king piece by switching it with the remaining rook.

I next rose to my feet and walked towards the battlements to ensure that no enemy had approached our fortress. By this time the heads upon the crenellations were in an advanced state of decay, and I covered my nose with my sleeve to spare myself the terrible odour of rotting flesh and the bad humours which it exuded. A low tutting was heard as Geraldine hurled the freshly soiled parchment through two gabions. He returned to his feet and pulled up his trews.

'A wise move, friend Juan,' he said, walking back to the board, 'yet you have only delayed the inevitable.'

With that he leaned over and claimed the rook with his second knight, chuckling aloud as he returned to his cross-legged posture upon the ground.

- XXX -

'Let us hope your defence of this castle fares better!' he added, and I winced at his dark humour before also returning to my place at the edge of the board.

It was not long before he defeated me, but not before I had halved his remaining pieces with my queen. Thereafter we played yet another game, during which Geraldine seemed content to engage in further debate.

'Have you ever been under siege before, Spaniard?'

I raised my eyebrows in weary confirmation, before saying the word that I knew would catch him by surprise.

'Yes, in Malta.'

'By my bones!' he marvelled, as his eyes widened in momentary wonder. 'the Ottoman siege of '65?'

'Yes.'

"Zounds! You must have been but a mere lad back then?'

'Yes,' I replied, 'no older than you were when you fought with Silken Thomas. The Turkish onslaughts were terrible and lasted over three months. I aged many years during those dark days.'

'There can be no doubt of that,' said Old Tom, 'given the stories I have heard from survivors. Yet, what glory was won for the cross against the crescent! But alas, my resistance of the heretics has never met with such triumph. After Kildare was slain, Dublin lost over a third of its population. My last siege also met with disaster, for when San Giuseppe and his five hundred Spanish and Italian troops retreated to *Dún an Óir*, I was also among their number.'

'Spanish troops in Ireland?' I asked in bafflement.

'Yes, paid for by His Holiness in Rome. They were sent to Ireland but eight years ago, with orders to aid Desmond during his second rebellion. But alas! George Bingham himself commanded the English cannon, and after a three-day barrage we had no choice but to surrender.'

'How did you live to tell the tale?' I asked, finding myself both amazed and also somewhat suspicious of his account.

'I hid myself inside the keep's privy after the decision to surrender was taken, then slipped past the enemy due to my knowledge of the English tongue which I had been forced to learn as a youth in Dublin. News soon reached me thereafter, however, of how every last Catholic soldier from the Continent was put to the sword by the Sassenachs.'

'Typical barbarity,' I snorted before casting my eye over the defences in the event of any enemy approach.

'One can expect no less from such men,' observed Geraldine while helping himself to another pawn. He then looked carefully over both his shoulders before leaning towards me and speaking in a low voice.

'I have told you that I myself lived for a time in England. I fled there following San Giuseppe's surrender, thinking it the last place the enemy would search for me. I reached it with the aid of a smuggler known to a Catholic ally.'

After telling me how he had outfoxed the Sassanas, he leaned back with a self-satisfied smirk on his face. This was shortly followed by a frown when I advanced my bishop alongside one of my knights, leaving his queen in a position of acute danger. A sly smile soon reappeared on his face, however, when a pawn of his ate one of mine, thereby shielding its sovereign from any further peril and allowing the Anglo-Norman to resume his story.

'I found myself an outlaw, renting a room with a poor widow. It was shocking to behold the way in which their paupers are treated. The woman received no alms and only earned few pennies for spinning the white warp. Yet although she was a Sassana, she had a kind heart and took me in as if I was her long-lost son. It was during this time that I saw what English society had to offer the more destitute among its number, with boys of fourteen years being soundly whipped and burned through the gristle of their ear with a white-hot compass, simply because they were vagrants who could not find labour. No more mercy was afforded to youths of eighteen that were charged twice for being felons, since they were immediately strung up.'

'Be that as it may', I replied with a shrug, casting another glance over the wall, 'the law has always fallen heaviest upon the weak and poor.'

'You speak in haste, friend Juan,' retorted Geraldine, 'for you are evidently unfamiliar with the laws of your hosts.'

I groaned in dismay when he proceeded to take my queen, then stared at him askance.

'The law of the Gaels,' he explained with another smirk, 'is also known as the Brehon law. It reigns over all men in this land, and only affords a penalty of fines. No limb is severed or life taken in its name. Furthermore, the Brehon does dictate that those in higher positions in society should pay higher fines for their transgressions, due to the position of authority they are expected to uphold.'

'Surely you speak in jest?' I replied.

His eyes widened at my reply, and he brought a bunched fist down upon the board, scattering the pieces upon the ground. I beheld this frenzied gesture in shock, partly also because I had just managed to trap his beleaguered queen between a rook and my second bishop. Yet Geraldine ignored the board as he leaned towards me with bared teeth, spittle dripping off the end of his lower lip.

'Do I appear to be jesting at this moment, Spaniard?'

'No,' I replied, as my fingers slid towards the dagger pommel at my waist, 'yet you should calm yourself, for I did not intend to cause offence.'

At my words Geraldine fell silent for a few moments and his chest heaved like a tidal wave as he sought to regather himself. After a while he regained his composure, his face regaining its normal hue.

'Your pardon, Spaniard,' he said at last. 'I am often left feeling incensed by the doubt and scorn poured upon my peoples by aliens of a heretic bent. For too long have Cambrensis, Camden and all those other liars cast an ill repute upon the Gaels, spreading cheap calumnies and petty falsehoods to garner favour in the queen's court in London where ignorance reigns supreme. All too often have I encountered men on my travels who have less regard for my people than they have for a moon-worshipping Caramine.'

I attempted to speak up, at his evident displeasure, to assure him that I held no such poor regard for the Dartrymen. Yet Old Tom raised a finger at me to keep silent.

'No, not a word!' he said angrily. 'I have myself fought in Flanders, and know how the Spanish regard the peoples of Erin. "Irish beggars," your fellows called us while we spilt our blood for your empire. And yet not a single man has been sent by your king to aid us in our struggle, even though you have promised us troops since the days of Silken Thomas.'

'But...' I protested meekly.

- XXX -

'Do not deny it!' continued Geraldine. 'For I know how the captain and his fellows regard us, and I doubt that your sentiments differ greatly. I have seen how readily you have discarded the clothes of your hosts to don the garments of the enemy. Yet if you shelter long enough in this land, Spaniard, you shall see that ours are a people that are true to the laws of God and of nature, unlike these heretical Sassanas that would sell both their people and their own God for a profit!'

The knuckles of his hand whitened as he formed a fist and clenched it tightly.

'Spain does ill to ignore the threat of our common enemy, for England is a kingdom unlike any other, and also has an eye on imperial expansion. Yet I shall not rest until we have thrown every last corrupting slanderer of theirs back into the sea. Their troops have ravaged our land, which once abounded in crops and livestock, enough for us to feed ourselves and fatten our purses from trade with the Continent. They have reduced our princes to paupers, yet we shall prevail for as long as we have our customs and our faith. For true wisdom and strength are best derived from suffering, Spaniard.'

I slowly nodded at him while doing my best to meet his impassioned gaze, then proceeded to pick up the fallen chess pieces. Another game was played in relative silence in the gathering dusk, until one of the Canarians appeared to relieve me from my watch. I staggered after Geraldine as we made our way back down towards the chieftain's hall. It was with great relish that I shared a cup of wine with the Anglo-Norman at the end of our long watch. My weariness was so great that I could almost feel my bones creaking as we retired beneath our mantles, soothed by the fire after so many hours spent buffeted by the wind and soaked by rainfall.

Yet my slumber did not even last halfway until dawn, for loud cries were heard in the night which announced the appearance of a different light. A deep moan of exhaustion left my lips as my eyes slowly opened, only to see Geraldine already back on his feet, snatching his large two-hander from the wall.

'What is it?' I groaned, as I pushed myself upon my knees.

'Fire upon the water!' was his swift reply as he ran off towards the stairs. 'Bring your rifle!'

My fingers were already closing about the Marquardt's stock. I slung it over my shoulder and proceeded to seize my sword as I hurried after Old Tom. The other Spaniards had also been alerted to the besiegers' latest devilry, and a great clink was heard as we made towards one of the loop windows which was guarded by Koldo. The Basque's eyes were wide as he stared at the lake, and as we pushed against him, we could make out the terrible vision of a tall pyre of flame, which slowly made its way across the water towards us.

'The Lord deliver us!' shrieked Juande upon spotting the red-orange glow. 'They have made a pact with Satan to consume us by hellfire! It is like Calais all over again, except that we are now stuck in a fort and cannot set sail!'

'What is all this wailing of women!' roared a voice behind us, which announced the appearance of de Cuéllar, followed by the loud cackle of the actual woman in his keep.

'Mishap and calamity, Captain!' cried Juande. 'For we cannot raise our swords against the very fires of hell!'

- XXX -

De Cuéllar retained his footing as he staggered towards us, which filled me with a faint hope that he might be sober enough to rally us.

'Out of my way!' he bellowed, and to a man we flew from his path as he pushed his face against the loop window and stared out at the water.

After a few instants he slapped the walls before him and pushed himself away from them.

'I cannot see a damned thing through the crack of these buttocks!' he yelled. 'Let us away to the roof!'

We made off up the steps after him, keeping a fearful silence because of the doom which approached us. Upon reaching the battlements we saw Pedro on guard, and the brightness of the approaching craft even allowed us to make out his pale face. Nightfall still lay heavy about us, with the sky a blanket of pitch-black save for the silvery sheen of the moon. The smoke which billowed from the burning structure was as dark as the sky above us, making the approaching fire all the more lurid as it drew closer. We looked on in speechless horror, and just when it seemed like it might strike the crannog that supported our keep, the fiery craft suddenly ground to a halt, filling our noses with the smell of its deathly fumes.

The crackle and hiss of the scorching wood was like the sound of a thousand vipers in our ears. For a few moments we stood in baffled awe before the flames which rose almost as high as our keep, amazed at the ingenuity of the Sassanas to construct a pyre and mount it upon a raft before sending it floating towards us.

'The palisade!' cheered Juande, clapping his hands together. 'Its stakes have barred the raft from smoking us out!'

'Fools!' coughed de Cuéllar, waving the smoke from before his face. 'They took our defences too lightly!'

I stared on in silence, wondering why so much effort had gone into preparing the floating pyre, by an enemy who had already encountered our stakes when crossing the lake to scale the roof. In that moment Geraldine cursed aloud, but none of the other Spaniards appeared to think much of it as he raced back towards the steps. With a growing unease I hurried off after him, questioning whether all Spaniards on duty had abandoned their posts. I found the Anglo-Norman at the bottom of the steps alongside the doors to Manglana's hall, kneeling and cupping his hand around one of his ears.

'Shhhh, listen!' he whispered at my approach, then pointed in the direction of the next flight of stairs which were carved into the wall of the tower-house.

Though I held my breath, I could not tell what it was that he had heard until he spoke again.

'The loud dripping...'

The realisation struck me like a thunderbolt, that one of the most annoying sounds within the keep had disappeared. We heard it once more before silence returned again.

'Hurry along and do what you can', whispered Geraldine. 'I shall summon the others.'

'Not again,' I groaned, but he was already running back towards the roof, leaving me to rush towards the women's quarters.

In the hallway I found Dal Verme, our appointed sentry, collapsed from exhaustion onto the ground after he had kept yet another day's watch without being relieved by one of de Cuéllar's cronies.

- XXX -

'Up, you dozy bastard!' I hissed, as the end of my curled toes sank into his backside. 'And bring your sword!'

His loud snoring was cut short when we heard bold laughter from within the room ahead of us.

'We are lost,' gasped the Milanese fearfully, 'I have failed you.'

I kicked him again in the backside, then drew my sword from its scabbard as I ran towards the open door.

'To me!' I roared as I stormed down the hallway, fear pricking my flesh when I saw five Sassanas standing beside the window.

The loud drops of heavy rainwater which fell from the edge of the window had been muffled by their entrance through the narrow aperture. Another Sassana was being pulled over the sill by his fellows, after climbing a rope which was bound to an iron bolt which had been flung through the window. I instantly realised the purpose of the floating pyre, which was a distraction while enemy skirmishers swam across the lake and climbed into the keep from its northern side.

Two of the Sassanas ran towards me with their wet feet squelching upon the ground and daggers glinting between their teeth. I instantly fired my rifle, felling the first assailant and filling the room with a thick, foul-smelling smoke that blinded us all for a few moments. As the fog of gunpowder cleared, I disabled another pair of intruders as Dal Verme grappled with another attacker.

My struggle brought me before the window face, where I was greeted by a brute with a huge head like a wild hog's. His wicked sneer was greeted with a thrust of steel, as my sword passed through his mouth and clean through the other side of his head. Within a moment he was falling to his death, yet the disabled attacker was so portly of bearing that he whisked me clean off my feet as I sought to unstick my blade. I was left clutching the window's edge as the sword pommel was wrenched from my grasp.

I had hardly regained my breath when my legs were kicked from beneath me. Another enemy pinned me to the ground, and I laboured to push away his dagger arm as the blade's point quivered before my eye. It was a desperate scuffle, during which another three intruders made their way into the keep, Dal Verme desperately falling upon them with his raised sword. My Milanese companion was soon beaten back, left to hold off four times his number. Meanwhile I struck my assailant in the crotch with my knee, sending him flying back over my head and towards the wall.

No sooner had I risen to my feet than I found myself standing empty-handed against a ring of grinning intruders who squelched towards me with large daggers circling before their evil faces. I feared that my soul would soon to be consigned to the devil, but plumes of smoke suddenly appeared in the doorway, and my ears were filled with a roar heard countless times upon the battlefield.

'For Saint James!'

In an instant I flung myself back upon the ground, and there was heard a sound akin to the cracking of sticks. The burst of shot was also accompanied by a volley of arrows, which barely left a handful of the intruders standing. A ring of steel and rushed footfalls announced the appearance of de Cuéllar and the other defenders, who laid into our stunned foes with broad strokes of their Irish blades. Desperate hand-to-hand fighting ensued, and I rolled across the ground to see Old Tom swinging

- XXX -

his large two-hander in sheer arcs over his head, hollering the battle cry of his noble house at the top of his lungs.

'*Crooooooooooom Abù!*'

One of the enemies in his path was sliced through the midriff and kicked off the blade before another swirl left another clutching his throat as he fell to his knees. Geraldine's blood-spattered face was rapt as he assailed his foes without any regard for his own life, the unleashed devil of Dal Verme at his side. With a thrust of his reddened blade, he skewered a heretic in the window before climbing upon its sill with breathtaking agility and dealing the ladder rested upon it an almighty kick, so that it flew away from the keep amid great howls below it.

As the last of the intruders hurled himself out of the window, we crowded about it, seeing dozens of the enemy scrambling back towards the lakeside like rats. The threat had hardly been snuffed out, and I was about to take aim at the foremost of their number when a thought struck my mind which had me tearing back out of the chamber while calling out to the two Canarians behind me.

'You two, stay at the window!' I gasped. 'As for the rest – follow me if you value your lives!'

The stairs were climbed two by two as we raced towards the southern side of the keep. Within instants we had reached the large window whence we had first beheld the large pyre upon the lake. We had arrived not a moment too soon, for gauntleted fingers were already curled over its sill, with the head of another enemy already visible. My rifle stock was immediately swung down upon it, leading the enemy to release his grip with a blood-curdling roar.

As he fell, he dragged two of his fellow tosspots down with him. My blood ran cold at the sight of yet another ladder below us, its rungs filled with another score of foes. Arrows clattered along the outer wall as I withdrew into the keep and turned to find Old Tom behind me. The Anglo-Norman had fetched a cauldron of pitch with Koldo the Basque, and with the help of Valdo and Dal Verme we emptied its contents through the lancet, which drew further screams of panic from the Sassanas below.

Captain de Cuéllar raced towards us with a faggot he had lit on the fire, then hurled it through the window onto the shadows below. Through this act he sparked off a great flame, which revealed men dancing madly in the night from the burning pitch on their clothes, with the more fortunate amongst their number hurling themselves into the lake. As de Cuéllar and the rest of the Spaniards withdrew chuckling from the window, Old Tom hurled insults at our fleeing enemies in their own tongue, before I nodded at the empty boiler upon the ground.

'That's the pitch gone. What will we use next?'

'There are some other rocks in the MacGlannagh's hall,' replied Geraldine, 'and when they run out, we can melt some of the pewter.'

De Cuéllar's band remained behind, laughing and slapping one another on the back as I trudged off with the Anglo-Norman and the Milanese mercenary to fetch the stones. When we had finally gathered a small pile of them along the window, I slumped against the wall, blowing small clouds of mist as I held my hands against my face. The captain and his cronies had by this time resumed their feasting in the great hall; Geraldine volunteered to watch the roof while Dal Verme prepared to gain some rest until dawn. Ahead of me, the Milanese condottiere crumpled onto the ground and wrapped his cloak tightly about him, whispering briefly to me before falling asleep.

'For how much longer can five of us keep this up?'

I wrapped my arms about my rifle as I sat silently by the window and mulled over his question, the hard-won silence interrupted by the odd pop and crackle as the last embers of the smoking pyre vanished beneath the water. As my breathing calmed, it became a labour of Hercules to resist slumber, and long did I call into the hallway for someone to relieve me, even as the laughter and groans of the captain and his fellowship reached me from Manglana's hall.

Thereafter I often nodded off, only to be wakened by Dal Verme's snoring. When the Italian eventually turned onto his side, his rasping subsided, allowing me to fall into a deep sleep against the side of the wall. I snatched up my rifle hours later when I shuddered awake, shocked by the blasts of a bugle which announced the first light of dawn and the speech that rose from across the water.

'Cowards! Animals! The most despicable and lowest of grovellers! You shall all rot behind your lord's walls until we throttle you with our bare hands!'

I immediately recognised the voice of the sheriff of Sligo, and I shuddered while peering through the window. I was hoping that I might put a ball in his head, yet a curse left my lips when there was no sight of him to be had, though his threats still boomed across the water in Castilian.

'We have offered you generous terms! A free passage to Spain! We have given you our word! Lay down your arms, and you shall be at peace!'

These last words were met by a hearty burp from the roof of our tower-house, which preceded a burst of raucous laughter. There soon followed a loud cry from de Cuéllar, who stood along the battlements with his roguish fellows.

'Begone with ye, devils!' shouted the captain. 'For the idle fawning of Satan's hounds moves neither heart nor mind!'

'We shall not leave this place until every last one of you is dead!' roared Bingham. 'Until you starve and thirst as you did on your ships following your embarrassment at Calais!'

I gritted my teeth in rage at the sheriff's scorn, angrily rising to my feet. The bore of my rifle passed through the window as I jerked my head from left to right to catch sight of George Bingham. I next heard groans and sighs from the roof above my head, and I instantly knew that some new horror had been concocted by our enemy.

'Hospitalarios!' shouted the captain, and I abandoned my post to join his band upon the roof.

My hand shielded my eyes as I stepped up into the grey light of day, to find the other Spaniards all gathered along the northern crenellations. When I joined their number, I could make out the cause of their dismay.

The northern bank of the lake which was visible to us consisted of a great tongue of land which jutted through the lake-water from the north-western end. I realised that the threats and warnings of the sheriff were issued from the tip of this headland, where the tiny forms of our enemies could be seen. To our horror, great cries in Spanish were also heard as two captive castaways were led towards the branches of a large tree over which two gibbets had been slung.

- XXX -

'Surrender!' roared the sheriff once more. 'Surrender if you value the life of your fellows! You have but a minute in which to announce your decision, before these men are rendered into the swinging corpses that you, too, shall soon become!'

None of our number proposed that we take up Bingham's offer, and we stared on in stunned silence as the two wretches were finally hung from the trees, engaging in a mad kicking of the wind as their captors strung them up slowly and tortuously. With a curse I tried to trap their heads in the sights of my rifle to deliver them from anguish, despite knowing that they were too far away.

At my first shot the men along the bank scattered like pigeons. Then a hand fell upon my shoulder as I reloaded my rifle, and as the smoke cleared, I turned to find Old Tom staring at me sorrowfully.

'There is nothing more that you can do for them, friend Juan. Save your shots for the bastards.'

When my attentions were returned to the tongue of land, I noticed the last tremble of the swinging Spaniards. The enemy had delivered a terrible blow to our spirits, so that we returned to our posts throughout the keep with a heavy heart and a heavier step. We could not help but reflect on how easily it might have been us dangling from the rope across the water, much less the likelihood of this occurring in the days ahead.

'We cannot keep up our watch forever' sighed Franco behind me. 'To hold to our oath will be to seal our fate.'

Had any of the captain's cronies spoken these words, I would have served them with a stiff rebuke. Yet it was impossible to do this to the young Canarian, due to the great commitment he had always shown when minding the defences in the way Old

Tom had first planned. From the first day, Franco had always stuck to our strategy, as did his brother Pedro, Dal Verme and Old Tom. Our vigilance only grew after the hangings we had witnessed, yet to our surprise the commitment of the other Spaniards towards our defence was suddenly revived by Bingham's vile display of cruelty across the water. De Cuéllar even abandoned mad Orla for long enough periods to observe Old Tom's first instructions.

After witnessing the hangings, I expected another attack on the keep to occur at any moment. However, for days thereafter, Bingham limited himself to sending messengers by boat towards the crannog, who delivered generous terms at the tops of their voices. Each declaration sounded more generous than the previous one, so that we were also offered our lives and safe passage back to Spain, on the condition that we lay down our arms. Yet each herald met with the same reception, as each touch of my trigger shredded the proud plumes on their helmets and punctured the horns in the hands of their trumpeters.

At least a half dozen of them were scared off this way, until another daring attempt at diplomacy was made by our enemy. Barely a week had passed since the scene of the hangings, in which the newfound zeal for the defence of our keep had started to wane amongst de Cuéllar and his *camarada*. This in turn meant that my shifts became longer and harder again, causing me much disgruntlement at being shaken awake towards dusk by one of the Canarians.

'What is it?!' I growled, giving him a stare accorded to the worst of trespassers.

- XXX -

Pedro was taken aback by my outburst, so that his voice trembled slightly when he spoke again.

'The captain ordered me to fetch you. Our enemy has requested a parley. They have asked to speak with you.'

'What the devil?'

'Come and see for yourself.'

These tidings filled me with as much unease as they did curiosity, so that I quickly rose to my feet and picked up my rifle, before following the boy down the steps. We arrived at the narrowest of slit windows which was situated but a storey high, so that it afforded us a clear view of the grassy ground of the crannog outside the keep. My anxiety only grew at the sight of the captain and his fellowship who were gathered upon the steps, with Geraldine standing a few feet away from them. When they moved aside, I made my way towards the window and peered out. My knees almost buckled when I made out the mocking smile and sallow cheeks of the man who approached the foot of the keep.

He had the sense of someone without a care in the world, sidestepping the corpses of other Sassanas with an almost casual air, as if he were taking a leisurely walk through the countryside during a time of peace. A large white banner with tattered ends was furled over his shoulder, flapping in the wind, and behind him I could see the skiff which had borne him across the water.

'Burke,' I gasped, when he stopped just below the window, and his eyes instantly darted towards the sound of my voice.

'Greetings, my rabbit!' he shouted cheerily. 'Can you manage a word in private?'

'I will do no such thing!' I shouted in outrage, while snatching up my rifle and placing his head in its sights. 'You have some gall, showing your face here again! The local drink has clearly dulled your wits!'

'Very well,' Burke replied, as he turned upon his heel and made back towards the lake. 'I warned him that it was all but a fool's errand. Yet the halfwit insisted that I speak with you. You would expect no less from the sheriff.'

In that instant the end of my cassock was tugged furiously, and I turned to see the captain's eyes blazing at me.

'Speak with him!' he hissed, prompting me to call out to the renegade.

'Wait!' I shouted, which cry had Burke stop in his tracks and hastily return to his previous place below the window.

'A sudden change of heart, I see,' he said with a wicked smile. 'Perhaps Bingham was right to send his devil to do his dirty work.'

'What do you want, cur?' I growled, feeling a burning itch in the forefinger that hovered over the serpentine.

'But some moments of your time,' Burke replied, 'that we may discuss a matter which is of direct concern to us both.'

'What matter?' I spat, calling his bluff, while dreading that he might reveal my secret to the rest of the Spaniards.

'Not a word about it shall leave my lips,' replied Burke, 'until you swear on your Romish falsehoods, that there are none else that can hear us.'

When I turned towards the other Spaniards, de Cuéllar was already beckoning to them to follow him back up the stairs. Amid a jingle of scabbards and scraping footsteps they were soon gone, so that I could resume my conversation with the man who had mauled me in the dungeons of Sligo.

'Speak cur, for we are now alone.'

- XXX -

For a few moments Burke appeared not to heed me, then seemingly spoke to himself as he stared at the ground with a weary smile on his evil face, prodding the rotting leg of a cadaver with the toe of his boot.

'All this strife because of one man,' he said with a sigh. 'When you think about it, an entire army has been gathered and bleeds for a single trinket. Meanwhile the tribesmen that hosted you suffer the brunt of winter because of a single soul they took in.'

He laughed at his own words, a long, hollow cackle which made me quiver with unease as I struggled not to fire the gun.

'To think,' he continued, 'that I usually need to only snap my fingers to snuff out a life. Are you feeling honoured, rabbit?'

'Your idle talk has left me wondering,' I replied, 'why I should not silence you with a shot to the head.'

Burke grinned at me hatefully, and I took solace in the desperate cast that I caught in his eye.

'You may despise me,' he said, 'yet you know that we are very much the same, you and I. I know your kind; we are cut from the same cloth. Indeed, I fear the war in Flanders has rendered heartless monsters of all those that survived it. And I know that you would abandon the MacGlannaghs the moment they serve your purposes. You would betray them as readily as I would, as indeed you have done already.'

I shuddered at his words, for it occurred to me that although I had spent months among the tribe, it was still an outsider who appeared to know me best. My trembling was not unnoticed by the renegade sergeant, who took a step closer to the window, seeming to study my face while he whispered to me again.

'Believe me when I tell you Spaniard, that for all his professions of devotion and loyalty, your protector the MacGlannagh will flay you alive when he discovers what you have hidden.'

I jerked my head over my shoulder at his words, as I sought to ensure that none of my companions were within earshot. When my eyes returned to the window, a chill gripped the pit of my stomach, I saw Burke staring right at me with a broad grin across his face. At the horrible sight I raised the gun back to my shoulder and took a step away from the window.

'Which is to say nothing,' he continued, 'of what you shall endure if my masters get their hands on you. For the Binghams always get what they want, rabbit, and their eye is on you. You shall never make it home alone, Hospitalarios, for I know this land like the back of my hand. God help you if I ferret you out again.'

'What do you want from me?'

'Return what is ours', he hissed, 'and the army will vanish. Bingham only wants the ring.'

'What ring?'

Burke exhaled impatiently.

'Listen to me, Spaniard. The sheriff has pledged that he will give you safe passage home. But first he must have the stone back.'

'It was lost in the river.'

He issued a choking sound, and his face twitched with great displeasure.

'You do not have a good hand, rabbit. Even if you survive this siege, which is unlikely, given the numbers, what then?'

'I shall play my cards to the end,' I rasped. 'Now begone with you, serpent.'

- XXX -

'Give it up or you shall not see out the next year.'

He cursed aloud as I swung my rifle back over my shoulder and made to walk up the steps, then shouted after me angrily.

'What choice do you have? You are surrounded! Do you think your stocks will last you forever? Ten defenders against hundreds of men? Do not make this any worse for yourself!'

His words echoed across the lake, but I ignored them, slumping alongside the window and only looking through it when I heard him grumbling to himself and the grass crunching beneath his feet. My eyes never left him as he trudged back towards the boat, its oars glistening in the growing moonlight while Burke cut a downcast figure upon its prow. When they left the crannog, the white flag was thrown to the ground, leaving me scrambling to take aim at the renegade.

Since the boatman obscured my view of him, I elected not to take the shot and risk further displeasing our besiegers. When I climbed back up the steps, I was surprised to find de Cuéllar and his cronies gathered on the floor just above me. None of the Spaniards spoke at my appearance, leaving me on edge, since I was expecting a flurry of questions. My whole body was as taut as a bowstring as I passed wordlessly between them; then the captain stepped out of the shadows into my path.

'What did he say?'

'Some desperate nonsense about surrendering in exchange for a reward,' I said with a shrug, as I walked past him. 'Just another pathetic attempt to sow suspicion amongst us.'

The captain's intense stare was unwavering as he lifted his head back slightly.

'Oh.'

When I returned to the chieftain's hall, Geraldine was outraged by the enemy's attempt at parleying.

'That serpent Burke! I was so tempted to drop a rock onto his head from the roof!'

'Indeed,' I replied. 'It was all I could do to stop myself from shooting him when he dropped his flag.'

'You should have done it!' exclaimed the Anglo-Norman. 'That man has more lives than a cat, and is more evil than the devil!'

'Alas, that ship has now sailed.'

'But why did he speak with you alone?' exclaimed Old Tom.

'I slayed one of the sheriff's kinsmen at Sligo,' I lied. 'He wanted to personally deliver Bingham's message of revenge.'

Upon hearing this, Geraldine unleashed a tirade of insults and accusations directed at Treasach Burke, which still echoed across the hall when I drifted off to sleep sometime later. Yet I was so worried about the ring being discovered that I did not realise the full impact that my brief encounter with Burke would have on me. My slumber was plagued by dark dreams of Sligo, filled with visions of a chain hanging from a dungeon ceiling and the Spanish spider atop the white-hot brazier, which made me rise with a howl as sweat slid down my forehead. This meant that my repose was fitful, disturbing my other companions who had sought out the warmth of the chieftain's hall.

My distress was not greatly appeased by the strange goings-on that occurred throughout the next day. It was upon resuming guard duty upon the battlements that I noticed a pair of prying eyes on the steps which I swore were Enano's. They vanished the moment I called out to him and he did not reappear. I was also unsettled by the visits of the captain's cronies to the roof, which were as surprising as they were frequent. Until Burke's parley, none of de Cuéllar's *camarada* cared for the sights of the lake or ever volunteered to guard the roof, since it was the place of least comfort and greatest responsibility. Their sudden appearances led me to suspect that they had eavesdropped on my exchange with Burke, and believed me to be in possession of something valuable.

My mind was therefore also occupied with how I could best hide the ring from prying eyes and fingers. Identifying a location would be no simple task, since there were only four floors in the tower house and I was closely watched at all times. In the end I decided that the trinket would be safest in the place where I had first hidden it. As I assumed my usual pose of sitting cross-legged at the edge of the roof, I slipped the ring onto my tongue and swallowed it down with a drink from my water skin, while my back was turned towards the staircase.

Thereafter I breathed easier, although my brushes with members of the captain's band in the corridors left me stiffening like a drawn bowstring. Yet none of them ever sought trouble or tried to obstruct my path. Meanwhile the days turned ever colder. Geraldine soon resorted to booting us to our feet in the morning, for we were reluctant to abandon our blankets alongside the hearth, where we often gathered to bare our frozen buttocks alongside the fire in the manner of the Dartrymen.

The weather further deteriorated after the first fall of snow, and at times there was no watch on the keep at all, so reluctant were we to abandon our places by the fire, where we sat wrapped in rags and shivering next to each other. On the following Sunday a huge snowstorm swirled as the hearths in the castle were made to burn higher. We had enough firewood to see us through Christmas yet still awoke with frost on our blankets, which I beheld in disbelief.

'I wonder how the enemy can stand it.'

It seemed incredible that the Sassanas would not abandon their post along the water, but they still engaged in desperate attempts to raid the keep. It was during these days that sharp eyes and a steady shot proved most useful to defence. Our enemies were often dressed in white sheets to avoid detection upon the snow, only for the ground to be reddened whenever my shot met its mark.

Time and again their attempts were foiled, as I lived up to my nickname of 'the Lynx of Haarlem', which had been assigned to me by the Duke of Alba in the Low Countries. Yet the moments seemed like hours as I sat as still as a statue in the piercing cold, spotting my targets and calmly waiting for them to assume a more exposed position. To make matters worse, a fire on the roof would only serve to betray my position, so instead, I draped many mantles across my body until I resembled some turbaned infidel. Long hours spent in the cruel winds soon made my frailties come to the fore, and every wound and injury suffered in war caused me to suffer varying degrees of pain.

Eventually even the captain acknowledged my efforts; he barked at his fellows to relieve me for a few hours from the watch on the roof and rewarded me with a half day of rest. Another time he ordered me to join him for dinner, and I sat alongside him at Manglana's great hearth, while Enano filled our goblets with wine and usquebaugh. A whole pig was turned on a spit, filling our nostrils with the warm smell of pork fat.

'Ahhh' sighed the captain as he took another long sip from his mazer. 'These joys are denied to the followers of Mahomet.'

- XXX -

'Truth,' I replied, taking a huge swig of a fine vintage which de Cuéllar had offered me.

Upon commencing our defence, the captain had been swift to inspect Manglana's cellar. I realised that whilst the rest of the defenders had been served with gravelly wine spiced with cinnamon or ginger, the captain had in the meantime been helping himself to casks from Greece and Languedoc, as well as the finest vintages from Cyprus.

I was highly irked by this discovery, yet not in the mood for any disputes following my travails on the rooftop. As far as I was concerned, there was no other defender who had endured as much as I did during the watch, so that I sat back as Enano cracked open yet another cask. A smile grew on my face as the claret was poured forth, and I was already feeling mellow while my beaker was filled with a fine red which was stout enough to rival the best years from Gascony.

'All we need is music', I said with a deep sigh of contentment.

'And women!' exclaimed the captain, readying to wake mad Orla with a loud clap until he noticed my glare of disapproval. His hands were quickly returned to his knees, leaving the long-abused crone to her rest in the corner of the hall.

'Ah, women,' he said softly, after he drained his cup and refilled it again. 'You would not believe what reached me this morning.'

'Oh?' I asked.

He leaned over towards a pile of his belongings and rummaged through them until he pulled out a page.

'There we are!' he said with a laugh, placing it upon the tiles between us. 'A personal message from Dartry's queen herself!'

'How did you receive it?' I asked, fearing that he may have broken our pledge and let a messenger into the keep.

'It reached the rooftop at dawn, bound to an arrow. The end of the shaft was blunted, which attracted our Canarian sentry's notice.'

I was filled with curiosity as I picked the letter from the ground and held it closely before my nose. The words were Latin and written in a fine hand.

'You know your letters?' asked the captain in surprise as his eyes narrowed suspiciously. His question was answered when I read the first few lines of the message aloud.

'Most worthy captain, who hath dared face untold perils that the bravest of men have fled, I write to thee from within the walls of my father's house, and I dare not imagine the dangers which lurk outside thy door. Even the ancients hath not seen the bravery thou hast displayed with unerring daring to withstand so large a force...'

The handwriting was as fine to behold as it was easy to read. Yet the message was boring, consisting mainly of veneration for the captain, which compared him to the likes of Hannibal and Scipio, while making thinly veiled professions of affection and desire. When the last of its lines was read, it was all I could do to return the page to de Cuéllar without retching at the impact of a woman's heart upon her wits. A self-satisfied smirk had by this time grown on the captain's face, and he passed his fingers over the letter with a mocking tone to his voice.

'Highborn is our lady, able to afford the softest scraps of vellum and the finest scents.'

- XXX -

'And clearly smitten by you. The archer who delivered that note was no mean shot; he would have charged a pretty sum to risk his neck for you.'

'I am not ungrateful,' replied de Cuéllar with a low chuckle, as he rose to one knee and then staggered off towards the hallway door, the letter still dangling from his fingers, 'for if I wipe my backside with one more dried leaf, I fear that it might fall off.'

I suddenly realised that his direction was the privy, and I laughed aloud at the fate of the letter, which had incurred such expense and toil for it to be delivered to its intended reader. My head had only just stopped shaking at his audacity when the captain reappeared with the satisfied grin returned to his face.

'Ah, Hospitalarios!' bellowed de Cuéllar, returned to his seat by the wall. 'What will people say when we tell them of our time spent in the company of the mere Irishry, warming our buttocks against their fires?'

'They will say nothing,' I replied, 'for we have no chance of ever leaving this land alive.'

We burst out laughing at our hopeless situation, then stared into nothing for a few moments. The grin on de Cuéllar's face had vanished, and for a few moments he was silent as he emptied yet another cup, then took a bite of pork from the wooden plate at his ankle. Thereafter he seemed to regain some of his normal cheer, and he proceeded to recount one tale after another, which were each as full of dark humour as they were lewd.

'Did I tell you, Hospitalarios, of that widow in Dunkirk who had two daughters? I was as young then as I was strong...'

I found myself roaring with laughter late on into the night, and I could not remember the last time I had given myself up to such merry abandon. My eyes began closing some time after midnight, as we shared memories of our years in the Imperial army.

'To think,' I muttered, 'how proud I was when I first enlisted.'

'It is all shit, my friend,' whispered de Cuéllar, as he fell back against the wall and started drifting off too. 'All shit...'

The following morning bore me a nasty shock. I awoke shivering with cold to find that my English clothes were all rumpled and torn. A thorough search of my garments had taken place as I was in a drunken stupor having imbibed such a quantity of wine the night before. The captain appeared in the doorway as I sprang to my feet, though he feigned ignorance of what had befallen me. I delivered a broadside of accusations and insults at the top of my voice, gesturing at him wildly until he ordered that all of the defenders be gathered before him in the hall, so he could discover who had rifled through my garments during the night.

He grunted in outrage upon discovering that Geraldine had not answered his summons. We marched out after the captain as he went in search of the old Anglo-Norman, and we found him curled up like a cat, slumbering idly in the middle of the dank hallway. Without a moment's hesitation, the captain strode up to Old Tom and kicked him in the ribs, which left the old warrior rolling over on the ground while he delivered a piercing howl.

'Thief!' shouted the captain. 'How dare you steal from one of my men?'

Geraldine swiftly rose to his feet and unsheathed his long skene dagger.

'Spanish lunatics!' he cried. 'I've had enough of your antics! What is the meaning of this latest madness?'

The captain did not betray a scintilla of fear as he cocked an eye at the Anglo-Norman, and he cut a daunting figure as he rested his hand upon the damascene pommel of his sword. De Cuéllar's skill with the blade was considerable, as had been witnessed during our last fight with the Sassanas, and his *camarada* gathered closely about him as he took another step towards the Irishman.

'Dare you raise arms against an officer, you pilfering son of an Irish swineherd?'

Geraldine's look of surprise was soon replaced by one of anger, as his face turned a hue of purple. I swiftly threw myself between him and de Cuéllar's band, urging each party to restrain themselves until the misunderstanding was solved.

'Did you search the clothes of Hospitalarios?' shouted the captain.

I rested a hand on his chest to check his advance upon Geraldine. On his part Old Tom shook his head and looked at me askance.

'You Spaniards are mad.'

I remained standing in front of him, for fear that the mood might worsen and spill over into violence. After all, the captain was not known to back down once he started a fight, and he was long used to picking scapegoats who had no choice but to accept his abuse. Yet Geraldine had resisted greater numbers all his life and was not likely to step away from the sight of five Spaniards, regardless of the danger they posed to him. My efforts at peace, however, were not appreciated by the captain, who jerked his head sideways as a sign for me to get out of his way.

'Step aside, or you'll swing for insubordination.'

I feared the worst, finding myself trapped between two deadly fighters. At any instant, cold steel could be drawn to spark off a fight which would only benefit our enemy. My lips parted as a cry of protest formed in my throat, but it was instantly stifled by the blare of a bugle.

XXXI

Rosclogher, Dartry, County Leitrim

1 – 4 December 1588

The trumpet was sounded again and again, and in the midst of all the fanfare we heard a joyous cry from the roof which had us tearing for the battlements.

'The Sassanas are leaving! The Sassanas are leaving! The siege is broken!'

It was a sight scarcely believable, yet across the water all tents had already been struck, as the enemy rumbled back towards the bog. The view stirred our hearts, and turned us mad with elation; Old Tom jumped upon the battlements and performed a merry dance involving a series of half steps, twists and leaps, while Franco fell to his knees and served the ground with an impassioned kiss. De Cuéllar raised his wineskin and laughed aloud, then staggered backwards and was caught by Koldo. Peals of laughter rose to the sky as Valdo stared across the lake in disbelief.

'Our Lady of Ontanar be praised!' he cried, tears welling up in his eyes as his voice echoed across bog and wood. 'We are safe a while longer!'

The fifes and drums of the enemy had all but died away, leaving us with the sound of slight breezes which whispered through the trees and the hillsides around us. By this time we had recovered our wits enough to notice the small pile of faggots which Old Tom had built on the roof.

'What in the name of the Holy Mother are you doing?' snapped de Cuéllar as he approached the Anglo-Norman, his wineskin held before him.

Geraldine stood up and served him with a look of outrage.

'Putting an end to your shameless lechery!' snapped Old Tom. 'At your protectors' expense!'

De Cuéllar's face turned scarlet, and he was speechless until some normal colour returned to his face again.

'Which reminds me,' he whispered in a grave tone of voice, before turning on his heel and making for the steps.

The captain's cronies swiftly made after him while Old Tom wordlessly returned to placing wood upon his pyre. He was soon aided in this task by the Canarians, Dal Verme and me, for we were keen to light the signal fire which would relieve the sufferings of our hosts in the mountains and return the chieftain to his lakeside seat of power. It took the better part of an hour to nurse the flames from wind and rain until they grew into a large fire, which then turned into a raging blaze to accompany the smoke from the chimney.

'And now to blacken the smoke' said Old Tom, before he walked off to fetch fresh straw stored below the stairs to the roof.

- XXXI -

Together we carried large armfuls of it back onto the roof, where many handfuls of it were soaked in the fouled cistern before being hurled upon the large flames which in turn delivered a fog to the heavens which was dark as pitch.

'We have a Pope,' laughed Dal Verme, and Geraldine smiled.

For a few moments thereafter we stood at the edge of the keep which had confined us for seventeen days, staring at the mountain range beyond the southern bank of the lake and wondering how long it would take for the sentinels to bear word of the enemy's departure to Manglana.

'Look!' shouted Pedro, pointing at the distant flames which appeared along the ridge of the mountain range ahead of us. 'Upon the summits!'

Geraldine nodded at the sight, before turning away from the crenellations.

'Our work is done. We may as well venture downstairs, although one of us should remain on the roof a while longer. I seem to recall that it was your turn, Franco.'

The Canarian looked crestfallen upon hearing this, then trudged off to his post as Dal Verme spoke.

'Do you think that it is a trap?'

'Unlikely,' replied Geraldine, 'yet who can tell? Besieged defenders have been fooled since the days of the wooden horse of Troy. Yet the MacGlannagh will have scouts trailing the English party. And if he does not appear after tomorrow, you will have had your answer.'

As the wood crackled and popped behind us, I was also warmed by the long-abandoned hope that I might see the ollave's face again. My heart quickened at the thought, and my steps seemed lighter and my bruises less painful as we made our way down to the chieftain's hall. The sight of broken brandy and mead casks greeted us. De Cuéllar and his men formed a tight ring and embraced each other, a scantily clad mad Orla among their number as they yelled old army songs at the tops of their voices.

They were getting drunk fast, and as we helped ourselves to some of the drink on offer, we watched them stumble to the ground and retch in dark corners while they passed out one by one. In the hours that remained until evening we drank in silence, weary of our great exertions from previous days and feeling the elation shared by all defenders after a broken siege, which was akin to having been afforded the gift of life again.

At last we slept, and I was woken by Franco at dawn. It was my turn to make my way back to the cursed roof for what I hoped would be my last watch. My snowy surrounds offered little interest as I sat swathed in my hooded cassock, but the tedium of sentry duty came to an abrupt end when Geraldine appeared with the Canarians and Dal Verme at his shoulder.

'Where is the chessboard?' I asked half hopefully, but Old Tom served me with a severe stare.

'Follow me,' he growled, 'and bring your rifle and your cassock.'

I glanced at the other men who returned my puzzled expression, but Old Tom only ordered them not to allow anyone else onto the roof until he returned. The Anglo-Norman ignored all of my questions as we hurried down the steps until the second storey of the tower-house, where we lowered the ladder to the bottommost floor and climbed down it. As our feet touched the ground, Old Tom pulled the ladder down after us.

- XXXI -

'Now, Spaniard,' he said, 'our guard shifts from enemies without to fools within.'

He would say nothing more, other than to drag the ladder along its side to the iron door which barred the entrance to the keep. He next beckoned to me to sit down alongside him, and it was not long before we heard cackles of laughter and loud speech above our heads. The noise ended when footsteps were heard on the floorboards above our heads, and Koldo's shrill voice could be heard amid the cursing and swearing which followed.

'Where in the Baptist's name is the ladder?!'

Some scuffling sounds could be heard as a desperate search ensued. Then the captain's head popped through the hole in the ceiling; he scowled openly at the sight of us when he turned his head towards the iron door.

'Return the ladder to us, Hospitalarios! That is an order!'

'He will do no such thing!' shouted Geraldine, springing to his feet and drawing his two-handed sword. 'We shall hold to our oath until the end!'

'Motherless Irish beggar!' retorted de Cuéllar. 'I do not take orders from you! Return those rungs to us, and do not make us come down there!'

'Withdraw your head, serpent,' replied Old Tom, 'if you value your life! And if any one of your underlings dares to descend, they will earn a ball through the throat for their pains!'

'You would not dare, Hospitalarios!' yelled de Cuéllar, though his expression turned to one of worry as he fixed his stare upon my rifle. 'That is insubordination!'

'Shoot him!' snarled the Anglo-Norman.

'B-but...' I stammered, feeling hesitant.

'Shoot him!' he howled, standing with his feet apart and raising his sword above my head. 'Otherwise I will rend you from shoulder to midriff!'

He assumed so savage an expression when he said this, and his stance so resembled that of an executioner, that I instantly did as I was bidden. As the captain stared at me in shock, I fired a ball but a handspan away from his face, the shot filling his face with sawdust.

'Ah, my eyes!' he cried, as his head was swiftly withdrawn and he kicked the planks overhead. 'Bastard got me in the eyes!'

There soon followed a whole litany of swear words and curses directed at Old Tom, yet Geraldine ignored them all. Any other man might have betrayed at least a hint of concern after angering the five seasoned killers above our heads, yet Geraldine retained an unnerving calm about the situation he had placed us in.

'You should get some rest now,' he whispered to me, 'for one cannot tell how long it may be until we are relieved. Keep your gun close, if one of them drops through the murder hole I shall rouse you.'

Despite his invitation to sleep, my agitation was such that it took almost an hour for my eyes to fall shut. It was the sound of cheers and horn blasts that had them open again, and I stirred to find Geraldine unbarring the heavy oaken door. Together we squinted at the daylight which rushed through the bars of the steel *yett* behind it. As our eyes became accustomed to the daylight we flung the gate open with a crash, allowing a flood of bluejackets to stream through the entrance, seizing up the ladder and climbing to the upper chambers of the keep to secure it. At least two score of the bodyguard had run past us before the tear-streaked face of Manglana himself appeared in the doorway. He walked towards us slowly, staring about him in disbelief.

'Verily men spoke,' he muttered, 'that our salvation lies with Spain.'

The tanist Cathal *Dubh* was next to appear in the doorway, and he could not help grinning hideously as he grasped my forearm.

My skin crawled at his touch which felt like snake scales, yet I forced myself to smile warmly in his direction after I had engaged in a slight bow.

'So we meet again, after all, Spaniard. You have displayed bravery of which the ancients would be proud.'

After engaging in some conversation with Old Tom, the tanist recommended that the Spaniards within the keep accompany him across the water back to the town, while Manglana and his wife inspected the tower-house and readied it for other guests. The long days spent confined in the keep caused our knees to buckle as we walked outside it, and the lakewater seemed to rise and dip as I struggled to keep my footing. A raft had been lifted upon the edge of the crannog, and as we approached it, we heard the captain cheering behind us with his cronies in tow. Geraldine turned and raised his sword with a curse, yet the captain saluted him as if our armed standoff within the keep had never happened.

'Do not tarry Irishman! We must stretch our legs across the water!'

The chieftain himself joined our number as we made our way back towards what remained of Manglana's town. Tribesmen crowded along the bank at our approach, waving madly in our direction and cheering at the tops of their voices. Their beards were longer and more unkempt than ours, with twigs stuck in their hair and rings encircling their red eyes. Nearly a score of them limped badly over the snow, as Cathal told me of their time spent in the heights of Dartry, his voice sounding hoarse from his great exertions in the mountains.

'We had a terrible time of it, being hounded almost daily by foes and wolves alike. The treacherous O'Reillys were ready for us, and some raiding parties made away with our prize bulls. Yet worse still, many suffered frost burns while half the cattle were lost. Indeed it has proved a hard winter thus far, yet it would have been far worse had the tower-house been taken by our enemies.'

When we got off the boat we were surrounded by Dartrymen, and the more able-bodied among them cheered as they hurled us into the air in jubilation. Joyous cries of '*an Spáinn*' were heard as we were hurled towards the heavens again and again.

'To think that they wanted us banished!' laughed fat Juande amid heavy gasps.

We were returned to our feet and a great slapping upon our backs commenced. It was clear that we had become the toast of the returned townsfolk, with our presence among them no longer open to question or met with resentment. De Cuéllar's gamble had paid off better than I could have ever anticipated, and I dreaded to think what would have become of the people of Rosclogher if our defence had not succeeded. Cathal *Dubh* had not spoken idly of their sufferings in the wild, for at least a dozen of the common folk were seen limping on blackened

- XXXI -

toes, thanks to the meandering goat tracks covered with sleet and heavy snow.

As we wandered about the ashen remains of their dwellings, it was clear that the merciless frost had also worked in our favour, and that cold and disease had been our greatest ally during the siege. Piles of dead Sassanas lay upon the green with their garments frozen upon their lifeless limbs, having succumbed to cold and disease. The risks of illness from so many rotting carcasses was too great to be ignored, and a number of churls was soon hard at work, carrying out the unenviable task of dragging the putrid corpses towards a far end of the bog, shielded from the town. Meanwhile a large number of tents had already been erected to shelter the returning families, and the townsmen toiled to erect hovels of wattle and daub to better protect their women and children. Stout fences had been raised to contain the cattle and horses also returned to Rosclogher, and a score of bluejackets prepared the ringfort as best they could for the night, also allowing a number of displaced tribesmen to temporarily reside in it.

As I trudged through the town and observed these labours, I could not help but feel a flicker of satisfaction at the memory of my struggle against the enemy during the siege. Although I had almost reached the twilight of my fighting prowess, I recalled my pride at joining the Spanish army in my youth, a fighting force which I once believed existed to protect the weak. My mind raced back to the days when I was a barefoot boy on the island of Malta, covered in blood, dust and sweat, and rejoicing with my fellow islanders as the Turks fled the large Spanish force sent from Sicily. It had kindled my fascination for the imperial army, which I had first observed as liberators and not oppressors, a perception which was to be entirely dashed by my time spent in Flanders.

Children slipped to the snowy ground about me as they pelted one another with snowballs. One struck me on the shoulder as I walked past a group of Dartrymen, who busied themselves erecting a hut under the watchful eye of the chieftain and his steward. The Abbey of Saint Mel next greeted me, looking as wretched as the rest of us, with its smashed windows and the icicles hanging from the eaves. I heard a loud grunt behind me, and I could not help but chuckle when I saw the Jesuit O'Ronayne bent over what remained of the outhouse that I had shared with Nial. He dragged a charred log from the burnt wreckage, yet upon hearing me laugh a wry smile spread along his blackened face.

'Come and help me, you idle whoreson,' rasped the Jesuit, and before I could laugh again someone grabbed me from the neck and shoved it under his armpit, then ruffled my hair with a bunched fist.

I laughed aloud when I was finally released from the strong grip, for I had missed Nial's company during the siege.

'All honour is yours, Juan,' said the bondsman at last, slapping me on the shoulder. 'Your bravery has the chieftain in high spirits. For too long had Donal poisoned the tribesmen's minds against you, yet his words shall no longer bear weight.'

His words left me feeling further elated, and I was nearly an hour long in debate with him and the Jesuit when Old Tom approached us.

'Juan,' he called, 'the chieftain has asked that we join him.'

I travelled back across the lake with the chieftain's party in one skiff, while another bore de Cuéllar and the other Spaniards. As the boats were punted past the tower house, I realised that our destination was the opposite bank of Rossfriar, and my heart sank when I remembered the gruesome scene of the sheriff's execution. The bodies of the dead Spaniards still hung from the trees, their mortal remains riddled with arrows since they had been used as target practice. With drawn swords we cut them down, and as one body thudded to the ground, it was seen to be holding a scrap of vellum in a clawed hand. It was a handwritten message signed by the English viceroy himself, and the colour drained from most of the Spaniards' faces when Old Tom read it out to us.

'I will return. Until then, make sure that you do not come into my power.'

O'Ronayne led us in prayer after the bodies were consigned to the earth. Although there were no keeners to lament their passing, we tarried together in silence alongside their graves, bound by the realisation that we could so easily have met their fate after being shipwrecked in Ireland. After our respects were paid, we were taken back to the tower-house to thaw by the great fire in the hall, where to a man we rid ourselves of the morning chill in our bones.

Following the return of Manglana, the rebuilding of the town got underway almost immediately. Provisions and materials were daily brought in from Duncarbery and from the lands of the chieftain's allies. Great cabins reappeared along the lake, and a thatched infirmary was rebuilt near Saint Mel. Carpenters toiled like galley slaves to create as much shelter as could be provided for the winter ahead, and the loud hammering lasted until late at night. The resolve of the Dartrymen never wavered, with many buildings rebuilt or repaired by the time Lady Dervila reappeared three days later.

It was a large escort that accompanied the lady Bourke. Although I was dismayed by the return of the gallowglass, it was all I could do to prevent myself from running towards Muireann, when she rode into the town alongside her young red-haired son. Lochlain stared about him in awe, then clambered off his horse and ran towards me, crashing into my belly and seizing me in a large embrace. His display of emotion left me feeling both awkward and flustered, until at last I allowed myself to pat him slightly upon the back of his head. He lifted his face towards me and grinned broadly, then shocked me with a question that I had not expected.

'How many did you kill?'

I gently pushed him away with a frown and gestured towards the water where Dervila's retinue were boarding ferries bound for the keep.

'Your lord grandfather will be expecting you, my lord,' I said.

Lochlain beheld me in puzzlement for a few moments before turning away and running towards the boats.

'I will see you at the feast tonight!' he yelled over his shoulder.

'Yes,' I replied absently, never taking my eyes off the distant figure of his mother.

Muireann appeared as beautiful as I had last remembered her, and she turned to greet her son with a radiant smile before a boatman helped her to board a skiff.

The chieftain was so elated at having reclaimed his keep, that even the return of his queen did not dull his spirits as while he readied to celebrate the defence of his tower house. I found it a great irony that de Cuéllar's band were invited to Manglana's

- XXXI -

hall with the rest of the defenders, yet they had also played their part to a degree. All memories of our sufferings during the siege vanished when we stepped into the hall, to find a large crowd gathered and cheering. Wild flowers were even hurled towards us by highborn women who cried their approval.

I could see that the chieftain's boar heads and other hunting trophies had been returned to their rightful place, and the arms of his forebears were hung from the walls once more. For the first time I saw the chieftain and his wife both smiling together in their seats of power, with expressions that were full of relief and contentment. Our protector's banner hung from the ceiling as burning pines crackled upon his great hearth. Candles eight fists long flickered about the room, filling our noses with the scent of beeswax as we sat at long, linen-covered tables supported by iron trestles. There followed a feast fit for those of high birth, with plates of pewter and ash filled with wild garlic, cabbage and onion. The bondsman sat at my right, pointing to red seaweed that glistened with freshness and was smeared with butter.

'That is dulse, Spaniard. You must have some of it, for we consider it a great specialty.'

Cowflesh seethed in great hides as large oxen were roasted on endless spits and geese simmered in lakes of gravy. The resulting smell was so heavenly that my mouth watered while the tribesmen recited a prayer of thanksgiving. O'Ronayne next stepped into the centre of the hall to deliver a slow exhortation. It was torture to sit still while his words were recited, and when the missive was finally finished, we all fell upon the food like a pack of wolves. The choice cuts of beef had already been served to the chieftain and his bard, in accordance with age-old customs, but many large slivers still remained. They were hacked off with knives before being flung onto plates, and big, wolfish grins appeared on bearded faces as fat dribbled down hairy chins. A tribesman shouted between mouthfuls, his face the picture of utter contentment.

'There is no place more beautiful than Rosclogher! Here we have all that we need!'

A clash of horns was heard prior to long swigs of usquebaugh. This ritual was performed several times thereafter, until the chieftain wobbled to his feet with a roseate face and his cup held aloft.

'I declare the Spaniards honorary natives of Dartry!' he cried. 'For as long as ye draw breath, ye shall always be welcome in Duncarbury and Rosclogher!'

He tumbled back into his seat to great roars of approval and the banging of trestle tables, some of his spilt drink dripping off his sleeve. Fearghal left his side and walked towards the hearth, with Miler the harpist limping towards him while clutching his brass-stringed harp.

'I hath composed a paean of triumph,' declared the bard, 'one which shall strike terror in the hearts of all traitors who hath forgotten our forefathers! Whose heads hath been turned by heretical silver! 'Tis a song of the eight sons of Golam, that father of all Milesians!'

A tribesman's fist crashed onto the side of his plate, flinging the remains of his food into the face of another and toppling his mazer onto the ground.

'A fitting ode by our bard!' he cried in Latin, fixing us with a reverential stare, 'in honour of our Galician brotherhood!'

- XXXI -

A number of other men scolded and hushed the loud tribesman, for no one had accorded him the freedom of the speech, and all of us Spaniards stared at him askance, finding ourselves unable to understand what he meant. Old Tom hissed a swift explanation to us before Fearghal's voice rose in the hall.

'All Gaels believe themselves to be the son of the Milesians, a race of men who hailed from Galicia.'

Fat Juande raised an eyebrow at the mention of his country, but then the first chords of the lyre were struck and the hall filled with a loud recital. No sooner had it ended than more poetry followed, and de Cuéllar and his cronies rose from their seats to help themselves to more cuttings of beef. Meanwhile I marvelled at the utterances of O'Dalaigh, and I was also surprised to understand a fair few of his words. After the third ode was delivered, I caught Old Tom watching me with a wry grin.

'You understand the words, friend Juan!' he observed in Gaelic.

'How long will he sing for?' I replied in Spanish, since I still lacked the confidence to use the vernacular of my hosts.

Geraldine shrugged as he picked up his knife and helped himself to a side of boar.

'One cannot say. Sometimes these feasts can last for days.'

As the night wore on, Fearghal broke into yet another paean of triumph, which he first declared in his best Latin to be dedicated to Captain de Cuéllar. The poem was also recited in Latin and told of a Gaelic messiah bearing the name of 'Aodh' who would be proclaimed by nature herself, and would be identified by signs in the sky. The captain appeared to swell in his seat as Fearghal proclaimed that he would rebuild the walls of ancient Tara, the old seat of Gaelic power, before expelling the foreigners from Ireland. At the end of his delivery the bard finally returned to his place at the chieftain's side, while behind me O'Ronayne could be heard muttering darkly below his breath.

'It will be God who delivers us and not Aodh.'

A band of travelling musicians next set about making merry with drums and pipes, while men stood and conferred with one another, mostly glad to be back to the comforts of their tower house. As I conversed with Nial and Geraldine, I could make out the tanist Cathal striding towards us with a smile playing over his stretched lips. After clapping me on the shoulder he rested his arm on it, smiling as he spoke into my ear above the noise of the crowd.

'They must have thought you were a hundred Spaniards in here.'

The bondsman heard him and laughed.

'Indeed, you put up a stout defence.'

I cleared my throat awkwardly.

'Hardly, for the enemy knew that we were only ten. A renegade among their number shouted it at me through a loop window.'

'Which is not to mention,' added Old Tom, 'that someone fouled the water cistern on the roof, which all but killed one of our men.'

Cathal appeared disturbed by our claims and shook his head in bafflement before he replied.

'Someone's head has been turned by the enemy. We must warn my lord MacGlannagh when the feast is over.'

Suddenly loud shouting was heard across the hall; then silence fell across it like a curtain as we turned to face the group

- XXXI -

of men who had appeared in the doorway. Donal MacCabe stood with five of his men, scowling in our direction with a raised finger.

'The Spaniards exceeded their siege rations! Such disregard from our allies in the face of a cruel winter!'

The Scot's claim was true, and I feared that we Spaniards had compromised our position again despite all the goodwill we had secured after the siege. Yet my fears were unfounded, for the constable was waved away by the highborn tribesmen, with a few even booing the Scots loudly. MacCabe stared at them in outrage, for he was unused to being so lightly dismissed. Whatever attentions he had secured were quickly withdrawn when servants entered the hall bearing more dishes full of roasted fare.

'Badger!' cried the Manglanas who could not believe their luck, as they rushed back to their seats to taste the flesh of the creature they considered a great delicacy.

Irish bagpipes were played thereafter, and when great oaten cakes had been rendered to crumbs, Captain de Cuéllar stood on his table to deliver a fine speech amid the great mirth that surrounded us.

'In Spain we always frowned on the north, which we considered the font of heretics, but here among you our faith has been restored. Indeed, your devotion instils me with hope and wonder. It brings to mind the courage of the first Christians who had to die for their beliefs. We are most fortunate in Spain to have freedom of worship without fear of death!'

He was nothing if not a great orator, and all present were in raptures before the chieftain also rose to his feet, praising de Cuéllar and all Spaniards for the bravery we had displayed. It was evident that the drink had muddled Manglana's wits, as he also proclaimed de Cuéllar an Aodh once more, then compared our defence to David slaying the giant Goliath. When this was done, he even proceeded to offer de Cuéllar the hand of his sister, who, although fair, was also somewhat big-boned. Although the lass appeared well besotted by the prospect of being wed to a Spanish captain, de Cuéllar got out of it well.

'My thanks, O worthy lord! But I must first deeply ponder the consequences of your offer. For after our holy victory, I have considered becoming a hermit one day, to retire into the mountains and devote myself solely to prayer.'

Manglana was at once awed and appeased by this revelation, which had hardly been delivered when the captain snapped his fingers at Enano. The short Spaniard instantly scurried over to one of the travelling minstrels who had taken their place by the fire, where they quietly fed on some beef cuttings which they had received as payment. The fiddler among them was shocked when Enano snatched up his instrument, then proceeded to strike up a tune.

It was all the cue de Cuéllar needed to grab Manglana's sister by the arm and lead her in a merry galliard. The poor maid did her best to match his movements as de Cuéllar hopped lithely from one foot to the other. His partner stumbled time and again to keep up with him, although his arm was wrapped around her back. Few if any of the onlookers cared, and Manglana remained standing as he observed the spectacle with a foolish grin, while Dervila stared on longingly at the captain.

Loud cheers resounded across the hall at the end of the spectacle, which the captain duly acknowledged with flourishing bows while his partner was led off with her head spinning by

- XXXI -

Muireann and Saorla. It was next the turn of our Irish hosts to engage in their revelry, with the minstrels back to striking up a tune. Enano and the rest of de Cuéllar's band observed the natives' medieval carolling with unmasked disdain, as freemen both young and old held hands and undertook simple steps. When their dance was over, Koldo the Basque waded amongst them, starting on a devilish shipman's dance with de Cuéllar.

Old Tom was next to throw himself into the merriment, as well as the younger natives who tried their hand at the alien dance to the horror of the onlooking bard. Shadows flickered wildly against the walls, and proceedings took an even livelier turn when the revelry, which had lasted for over an hour, came to a pause. A great contentment and gasping of breath ensued by the end of it, and thirst was slaked as ewers of usquebaugh and beer were brought round by serving knaves, together with stout flagons of wine.

Amid the odd burst of laughter, many heads were turned at the sound of the fiddle taken up by Enano. De Cuéllar stood with his arms parted, as his thumbs and forefingers proceeded to form a circle. As the strings of the violin were struck, he undertook the unholy movements of the sarabande, which drew a sharp intake of breath across the hall. Men and women flocked about the captain once more, laughing as they sought to emulate his gestures with looks of undisguised desire cast between dancers, no doubt aided by their heavy drinking and the devilish movements that ensued.

'Madness' chuckled Nial at my elbow, then looked surprised when I rose to my feet after draining my horn.

'Indeed,' I replied, and staggered towards the flurry of bodies.

I did not know how to play a single note, but the sarabande was not alien to me. I had danced it in my youth, so that my awkward shuffling was still better than the movements of our hosts, who had only just familiarised themselves with it. A few of the younger freemen parted and cheered so that I found myself alongside the captain, engaging in a sort of duel as we each sought to outdo the other's movements and regarded one another with undisguised contempt. So furiously did I commit myself to this contest that it was almost another hour before I noticed the eyes of Muireann watching me from alongside Dervila's empty throne.

It was a stare both keen and bewildered, withdrawn the moment I met it. A howling tribesman blocked my view of her face for a moment, which was all the time it took for her to disappear, leaving me with de Cuéllar, though my mind raced with visions of her. It must have been well towards midnight that the music ended and Manglana was helped to his bedchamber. Yet logs were still thrown upon the fire, and many still lingered on the benches as our cups were magically filled once more. One by one Irish noblemen passed out on the straw strewn floor. Huge hounds beheld them in bafflement and then licked their faces, until knaves and servants appeared from the shadows to bear their masters away.

As another wine-filled goblet reached my lips, I made out the tanist Cathal and young Lochlain, who were staring at the captain in wonder while he recounted his role in the siege. Of course the account was greatly embellished, and our defence made to sound like a feat that rivalled the defence of the island of Malta or the famous Christian victory against the Turk at Lepanto. Yet both tanist and prince listened to the tale in awe, which left me to recall my own boyhood enthusiasm for the feats of the imperial army.

With a shudder I rose to my feet, keen on fresh air and solitude in which to forget the disappointment of my past choices. A splutter left my throat when I noticed Dervila sitting cross-legged on the floor before de Cuéllar's band; she regarded the captain with undisguised admiration. This sight was swiftly forgotten when O'Ronayne spun towards me with a horn of mead in each of his hands. A frothy moustache had sprouted beneath his nose, and he shouted with his eyes wide, 'Only the righteous shall prevail!'

In an effort to help him along his confused path, I seized him by the shoulder and flung him about. He was left whirling like a top towards the hearth, and loud gasps were heard when he kicked up a red shower of embers. Laughter erupted as the Jesuit proceeded to fall onto his backside, and servants hurried towards him to beat the flames out of his garb. As I turned to the doors I saw that Old Tom had appeared, his speech slurred as he tried to throw a punch at me. The blow was easily dodged as the Anglo-Norman also fell onto the ground, and in that moment a scuffle broke out amongst the remaining stragglers. I stepped over Old Tom and made for the staircase.

I was weary of the heavy feasting as I climbed onto the roof, and keen on the fresh breeze which reached my nostrils from the battlements. My shoulders bounced off the walls of the keep before I was greeted by the heavenly sight of the stars which littered the black sky. My head cleared enough for me to notice the approach of two figures. As they drew nearer, the glow from the hall behind me allowed me to recognise Muireann and Saorla. My breath was heavy with brew as I stepped before them without second thought, barring their path.

'You owe me an apology,' I slurred in poor Gaelic, while trying my best not to fall over.

The women exchanged a look of puzzlement before Muireann herself replied in Latin.

'Whatever for?'

'For doubting the valour of your Spanish allies.'

I noticed that she was flustered by my assertion, and for a moment there also appeared to be three of her. Despite the fresh air, it was all I could do to keep on my feet, and Muireann smiled hesitantly before Saorla spoke up instead.

'My lady's late husband never doubted your courage. My lord Aengus -'

'Who is this Aengus?'

My lip was curled with disdain when I said this, and I tottered from one foot to the other even as Muireann appeared startled. Saorla beheld me in fear when I stumbled towards the ollave and planted a chicken greased kiss upon her cheek, then held her stare.

'The time for mourning is over!' I blurted, then grabbed her waist and drew her closer to me.

She tried to push me away as I made for her face, then slipped free of my clutches so that my lips met thin air and I collapsed onto the ground. The call of a sentinel was heard behind us, followed by Muireann's swift instruction to her fellow maid.

'Not a word to anyone, Saorla!'

My last memory of the night was the scrape of their brogues against the stone steps, as they hurried away and I passed out upon the ground. I stirred hours later in the first rays of dawn, then remembered the ollave. My hand reached out to the empty space beside me, and with a twinge of sadness I rolled onto my back, taking a sharp breath of crisp air which made me gag.

'You're a fool, Abel,' I croaked.

Some coughing ensued, followed by deep breaths of fresh air as I got that fleeting feeling of joy at still being alive. This was quickly replaced by misery when a great pain tore through my head. I somehow staggered back to my feet, then shuffled to the hall where the blare of pipes could be heard once again.

Another day of feasting had commenced, and I had hardly stepped through the great doors before one of de Cuéllar's band laughingly showered me with mead. Given the throbbing in my head I was in no condition to avenge this misdeed, determined as I was to clear my head with a cup of wine as food was handed out freely once more. As the merriment recommenced, the bard recited countless odes, and the same dances and scuffles from the previous day resumed. Yet in vain did I seek out the ollave amongst the great gathering in the hall, for she was nowhere to be seen, although Saorla, sitting by Dervila's elbow, often cast me looks of undisguised contempt.

In truth I was relieved when the feasting finally ended, and the assembly's attentions turned back to the rebuilding of the town. The growing cold of winter was all the spur that was needed to ensure that a fair portion of this work had already been performed by the lower-born and the churls. Most of the mud and wattle huts and cabins were restored, and a large bawn for the cattle was already half built to protect valuable livestock from the elements. Dervila promised to restore the infirmary from her own purse, and O'Ronayne's servants had not been idle either. A number of outhouses were restored through the toil of worthy carpenters, and the Abbey of Saint Mel had been cleared of the filth left in it by the heretics.

Meanwhile word of our exploits during the siege travelled far and wide, carried by tribesmen to lands beyond Dartry. Unexpected tributes were received from neighbouring chieftains, for clearly a hope had been kindled by our unlikely defence of Rosclogher. Many envoys were also received by the chieftain. Manglana also received gifts of muskets and goatskin cloaks. O'Connor's sub-kings were among the first to arrive, followed by those of the O'Dowds and the O'Harts. Each regarded Francisco de Cuéllar with wonder, rendering the captain a mainstay in the chieftain's hall. All visitors listened to his stories with silent nods, then bowed to him deeply and declared themselves loyal subjects of King Philip II of Spain. I was often left rolling my eyes at these proclamations of loyalty, for it was not as if de Cuéllar had any sway in the king's court in Madrid. One even recited part of a papal bull, in which the pope had pronounced Philip II of Spain the rightful king of Ireland.

The greatest reception was of course reserved for the official envoy of Manglana's overlord, the mighty Brian *na Múrtha* O'Rourke. O'Rourke's kinsman Owen MacFelim appeared in Rosclogher with a score of raiders and as many heads of cattle to honour Manglana. MacFelim was lord of the castle of Carha and head of a lesser branch of the O'Rourkes. He was an old and wizened man yet said to be most wily, often consulted by *na Múrtha* on matters of rule.

MacFelim's links with Dartry also rendered him an apt choice; some of his sons had been fostered by Manglana, and the MacFelims had themselves reciprocated the honour. It was therefore with sincere joy that he was received by the chieftain, not to mention Dervila, who also happily received her husband's fellow sub-lord. As I witnessed their happy exchanges, I noticed a large swarthy man with sunburned skin who clung to the lord of *Carha*'s back like a long shadow and who bowed to no one. Yet his head swiftly turned towards us when he heard the voice of Old Tom.

'Geraldine, you old rogue!' he bellowed in flawless Gaelic. 'The master wants you back.'

The Anglo-Norman bowed respectfully towards the armoured giant.

'If it pleases the lord MacFelim, I shall return with his party, Dario Ohmunevic'.

His mention of the soldier's name suggested Slavonian roots, so I was not surprised to learn that Ohmunevic was a forest Croat, one of those dreaded mercenaries renowned for their deadliness in the skirmish. A fellow castaway of the Armada, he listened intently to Geraldine when the latter described some of the happenings during the siege, then raised an eyebrow in concern when mention was made of the poisoned cistern. Thereafter he broke away from us, and we took our places as the feasting ensued. De Cuéllar was summoned to recount the tale of the siege, and most of the company of MacFelim listened in awe whilst the captain embellished our exploits, greatly exaggerating his involvement in the defence as he waved wide strokes in the air with his sword.

After his usual lies had been shared, many of the younger freemen gathered around the captain to pepper him with questions. They hung on his every word. In the meantime, the lord MacFelim was seen whispering with the forest Croat, who gestured to Old Tom that he should make his way towards him.

As Manglanas and MacFelims mingled, Geraldine's approach went largely ignored, and after MacFelim had exchanged hushed whispers with him, too, I could see the Anglo-Norman beckoning for me to join them. My attentions were torn away from Muireann as I walked over to the three men, and a gentle smile flickered between the MacFelim's scarred cheeks when he spoke.

'It would appear that your efforts have been understated, Spaniard.'

'It matters not. I did what I had to sire; I was bound by oath.'

'As were others, although it appears that that did not suffice.'

'Officers,' I sighed 'I have served them all my life. What turns a boy into a man is serving men who act like boys.'

MacFelim chuckled at my quip before sitting back and raising his horn of brandy. Meanwhile Ohmunevic's hard expression remained unchanged.

'Who are you?' he asked me.

'My name is Juan.'

'That much I have already learned. But Thomas here says that you are also possessed of a marksmanship which even the good captain appears to lack.'

His brow darkened as his gaze darted towards de Cuéllar.

The captain still gestured wildly in a corner, watched in awe by Dervila, Cathal and Lochlain.

'I have had experience in the army,' I said.

'That much is clear,' said MacFelim, 'but whereabouts?'

'Wherever it has been, I have a knack for ending up in the thick of it.'

The O'Rourke's elderly envoy laughed again.

- XXXI -

'Old Tom has told me as much. How does our struggle compare to others you have witnessed?'

I calmly summed up my thoughts before I replied.

'As far as I am concerned, the only difference is that the boot is now on the other foot. In the Netherlands it was the heretics who were considered the rebels.'

Ohmunevic and MacFelim stared at each other before the Croat fixed me with a steely gaze and spoke again.

'All of which makes you invaluable to our cause.'

I did not reply, for his stare made me feel uncomfortable, and I inwardly cursed myself for having spoken too much. MacFelim's eyes narrowed as he also studied my face, and when he spoke again I could not help but feel that he had read my thoughts.

'Troubles brew west of Dartry MacGlannagh and Breifne O'Rourke,' he said, 'troubles which may well embroil us all before long. Our enemy always finds us divided, yet the defence of Rosclogher has stirred many. It might be the chance we need, to unite the whole of Connacht behind one man.'

He gestured with his cup towards de Cuéllar, then chuckled when my jaw dropped.

'The leader of a force does not matter, if the guidance of those that matter is executed. Old Tom here served Desmond, who spent many years as a beggar in London before finally rallying to the cause of his people.'

Geraldine frowned awkwardly at the MacFelim's reference, though he did not deny the assertion which had been made.

'De Cuéllar is not a man to be entrusted with power,' was my terse reply.

'That is not of concern,' said MacFelim quietly, 'for my lord O'Rourke would have him tightly collared. All that counts is harnessing the popular imagination of the common folk, for they might readily forget their petty squabbles to unite behind a man whose only fame is military, and who has no ancient claim to their petty lord's lands.'

He served me with a stare of sorrow and weariness.

'It has been our bane in this land, Spaniard, that our deep-rooted divisions are often given precedence over our resistance to the heretic. Yet we must adapt our traditions as well as our fighting ways. We cannot run like wolves forever; we must stand our ground on the field.'

A burst of raucous laughter assailed my ears, as a trestle table collapsed. Geraldine's eyes narrowed as he peered over my shoulder with a sigh.

'De Cuéllar has still not learned how to handle his drink. Another table has fallen beneath him.'

The MacFelim ignored his words, his eyes still fixed upon me as if we were both upon the peak of Mount Truskmore, with no other living creature around us for miles. I met his severe gaze with as serious an expression as I could muster, although my temples pounded from the tuns of wine which had flowed down my gullet. When he spoke again I strained my head forward, and his words were as crisp and as clear as his mind.

'The bards hail you the sons of Golam reborn. Your Captain de Cuéllar, regardless of his true nature, is being hailed as the new Aodh. The entire land could well burst into rebellion at the snap of his fingers, and together you could unite the northern rebels behind one banner.'

'Down with the heretics! *MacGlannagh Abuuù!*'

- XXXI -

De Cuéllar's cry behind us left me wincing in embarrassment, as he hacked at thin air with his drawn sword, then stumbled over one heel and careered into yet another trestle table. A loud yelp of dogs was heard as more food fell onto the floor.

'There goes the last table,' groaned Geraldine, 'just as I was yearning for another mutton leg...'

As always the feasting lasted late into the night, and the next day MacFelim's band of riders prepared to leave Rosclogher at dawn. While pulling on my shirt, I caught sight of Old Tom boarding a ferry and called to him through a window. The ends of his lips twitched with amusement as Geraldine raised his sword to me in salute.

'I must leave you now, friend Juan, for I have other duties to attend to! Look to your welfare; I suspect that we shall meet again before long!'

With that he was gone, boarding a little boat which swayed from side to side as it glided towards the eastern bank, leaving a stream of ripples in its wake upon the face of the dark water. For days thereafter I pondered my exchange with the MacFelim, for I already suspected that the siege of Rosclogher had been a small prelude to the desperate struggle yet to engulf Connacht.

XXXII

Rosclogher, Dartry, County Leitrim

4 – 25 December 1588

'Will we see out the winter?'

Manglana's face was pale when he asked the question. The long unspoken truth had finally been raised in the assembly. November had turned into December, and the elation following the siege had ended with the visits from neighbouring chieftains' envoys. Although the rewards in weapons and trinkets had been generous, the gifts of livestock had not sufficed, and the assembly feared that many tribesmen would go hungry. Cathal the Black's previous appeals to reduce the banqueting had fallen on deaf ears, since Manglana would not dream of denying hospitality to his distinguished guests, even if he were down to his last chicken.

So it was that I found myself being summoned with the other Spaniards to the chieftain's hall by Cathal the Black. We were asked to provide our account of Dal Verme's poisoning to the chieftain in person, that he might believe that the rot of sedition had set in amongst his fold, a sedition which would only grow worse if tribesmen starved. As we entered the hall and awaited our turn to speak, I stood silently between the Canarian brothers, being the only Spaniard who could understand the debate in Gaelic, which still raged in the hall.

'Any further feasting must be stopped,' said Cathal, 'for your own steward fears the low quantity of our stocks. Your people shall suffer great torment if any further setback is endured before the fighting season'.

'People must suffer for their king,' replied Manglana tersely, 'if they are to respect him and earn his protection.'

'The people's patience for suffering is not without its confines,' said the tanist gently, 'and their loyalty is required more than it ever was before. Many a subject's fealty to you has been strained by the siege of the English army from Dublin. The protection which you offer is provided by other mouths that must also be fed.'

Manglana scowled openly as he shifted awkwardly in his seat.

'And do you question my power, lord *tánaiste*?'

'Not now or ever, my lord!' exclaimed Cathal, with his scarred arms held apart before him for emphasis. 'Yet to what end do I conceal the truth, if it might threaten your reign?'

'My steward shall gather more tribute,' growled the chieftain, 'coshery, livery and whatever else he would call it. Our revelry is to be maintained if we are to secure good allies.'

I could see the steward Malachy bristling at his master's suggestion, but a look of hope appeared on his face when the tanist boldly emphasised his concerns.

'It is the people's devotion that must be secured first and foremost!' he said. 'They cannot pay any more rents than they have already rendered! Your subjects must be treated with care, my lord, for I fear that some heads in our fold have already been turned by enemy silver! I have gathered the Spaniards to bear witness to this very fact!'

'There are always those who wish for an end to the reign of chieftains!' snarled Manglana, 'and what of it? We have laws with which to punish sedition!'

'Yet we are in no position to further fan any flames!' insisted the tanist.

I marvelled at Cathal's bravery as his lord's face turned scarlet.

'Then what would you have me do?'

'It seems to me that there is not much that can be done. Yet what little there is should be undertaken without hesitation.'

'Such as?'

'The new keep being built at Derrylihan. There is little scope in furthering its construction, since our resources must be devoted to securing the keeps that already stand.'

'That keep has been promised to the constable MacCabe!' cried Dervila as she suddenly rose from her seat amid a great swirl of her garments. 'It is part of a payment long promised to the gallowglasses, and one on which we cannot renege!'

'I do not speak of reneging but delaying, my lady,' replied Cathal softly, with a short bow.

Dartry's queen beheld him as if he were a mound of offal which had suddenly become possessed of a voice.

'Who knows what speech can be trusted, when it comes from the mouth of an unsightly cur!' she cried. 'Equivocation and petty feuds are well suited to motherless slanderers such

- XXXII -

as yourself. How you obtained your position with a face so blemished runs contrary to all Gaelic tradition, whether or not it is an Anglo-Norman who must remind them of it!'

My jaw dropped at Dervila's vicious tirade. She made no secret of her hatred for Cathal the Black. The tanist stiffened at her outburst, then managed to utter a terse reply.

'Fair looks shall not spare our people from hunger.'

'That much is true!' boomed the chieftain, quickly stepping in between his wife and tanist. 'Yet rest assured that the foundations of the new keep have long stood untouched, and no work has been undertaken on them since April.'

'Ah,' whispered Cathal, still reeling from the assault by the lady Bourke, 'that is fair tidings indeed, for little else remains to be cut, save for the endless revelry.'

The chieftain held his face in his hands.

'Not a day passes that I do not curse myself for allowing Aengus to attend that cursed bard contest! He is fortunate not to have seen these dark days, yet I do wonder what he would have counselled were he still with us!'

'We live in a new time, sire,' said Cathal, with a renewed vigour in his voice, most likely having been stung by the reference to the previous tanist, 'one unlike any other faced by our people. We face an enemy who is quick to seize up on the discontent of your subjects. Aengus himself -'

'Don't dare mention my son's name,' hissed Dervila. 'A fawning hound such as yourself, who assumes to know the mind of one who was so wise!'

All eyes fell upon her as she readied to continue her tirade. Yet in that instant the doors of the hall burst open, revealing Constable Donal MacCabe and five of his men. The Scots bore great Lochaber axes, and their chain mail clinked heavily as they strode towards Manglana's throne. The sight was truly an ominous one, so that Nial and six other blue jackets formed a shield before the chieftain, with their spears raised and swords half drawn. The Scots' advance came to a halt but a couple of feet away from them, and MacCabe's knuckles whitened about his axe handle when he addressed the chieftain.

'For days we have awaited your return from the heights of Dartry. Our lady Dervila's father offered us refuge, but little else. Our babes were lost in their mothers' arms, and a fair few of my men were bitten by frost. We are hungry and our food has dwindled. Your payment is owed to us in arrears.'

As the chieftain shifted uncomfortably in his seat once more, I resisted the great urge to cry out and reveal the existence of the emerald ring which burned inside me. Yet I remained silent, bridling my screaming guilt and resolving to only speak of the trinket when I found myself in a situation of life or death. At last, Manglana raised his hand.

'With what shall I pay you? I have no beeves to spare for my own men. You must tighten your belts and go out and forage.'

The MacCabes stroked the edges of their axe blades with their thumbs, while their scarred leader pointed an accusatory finger at the chieftain.

'I wanted to disband in October and return in May. It was you who insisted that my men stay on through the winter.'

Manglana turned his head from side to side, as if seeking an answer which had eluded him, then offered a response.

'I have always made good on my debts to you, Donal, yet at present I must recover my losses. I sniffed trouble during the

- XXXII -

winter months, yet who would have expected the whole of bloody Dublin to empty upon the land at Samhain?'

'Then we shall have coshery and claim direct tribute from your town!'

'Do not get ahead of yourself,' snapped the chieftain, 'for that is my right alone to give! My people have suffered enough already!'

'They still need protection! How else should I make good on your word to my men and their families? They journeyed far from home to fight for your people!'

Manglana grimaced and his eyes closed for a few moments as he visibly struggled to bridle his rage. When he spoke again, his voice was low and resolute.

'They shall just have to wait. Otherwise they can go and work in the mines abroad.'

MacCabe grabbed his belt and laughed aloud, his expression incredulous.

'You would have us wander forest and mountain like beasts? A band of desperate Scots roaming the land? Would you truly answer to what might happen then? Even I would be powerless to stop my men's looting and depravation.'

The chieftain barely restrained a shudder at the thought, resting his mouth upon a twisting fist in frustration before Dervila finally spoke.

'Donal MacCabe, you have been a servant both loyal and true to this land. Your men may share lodgings with our townsfolk, and shall be accorded first ranking as debtors. The lean months will be gone by the summer, and the fighting season promises to be bountiful.'

MacCabe gave no sign of acknowledging her words, and stared straight at the chieftain when he issued a low threat.

'Hear me well, Tadhg *Óg* MacGlannagh. You have one season in which to make good our debts. If not, my axes shall be forced to seek a new buyer, whoever that may be. Do not forget that we fight for a living and that your battles are not about blood to us.'

Upon delivering his threat, he stormed out the hall with his glowering Scots on his tail. When they were gone, the chieftain sat for a few moments with his face in his hands, and I feared that he might be reduced to tears.

'Would that I had never taken the constable into my service,' he sighed.

'The constable and his party were part of the dowry which you were gifted by my father,' exclaimed Lady Bourke.

'Would your father have them back?'

Dervila gave her husband the dirtiest of looks, for she was clearly not impressed by the suggestion. Since the arrival of Captain de Cuéllar, her disposition towards the Scots had cooled, yet it was clear that she found the slight on her father's gift hard to endure. Then the tanist stepped in again, seeking to seize on the chieftain's despair to dismiss his detested rival.

'Disband the gallowglass troop, my lord! The town cannot endure such an imposition! They have suffered much in the mountains without the constable's men to cheat them and rape their daughters! We now have Spanish heroes in our fold, who shall draw men across the land to our banner! They can train us how to stand on the field, for the Scot's way of fighting is almost as outdated as our own!'

- XXXII -

'Stay your tongue, serpent!' screamed Dervila, as she rose to her feet again. 'Our lands have been kept safe by the presence of MacCabe's axes whenever you rode off to raid beyond our borders!'

'Our safety has only been preserved by the divisions amongst our enemies!' retorted Cathal, who had finally lost his composure, enough to risk open disagreement with the queen of Dartry. 'It is no secret that the English viceroy in Dublin hates his servants the Binghams for their duplicity and barbarity!'

'So much so,' sneered Dervila, 'that they rode together across Connacht and travelled with the same army!'

Cathal had no response to this, for indeed the unlikely appearance of the viceroy and the Binghams in the west had baffled many. Ample rumour had also reached far-flung Connacht, that the English queen's viceroy in Dublin and Bingham in Connacht detested one another, being each affiliated to rival parties in the English court in London. I suspected that the cause of it lay in my insides, since the emerald ring appeared to be the one likely reason for their unlikely joint appearance.

'Silence!' bellowed the chieftain in exasperation. 'The decision on the gallowglass has been taken and shall stand.'

With this he buried his face into the palm of his right hand once more, then summoned his steward to his side, issuing an instruction that his servant repeated to the rest of the hall.

'Leave us, all of you.'

We had barely cleared out of the hall when Captain de Cuéllar leant over towards me.

'It appears that our stay has lasted long enough.'

'How do you mean?'

'It appears that Manglana is losing his grip.'

I said nothing, keeping my silence until I had reached the town and made my way back to the outhouse. Weary from worry and the heavy guilt that weighed down my soul, I collapsed onto my blankets, only stirring when the bondsman's movements awoke me at dusk.

'How goes it, friend Juan?' he asked. 'I have not seen you all day.'

I was surprised by the glare which had replaced the usual smile on his face, as he lit a taper upon the ground.

'Recovering from the siege,' I replied as he unslung his swords and removed his brogues.

'Yes, it is weary work keeping watch; it was often my lot in lives past. Yet seeking to keep the peace between mercenaries and townsfolk is even more taxing.'

Nial spoke to me of the day's events which had followed the fruitless meeting of the assembly. Cathal the Black had been ordered to ride to Breifne to request aid from Manglana's overlord the O'Rourke. Lady Bourke had been sent to her father's lands, with the same request. My heart sank like a millstone when he told me that the gallowglasses had taken up residence in the town. This was openly contested by the Dartrymen, who made their feelings clear to the bluejackets who sought in vain to keep the peace.

'Our lord will do well to steer clear of the town for a few days,' he said, 'and he rides out to Duncarbery at dawn. I have been asked to join him, so you will have to keep the company of your countrymen for a time.'

Nial's absence was as keenly felt as the cold which set in as Christmastide approached. A constant smell of peat smoke lingered over the town, together with a great calm that was only broken by the odd scuffle. These scrapes often broke out whenever the gallowglass made a nuisance of themselves with the despairing townsfolk.

All in all, it was a lonely, wretched time, for de Cuéllar's band had not warmed to me after the events of the siege, and the Canarians made for poor conversation despite their good intentions. Meanwhile Dal Verme always preferred his own company, given that he looked down the end of his nose at everyone. As I sought to avoid both Scot and Spaniard, I found myself wandering alone with a loaded rifle along the edge of the lake, at times even crossing the bog and daring some walks beyond it, for as long as I could stand the cold.

Over five days were spent in this manner until I found myself drawn to the newly restored structure which served as O'Ronayne's new residence, which had been constructed against the abbey's western sidewall. The guards before it did not stir at my approach, and as I dared to open the door they nodded to me with a smile. Finding my way unbarred, I was surprised to find how similar the new home of the Jesuit was to the old one which had been burned to the ground. I was once more greeted by a table and chairs, and with fresh straw strewn across the floor. A new fireplace had also reappeared, and I basked in the comfort of its hearth as I eyed the large wooden shelves filled with books.

The works were chiefly in Latin and Spanish, with a couple of French books also included. I dared not think about the price of the books in terms of cattle heads, which would have probably seen the tribe through a decade of winters. I grinned at the sight of Erasmus's Adagia, which brought to mind the memories of happier days spent in the village of Willebroek, a time when I was often the guest of Elsien's father Reynier, an educated man who had kindled the flame of interest I had shown in his own library. The old miller had allowed me to spend days in his house, reading works by the greatest minds of Europe.

'Time heals all wounds,' I said half aloud. Tears formed in my eyes when I heard a scrape of footsteps behind me.

I turned to find the unexpected sight of Muireann, who also beheld me in surprise. She clutched a vellum-wrapped book in her hand.

'Ollave Muireann,' I blurted with a swift bow, then lifted my head to still find her staring at me in confusion.

Her ochre eyes smouldered beneath her brown fringe, and the book was still held before her. When she still did not answer, I thought that an apology was perhaps in order, following my indiscretion during our last meeting.

'My deepest apologies for any offence caused,' I managed, 'I had more than my fair share to drink, and -'

'Do you still love to read?' she asked suddenly.

'Why, of course,' I replied, taken aback by her question. 'Of course.'

She placed her book back on the Jesuit's shelf, and reached out for the one I held.

'Have you read this?'

'Yes, many years ago. In Flanders.'

She clutched it tightly to her bosom and stared away from me with a sorrowful look clouding her face.

'It was a gift to Redmond, given to him by Aengus.'

The reference to her dead husband left me uncertain what to say, especially given my last reference to him on the roof.

- XXXII -

'A worthy gift, my lady,' I managed at last, 'and most dear to come by, I would imagine, in this far-flung corner of the known world.'

'Alas, a memory of joyful days long past,' she replied, 'of times of peace and plenty. Our herds have grown thinner with each passing year. Much of our wealth goes to war nowadays, with little left for craft or for learning.'

'Did these books all belong to your husband?'

'No Spaniard, only the more recent titles. Before O'Ronayne appeared in Dartry, he would not stomach the teachings of humanists. He believed that they encouraged conciliation with the heretic. It was his friendship with Aengus that changed his view of Erasmus and his fellows, for my husband brewed him the finest mead, over which they held lengthy discussion. Aengus gladly learned much of what Redmond taught him, yet he always rejoiced whenever these books arrived, for he always delighted in learning of things beyond this land.'

'He would have learned much from this library, for 'tis a kingly collection,' I said, nodding in approval.

'Your words are most kind, Spaniard, although hardly true. There are barely thirty volumes in all.'

'That is true, my lady. Yet in the land of the blind, the one-eyed man is king.'

A small smile grew on Muireann's face when I quoted the famous proverb.

'And what is your own view of the humanists?' she asked.

'I find little to dislike in their views,' I replied, 'in a world full of atrocity and injustice. Peace is certainly better than war wherever a choice presents itself. But what are your thoughts?'

Muireann smiled once more at my question.

'You are certainly of a humanist bent, to be curious about the opinions of women! And as a woman of letters, I agree with their teachings: that women should be educated and articulate, learning should be enjoyable, and that the act of love-making is not an evil. Yet what I most admire is their stance that one should be possessed of a questioning mind.'

'And of peace and war?' I asked, noting that she had not referred to it.

Her lip was pursed at the question, and she was wrapped in thought before she replied.

'I could never fathom conciliation with the heretic. Not after what my people have endured.'

There appeared scant reason to dwell on the subject, when one considered the price she had paid for her tribe's struggles against the Sassanas. In fact, Muireann gladly spoke of other topics instead. The hours passed like minutes as we shared ideas from the countless books we had read, like Macchiavelli's *The Prince* or More's *Utopia*. Not since my exchanges with Elsien had I met a woman so enthralling, who knew of serious works on Platonism and the humorous satires of Rabelais. In the end, I could tell that it was to her evident displeasure that our conversation ended. With a large frown on her face, she told me that she had been summoned to Manglana's hall to sup with Lady Bourke who was due to return that night.

When she was gone I found myself feeling both serene and content. I thought that I had made an impression on her and suspected that she would no longer refrain from seeking me out. Yet as I walked back to the outhouse on the periphery of the abbey's fence, I was quick to warn myself against becoming too close to a woman whose qualities I greatly admired. I feared she might jeopardise my plans to flee to the Continent, where the ring might secure my passage to the Indies.

My sense of foreboding was not wholly misplaced, since an opportunity to return to Spain presented itself more quickly than I had expected. With the townsfolk's resentment left to cool for two weeks, it was not long before the chieftain showed his face in Dartry again. Upon returning to Rosclogher, Manglana requested that the Spaniards earn their keep on days which were clear from rain and snow. We were ordered to provide martial training to his troops, and show lowborn herdsmen how to use both blade and firearm.

There was no better way to break up the monotony of the long winter months. Any clement weather found us out on the green, with Dal Verme adding finishing touches to the sword strokes taught by Nial whilst Enano and Koldo showed the darker arts of close combat to their fresh-faced charges. My lessons in marksmanship recommenced in earnest, and the troops in the ringfort trained towards midday. I also provided training outside the tower-house, which had been requested by Dervila's ladies upon their recalling the wager between their mistress and de Cuéllar. Rumour of the contest grew across the town, so that with the approach of Christmas I found myself summoned to the keep almost daily to train the highborn womenfolk.

With dexterous hands I showed them how to load the rifle with the scouring stick, again and again, until my nostrils could not smell anything but rotten eggs for hours afterwards. The end of these sessions wore me out, so that I was often found by myself outside the outhouse cleaning my gun. It was on one such occasion that the captain found me, bent over my muzzle as I sought to pluck a scrap of wadding from within it. Of late de Cuéllar had become a less cheerful and a more brooding figure, with unknown matters clearly weighing upon his mind.

'Do you have refreshment?' he growled, before making straight into the abode that I shared with the bondsman.

I was irritated by his arrogance, yet sought to keep calm.

'Only some brandy from last night. At the foot of the bed.'

The captain issued a loud grunt as he bent over to pick up the carafe, followed by the usual snuffling sounds he made whenever he drank. A loud burp followed as the captain emerged from the hut, wiping his mouth on the edge of his sleeve. When his arm came away from his face, I could see from his eyes that he was in a dark mood and that his thoughts were elsewhere. It was a fair while before he finally spoke to me.

'I do not understand this man. I offered to relieve him of our presence and promised to lead his Spanish hostages to his allies in Ulster. Let's face it Hospitalarios, we have proved more trouble than we're worth, what with the tribe having to feed the Scots and the whole of Dublin's garrison passing through. Yet again Manglana has refused my offer.'

He sighed aloud in frustration, staring at the peaks beyond the lake.

'He says the enemy has doubled its guard in the north. Yet I am starting to believe that it is just an excuse. An excuse to keep us from leaving.'

'Perhaps it might be best to see out the winter here,' I replied, as I looked up from my rifle. 'At least until things die down.'

De Cuéllar groaned as he sat down beside me.

'For how much longer will we wallow among these miserable beggars?'

- XXXII -

'Yet why not winter here?' I asked, since that was my intention. 'At least until spring? Our leaving would meet with more clement weather.'

'What? And live like savages?' protested de Cuéllar. 'Besides, it shall be the fighting season then, and the perils we face will only worsen. The English ships will be out in force as the months become warmer, cutting us off by sea.'

I realised that the captain expected me to flee Dartry with him. This did not sit well with me, following his erratic behaviour during the siege of the tower-house, so I thought I would try to persuade him of the benefits of remaining in Ireland.

'Why should we hazard a winter voyage by sea, Captain?' I said. 'We have everything we need here. You could persuade de Leiva's force to join with the rebel chieftains. Together we could drive the heretics from this land, and we shall not want for women and meat!'

De Cuéllar scoffed at my appeal.

'And live as savages?' he laughed.

'Is it any worse than sharing a rotten egg in a Flemish trench? With rain pouring down your neck while officers pocket your pay? If this is a savage life, then I can find no issue with it!'

De Cuéllar's eyes narrowed whilst he mulled over my words.

'I do not think I like your tone, Hospitalarios. Are you forgetting that we are sworn to the service of our king? These matters here are of no concern to us.'

'But I thought that we fought for the faith!'

De Cuéllar growled and grabbed me by the scruff of the neck, shaking me with a great rage.

'It is the king who decides who we are to fight. We will bear arms against Rome itself if he so demands, and drop the Holy Father to his knees.'

'It's happened before,' I gasped.

The captain snorted and flung me away.

'Then cease your womanly rant, you mutinous whelp. You will leave with me whenever I command it. The duke of Parma will do all he can to return us to Spain, back to a civilised life in the king's service!'

'They say it is dangerous,' I replied, as I staggered away from him, 'and they have never lied to us. Cathal the Black himself left for Breifne with a large force of mounted freemen, and he has still not returned.'

De Cuéllar scowled at me.

'They also said that the castle could not be defended! Why will you not heed me? De Leiva knows better than to waste his men and his time among these medieval tosspots! His ship will be repaired any day now, and we shall miss the boat if we do not leave soon.'

'And risk a journey home in the winter months? The year is still 1588, Captain. Are you forgetting the squalls we met when we set sail from home? And that was during the sailing season! De Leiva himself must know that. Surely he will not set sail until the year is out!'

'I would rather brave the elements,' he growled, 'then be hostage to Manglana for another instant! What is the matter with you, Hospitalarios? Have you gone soft, spending time playing the Adonis whilst you talk books with that poet woman? In any case, have you bedded her yet?'

- XXXII -

To my surprise, I found myself bristling at his reference to Muireann. Yet de Cuéllar droned on in the gathering dusk, his voice boring into my ears.

'There are still those to whom honour is worth something, no matter how far they are from home!'

I rose suddenly to my feet, met by his contemptuous glare as I trembled with rage.

'You have the gall to speak to me of honour!' I replied. 'An officer who swears an oath to the chieftain, only for other men to have to uphold it!'

'I do not forget my oath to serve my king,' he spat, 'and would risk life and limb to return to his service!'

He turned a hue of scarlet as his dagger was drawn at my outburst, and things might have gone poorly for me were it not for a small band of bluejackets who passed by us on their way to the abbey. When they saw us, the men called out to us and waved. De Cuéllar returned his blade to its sheath as he smiled back at them and nodded in salutation.

'They revere you, Captain' I said. 'Fleeing like a thief would leave them devastated. These people would die for us. Can you say as much of our own officers?'

De Cuéllar fell silent, and his eyes were clouded with confusion as I pressed on.

'We could live as lords among them and teach them everything we know. Be the chess players not the pieces on the board.'

The captain appeared tormented by my pleas, then whirled upon me suddenly.

'And run barefoot through the bush like outlaws? No, Hospitalarios, our place is with Spain! She is the mother whom we are sworn to protect. I wonder at the thoughts which pass through your head, Hospitalarios, yet I do not forget who I am!'

His accusations cut deep, so that I struggled for a reply before I was snared by his next accusation.

'I think that you do not want to leave. I also do not believe that you are Juan de los Hospitalarios.'

'What do you mean?' I asked, feeling entirely stunned.

'I know who you are, where I have heard of you before. You are the man Ramos wanted. I heard mention of you at his office in Seville.'

My jaw dropped as de Cuéllar smirked and leant towards me.

'I have met few men who can hit the mark like you do. Fewer still bear the mark of a chain upon their left ankle. There is no doubt that you are the Lynx of Haarlem.'

The captain shook his head in disbelief as he drew closer to me.

'Alba's own marksman, Abelardo de Santiago. I have long suspected it.'

When I looked at him again, his voice was lowered and overcome by an understanding tone.

'I know who wants you dead, but none need know that you are alive. My own doom was also decreed at sea, when a stupid officer condemned me to death. But who cares now? Those that falsely accused me lie beneath the waves, where all those who know you also believe you to be. You can take up a new name, and I shall personally vouch for your new identity.'

His proposal was met with a weary reply.

'And what of the wager of Cathal the Black, Captain? He risked much to defend us, when most of the assembly wanted

- XXXII -

us gone. The gallowglass constable will claim many heads of his cattle if we leave before the spring.'

De Cuéllar looked at me in wonder, as if I had uttered the most incredible nonsense.

'I have said it before to you, man: that wager is no concern of mine, for it was taken before I even reached this land. Besides,' he added, serving me with an expression that dripped sarcasm, 'you broke your oath to the king of Spain. Why should the wager of a scarred tribesman mean anything to you?'

His words left me feeling distressed, but he persisted further.

'Listen to me, Santiago. Disappointment and sadness are a part of life. My father died before I knew him, and I was pressed aboard ships before I was even drawn to women. It was no place for boys, and I wish that I did not see most of what I did. Yet what does it matter? Am I to abandon my rank and country because of a gamble taken by a highborn tribesman? In time the tanist will make up for the lost heads, and what of it? The enemy will end up claiming them anyway. You have seen the way the natives fight; they shall be slaughtered like lambs before the summer's end.'

At these words I could not help but think of the chamber in Sligo and of what would befall the emerald ring if and when the captain's prediction came true. It was then that I resolved to desist from convincing him to linger longer in Dartry, since another opportunity to reach the Indies via the Continent might not present itself for months thereafter.

'Very well then,' I uttered at last. 'I shall attempt flight whenever you order it.'

An evil smile spread across his face, which I had not seen since the chieftain's return.

'You see reason at last, my friend. Stow away as much food as you can spare, and whatever powder you can carry. I have the beginnings of a plan forming in my mind, and we may not tarry a fortnight hence.'

He had trudged off and I had returned to cleaning my rifle when a low hiss reached my ears. I lifted my head and saw the captain staring back at me as he whispered an afterthought.

'And steal whatever you think might aid us in our flight,' he said, then limped off again.

The captain's orders were barely two days old when Cathal the Black finally made his return to the village. It was some hours after midday that shouting and laughter were heard near the bog, and I emerged to see the tanist leading his horse behind him. His riders were covered in sweat as they also led their mounts by the reins. My heart leapt at the great lowing behind them, as a score of horseboys led as many black cows after the tanist's force.

Nial and I mingled with the townsfolk and gallowglass who crowded about the returned horsemen, calling out praise and plaudits as Cathal the Black raised his hand to them in salute.

'A fitting return, my lord!' shouted the bondsman behind me. 'It appears that your travels abroad were fruitful.'

Cathal turned his head towards us, and his yellowed teeth glistened as he acknowledged the greeting.

'Both fruitful and fortunate, friend Ne Dourough. O'Rourke has himself fallen on hard times and could only render us nine heads. "In honour of Aodh and the sons of Golam," he said. Yet upon our return I skirted his borders and fell upon an unsuspecting *tuath* of the O'Reillys. They never expected MacGlannaghs to venture so far east at this time of year.'

- XXXII -

'A triumph befitting a poem from the bard!' laughed Nial, but Cathal *Dubh* shrugged.

'They were all too easily overcome.'

Manglana had since retired to Duncarbery once more, where he was locked in long debates with some neighbouring allies to the north of his borders. Dervila, however, had remained in the tower-house on Lough Melvin, and so Cathal decided to throw a feast that night in his long, wooden cabin along the banks of the lough to mark his return. It was not to match the banquets held at Rosclogher, for Cathal only invited his closest subalterns and Spanish allies. De Cuéllar's plans weighed heavily on my thoughts. I buckled my sword belt and set off from the outhouse alone when a familiar cackle of laughter was heard from the peripheral huts along the green.

When I looked to my left, I could make out the dim figure of a young harlot who limped with a grimace back towards her own lodging. Catcalls and jeers were hurled at her back as de Cuéllar's band emerged from their lodgings, and the woman's movements revealed that they had all had their fill of her. I shook my head in irritation, for despite our exalted status it had not taken long for the ragged fellowship to resume their wicked ways once the town had been rebuilt.

I quickened my pace as I sought the tanist's lodgings before de Cuéllar and his men could appear. My mouth watered upon entering the cabin. It was so smoky that I could barely made out the tanist and his men. Their mantles were furled about them as they sat back against the wooden walls, helping themselves to the finest cuts of meat cooked over a fire outside the hut. Cathal appeared in high spirits as he took another swig from his cup, which was swiftly refilled by a serving boy. His sores were barely visible under the black hair which hung over his face. As he sat back, his gaunt profile reminded me of one of the champion cattle raiders of old that were often hailed by the bard.

'Greetings, friend Juan!' he hollered as he raised his cup. 'You are always welcome at our hearth!'

I bowed deeply to him before taking my place at the edge of the gathering, where I was swiftly served with a shank of bull meat and an overflowing goblet. An even heartier welcome was reserved for the captain and his men, when they entered the cabin with broad and satisfied grins. Cathal even rose to his feet to embrace de Cuéllar, who chuckled amiably before taking his seat. All five of his band ignored me as they helped themselves to the fare on offer, and did not so much as acknowledge the Canarians or Dal Verme when they appeared.

As the evening wore on, a travelling harpist played a lyre while we sat back and drained a small barrel of mead. The tanist laughed aloud at many of the captain's tales and recounted some of his own adventures. His voice was pierced by sadness when he told of the destruction of Munster, which he had witnessed years earlier. This had followed the Desmond rebellions, when the enemy had inflicted great hunger and poverty upon the south of Ireland, razing it to the ground and rendering it a wasteland.

'Thou wouldst not have travelled far if thy ship had been wrecked upon its coast,' remarked the tanist. ''Tis most fortunate for ye that the northern rebels still hold sway in Connacht.'

'The Sassanas are an enemy both vile and ruthless,' remarked de Cuéllar, shaking his head in mock outrage and glaring into

- XXXII -

his cup, 'yet we do not fear them, and shall always remain true to thy cause.'

Despite the dim light, I could see that the tanist had been warmed by this remark. He raised his cup towards his honoured guest.

'Verily do I feel more emboldened by thy presence,' he declared, 'for with allies as brave and as seasoned as ye, we cannot but learn to prevail against the heretical scourge which afflicts our lands like the wolf *An Faolchù*.'

All cups were drained to loud growls of assent, and when we were finished, de Cuéllar spoke up again.

'What of this wolf *An Faolchù*?' he asked, seeming genuinely intrigued.

Cathal was as surprised by this sudden interest as he was keen to share knowledge on a subject which had appealed to the officer he revered. I listened on as the captain learned of the creature that had long afflicted the herdsmen in Dartry and who had been accorded the nickname of its previous bloodthirsty chieftain, who was also Cathal's father. De Cuéllar's interest hardly wavered as he listened to each word with the greatest attention. He proceeded to scold me when he heard how I had missed my clear shot at the beast, while riding in the company of the lady Bourke.

'Alas!' he cried, when Cathal's account was ended. 'Would that I had formed part of my lady's party! For I have had great experience in snaring these creatures.'

'Truly?' exclaimed the tanist.

'Oh, indeed,' said the captain, reassuring his listener with a brisk nod. 'I was but a young boy when my father sent me out to slay them, armed only with a staff and a sling.'

'I thought you grew up fatherless,' I said in Spanish, but the captain served me with a dark stare, before addressing the tanist again in his best Latin.

''Twas a great talent that evolved in me then, learning the prints of the beast and tracking them back to their lair. I could move for leagues unseen, running from shadow to shadow. I would stir them from their holes before leaving them dead with a well-aimed stone to the skull. Scores of the beasts were killed this way, and men from other villagers soon appeared at my father's door to request the use of my skills.'

''Tis indeed welcome news,' exclaimed Cathal, 'for the beast *An Faolchù* has long pilfered cattle and men from this land. Thy skill would be a great boon to us come the spring!'

'Why tarry so long,' said the captain, 'when with a handful of men I could slay the fell beast within days?'

'Truly!'

'Let us wait until the revelry of Christmastide, which shall further allow my leg to mend,' said the captain. 'Thereafter I shall rid thy people of this beast, for ye have long provided us with safety and comfort.'

'O, worthy Spaniards!' cried the tanist. 'That ye should rid us of so great a scourge! Happily dost thy offer reach mine ears! And to think that a sling shall so swiftly despatch the beast!'

A look of concern appeared on de Cuéllar's face at these words, and he cleared his throat awkwardly before he spoke again. I could not understand what his game was, so I was overcome by a great curiosity as I watched him like a hawk.

''Tis a beast of some repute,' said the captain, 'which shall require some days in deep brush, where a sling may not be the most adequate of arms. In my country the trees are well spaced out, but here my arm would hardly be raised to fling the stone, that it would strike wood instead of thin air.'

'Ah,' said the tanist, with a note of regret, 'then that makes the beast harder to kill.'

'Not unless I have crossbows and rifles,' said de Cuéllar, taking a sip from his mazer, 'as well as clothes and provisions to last me a few days.'

'Certainly!' cried Cathal with little hesitation. 'I shall provide thee with kerns to aid thee in thy venture.'

'That will not be necessary, my lord,' replied the captain with a gentle smile, 'for great stealth shall be required, and men who can speak volumes to one another with a mere expression or sign.'

'Indeed,' replied the tanist as he shook his head and beheld the captain in wonder, 'for after the defence of Rosclogher, ye should hardly explain thyself further.'

When this discussion was ended, Cathal *Dubh* raised his glass and repeatedly honoured the Spaniards and the impending death of the wolf. Meanwhile I noticed de Cuéllar exchanging sly winks with his band, who grinned like the lowlife bandits they were before helping themselves to more food and drink. When the feast was over, I staggered back with them to their hut, leaning over towards de Cuéllar who swayed drunkenly as he shuffled towards his hut.

'If you lied to the tanist,' I said, 'he will be distraught.'

'We must all grow up, sooner or later,' replied the captain with a shrug.

His duplicity left me feeling deeply disturbed, although further concerns were to weigh on me the following dawn. I awoke in fright when a heavy hand was placed on my mouth, and I was met by the sight of a gnarled gallowglass warrior who glared at me with five of his huge fellows at his back. I was pulled off my bed and pushed out of the hut, with hardly any time to wear my brogues. The half-dozen Scots closed in around me with their heavy axes held out before them, wordlessly leading me away from the town and towards the trees which lay east of the lake. They held me by the scruff of my tunic as we travelled deeper into the woods towards an unknown destination.

In vain did I attempt to talk to the men, for no reply was forthcoming. It was clear that the path they struck was well known to them, and when the trees receded slightly they would surround me again. Nearly half an hour passed, and we came in sight of a small cottage beneath an oak, with a plume of smoke rising from its chimney. A curtain of hide hanging before its entrance was quickly pulled aside as the leader of the Scots hurled me inside, leaving me to fall on my knees.

'My lady,' was all he said before bowing once and returning to the company of his men who stood outside.

When I looked up, I made out the stunning beauty of Manglana's wife, who stood between two long tables that were laden with all manner of items. She was accompanied by her handmaiden, Saorla.

'Art thou scared, Spaniard?' asked Lady Bourke.

'Of you? Of course, my lady, yet what have I -'

'Not me – not yet,' she cut in, 'although other dangers lurk within the tribe which you would do well to heed.'

I was confused by her words, and I did not know what to say until she spoke again.

'Rise to your feet, Spaniard. Help yourself to some brandy, for the morning air is cold.'

- XXXII -

Twigs fell from my knees as I rose off the floor and Saorla passed me my drink. I stared at the bottles and jars that surrounded me. I could make out the entrails and feet of various creatures within them, such as frogs and birds, the likes of which I had not seen before.

'What is this place?' I asked, as my head turned in astonishment from side to side.

'Why, this is my secret apothecary, Spaniard,' replied Lady Bourke, then smiled.

She seated herself in a chair at the back of the hut before beckoning to Saorla to serve her again.

'Where did you think all the rumours of my being a witch came from?' she asked me. 'Not to mention the medicines used by our Jesuit physician?'

'Are those his?' I whispered in awe, jerking my head at a stack of five books at the end of one of the trestle tables.

'No,' she replied curtly, 'those belong to me. They are works by Paracelsus. There remains more to be done to fully convince Redmond of their worth, although I must say that his understanding is growing rapidly, no doubt aided by my generosity towards his causes.'

I reached my hand out towards one of the volumes, then cast her a sidelong glance.

'May I?'

'Why, certainly,' she laughed, her face suddenly overcome by a look of mischief, and her cheeks coloured by another sip from her cup, 'word of your love of books has reached my ears, swiftly relayed to me by one of my birds.'

'And a most pretty bird at that -' I began, but stopped when I noticed the frown on her face.

I suddenly felt flustered, so returned my attention to the book, picking it up and holding it out before me. It was written in French, which was not my strongest language.

'Prognostications.'

'And are you surprised, Spaniard?' asked Lady Bourke, with a hint of amusement in her voice.

'By what?' I asked, although I was indeed amazed by the intellectual pursuits of a woman in so distant a part of the world, and by the appearance of more costly volumes.

'You look surprised,' was all she said, then issued a low chuckle, 'yet I was a bright young thing during my childhood, the darling of my lord father who ensured that I received the best education. He even provided me with a French tutor, not just one for Latin. He had high hopes for me then, up until my husband appeared at our keep in the company of that animal of his elder brother.'

I noticed her voice faltering at the mention of the tribe's former chieftain, and a look of angst overcame her for a moment before she continued with her account.

'It was the first time I had seen Gaels, and my husband was a wild sight as his eyes blazed at me from atop his saddleless stallion. The sight of him scared me, but not enough. I suppose I warmed to his unexpectedly courteous ways, which contrasted greatly with his elder brother's savagery. For Cathal *Óg* often humiliated and ridiculed Tadhg, addressing him worse than you would a churl. I suppose I felt sorry for Tadhg, and he was moved when I took a damp cloth to wipe the blood from his forehead after *An Faolchù* had served him with a blow from his sword handle.'

- XXXII -

This treatment of Manglana seemed almost unthinkable to me, and I marvelled at the tale as Dervila further described her lord's courtship.

'Thereafter he visited us often, bearing what paltry gifts he could afford. He was always strong and brave, and had the mind of a viper. He was greatly revered in this land before he became chieftain himself, which is why Cathal *Óg* tried to kill him.'

'His own brother?'

'Yes, his own elder brother', she said with a wry smile, 'Cathal *Óg*, whose own people called him *An Faolchù*, the wolf. Be thankful that you never knew him, Spaniard, for so vicious and barbaric a creature has never been witnessed. We were all of us relieved by news of his death. But I digress…where was I?'

Her lips were pursed in thought before Saorla spoke up.

'Your lord husband's courtship, my lady.'

'Ah, yes. He was relentless in his visits to my father's keep, seeking to court me no matter how many times I laughed him off. My father long warned me to resist his advances; he advised me to hold out for someone more powerful, who could afford large rents that would satisfy my love of learning. Yet love is blind, and I suppose that I was drawn to him. We often spotted him atop his horse in the rain as my cousins and I laughed at him from behind a slit window. He looked so formidable in his armour; I knew there was no man alive who would do more for me. He even went as far as to get his overlord, the O'Rourke, to arrange our handfast!'

A long, hollow laugh left her lips when she said this.

'To think how happy he looked back then! And I was so full of joy myself, intrigued by this man from the north, whose face shone at his every sight of me. Yet nothing prepared me for Dartry. That gossip Nial will no doubt have told you how I returned to my father's lands for over a year before coming back. The butcher *An Faolchù* had mercifully passed on by then, and my husband was declared chieftain. He was charm itself upon my return, racing to my side at each opportunity.'

Her face was suddenly overcome by sadness and resignation as she seemed to stare past me.

'Then I learned that there were other younger things, warming his bed and fathering his bastards. Yet it no longer bothers me, for I no longer want that pig to touch me. I suppose I could have divorced him, but I didn't. Aengus was already my whole world by then. God knows I almost died delivering him. So I poured everything I knew into my son, to ensure that he did not end up an uncivilised, fighting brute like his father. I was overjoyed by his handfast with Muireann, for although he could have brokered more power for us, their minds met the instant they met, and she was nothing but good for him. But alas, it all ended with the taste of yet more ash in my mouth.'

Her lost stare disturbed me as she held her cup out to Saorla and drained it in one gulp, then held it out twice more.

'We must all accept our fate Spaniard,' she said at last, 'and I shall be remembered as nothing more than yet another wife who waited patiently upon an unfaithful husband. Another unknown wife of another forgotten warrior-chieftain involved in petty squabbles on the periphery of the known world. Would that you had not rescued me when that marksman took aim at me. You should have worried about the wolf instead!'

'Sometimes the unlikeliest of events lay ahead of us, my lady,' I replied, 'landing us in situations we would never have imagined.'

- XXXII -

My reply seemed to pique her interest as her eyes shot towards me. She rested her chin upon her knuckles, with a long finger placed upon her cheek.

'Perhaps you speak true. The day may come when Dervila MacGlannagh may be remembered like Queen Maeve of yore, through an act of bravery to set me alongside the myth that surrounds Grania O'Malley.'

She stared at me for a few more moments, then spoke again.

'What are your feelings for the ollamh, Spaniard?'

'My lady?' I asked, surprised by the question and flushed with embarrassment.

'I have seen the way she looks at you and how you look at her. Yet the fate of the tribe is linked to her future. You must quell your feelings for Muireann, before they go too far.'

'What feelings?'

Dervila smiled gently and rose to her feet before walking over to me. I winced when she held out her arm, for fear that she might slap me, yet the palm of her hand rested gently upon my cheek.

'Any affections you harbour for Muireann shall not blossom in this world. You are a valiant man, Spaniard, but that alone shall not spare you from the higher workings of the tribe.'

'I shall heed your warning, Your Grace.'

She smiled faintly.

'By our laws a widow reclaims her dowry and has full control over her marriage portion. The ollamh also owns many heads of livestock, among other goods. Powerful men woo her already. The tanist Cathal has long divorced his last wife, while Donal shall readily take up another.'

'T-take more than one w-wife?' I stuttered in shock.

'Our ways may seem strange to you Spaniard, yet they exist nonetheless. Muireann's dowry will grant great power to whoever marries her. A landless alien will not stand in the way of her suitors.'

Her revelation rendered me speechless and she uttered her next words slowly.

'My husband has ordered that she reveal her mind to him soon. Her choice shall affect our own position. Do not cloud her mind with your affections, Spaniard. Would you rock the boat that keeps you afloat?'

I rose to my feet and bowed while thanking her for her advice. When I walked away I bent my head sideways to avoid the legs of chickens and sprigs of mistletoe which dangled from the ceiling. My face brushed against some hare skins as her last words reached me.

'Remember that there are eyes and ears everywhere. Beware your pride, man of Spain.'

I turned on my heel and bowed to her again to hide my grimace.

'You ask much of a Spaniard, my lady, yet your warning is heeded.'

'If you value your life,' she said, as I turned towards the door, 'for although the Scots are loyal to me, even I do not have full control over Constable MacCabe.'

'Then have no fear, my lady,' was my instant reply, 'for I care for no one more dearly than I care for myself.'

XXXIII

Rosclogher, Dartry, County Leitrim

26 December 1588 – 2 January 1589

Dervila's warning weighed heavy on my mind during Christmastide. The whole tribe was gathered in the restored Abbey of Saint Mel, with its freshly whitened walls and its new glass windows. While the birth of Christ was celebrated by the tribe, it was all I could do to avert my stare from the chairs at the front of the nave, where the *ollamh* stood in the company of the lady Bourke. After Mass, the highborn tribesmen walked off in their usual procession back to the tower house. I rubbed my freezing hands close to my face and blew hard on them. When my hands fell back to my sides I was surprised to see the ugly face of Enano in front of me. He snarled quick instructions before running off after his fellowship.

'Make ready to depart. Captain says that we will fly any day now.'

A sense of excitement and dread seized me as I walked back to the outhouse, realising as I did that I would soon be leaving the place which had been my home for two months. I was saddened at the prospect of leaving Dartry until I remembered the ring. I swiftly opened the eighth gourd of my bandolier and poked my finger into it, breathing a sigh of relief when I felt the edge of the ring which I had long since returned to the ampoule. I had carried out the miserable act of recovering it from my bowels not long after the Sassanas' siege of the Rosclogher tower-house was ended, in the cold, early hours of the morning, behind a tree.

After checking on the trinket there remained little to do, except open a small sackcloth bag I had hidden beneath my bed and ensure that it was still full of the scraps which I had pilfered away following every meal. I had also pinched a skin of water from the bondsman and concealed, together with a second brat mantle, away under my mattress. Upon inspecting my clothing I decided that there was little else I wanted for, since the English clothes taken during the siege had proved to be of good quality and more than adequate to keep out the winter chill after the lice had been smoked out of them. Otherwise there was little left to prepare, save for ensuring that I left Dartry with a well-sharpened blade and a cleaned rifle.

During the week following the Nativity the whole town keenly awaited the shooting contest between Dervila's chosen maid and Captain de Cuéllar. Targets formed out of enemy breastplates and helmets were erected upon the green, which had turned snow white, and Lady Bourke requested that her charges receive further training from me. She had still to choose her best markswoman to take on the captain, and was clearly taken up by the impending contest. This only served to spur the ollave to go to great lengths to master the firearm, and I could scarce imagine Dervila choosing anyone else to stand for all Dartrywomen during the contest.

It was barely a week later, with two days left before the contest, that Enano appeared at my door at midday. Nial had not yet returned from some business he had with Manglana's steward, so the wicked dwarf found me alone, causing me to start when I noticed his evil face.

'Your honeymoon is all but finished, marksman,' he snarled, 'and you shall soon return to your rightful command. We leave two hours before the first light of dawn. I shall return then.'

As he walked off, I was filled with unease; nothing felt right about the deceitful escape. Then memories returned of my ambition to sail for the Indies, and of the great riches which might yet be afforded to me if de Leiva did succeed in returning to the Continent, allowing me to find Elsien's brother, Maarten, and to pawn the emerald ring in Seville's underworld. Even at a quarter of its fair value I would still be in funds for a few years, and I could command a troop of men to defend my cattle farms when we finally reached the Indies.

'I am a lover of liberty,' I whispered to myself, quoting Erasmus as I checked my belongings a final time. 'I will not and I cannot serve parties.'

Indeed, Enano's instructions had filled me with a quiet dread as recollections of the iron discipline of the Spanish army returned to me, mingled with the fear of serving a buffoon like de Cuéllar. It was in vain that I reassured myself, as my tossing and turning persisted late into the night that joining the captain's band was but a temporary step which might ensure my dreams could be pursued in the long term. A sixth sense had developed within me over my years spent in the army, forged during the long hours spent alone in concealment, awaiting the perfect moment to strike my target. It was a feeling which I had learned to trust beyond my coldest reasoning, and it would give me no peace until late into the night. This meant that I only slept for a couple of hours before a jerk was felt at my shoulder and Enano's low whisper was heard.

'Up, whoreson! And follow me quick!'

With a gasp I snatched my belongings, then tarried in the doorway. I started when the bondsman snored loudly behind me.

'Hurry!' hissed Enano, and I thought the better of quietly saluting Nial. I hurried after the dim figure of my fellow Spaniard as we ran down towards the water. Obscure and hooded forms had gathered upon the newly restored jetty, clustered above two boats which readied to bear us across the water. I felt both bleary-eyed and light headed as I hopped into one of them behind Enano, too weary to ask questions as a familiar voice reached my ears.

'Have a care, my friends,' said Cathal *Dubh*, 'for the creature is as dangerous as it is cunning and has killed two huntsmen already.'

'Never fear, my lord!' declared de Cuéllar in the opposite boat. 'The beast shall be swiftly despatched, and we shall bring you its head before the contest.'

'Godspeed, O worthy Spaniards,' said the tanist. 'The whole land shall rejoice at its deliverance from the black wolf.'

Cathal's salutation prompted me to turn towards him. All I could see in the gloom was a dim, hooded figure who raised his

- XXXIII -

hand towards us and then shrank as our boatmen punted hard towards the opposite bank. A shard of silver moon hung low in the sky, barely revealing the vast expanse of trees before us. They stood silently, like a dark ocean ready to swallow us. As my head cleared, I fixed my eyes on the boat and tried to keep the woods out of my mind for as long as possible, preferring not to think of what lurked within them. The crannog and tower-house also offered a timely distraction, although I was sad to see them vanish over my shoulder, since I could not bear to think what the ollave and her son, Lochlain would think when they discovered that I had fled Dartry like a thief.

As we neared our end, I realised that I was seated at the feet of the Irish boatman, and the mumbling ahead of me revealed the presence of Juande and Koldo. Amid their talk and the muffled splash of water, I wondered what Dal Verme and the Canarians had made of the whole affair, and was relieved at the thought of their company during the march ahead. Yet when we were delivered on the tongue of land, I was amazed to find that there were only six of us, and that the other castaways had been left behind.

'What of the others?' I exclaimed, feeling disturbed by my sudden discovery.

'What others?' snorted the captain as he turned his head from left to right.

Our arrival upon the opposite bank had been greeted by the first glimmer of dawn, and in the growing light I could see de Cuéllar studying the trees before us for the best path ahead. He appeared entirely unconcerned by my question.

'Pedro and Franco!' I shouted, feeling deeply irked by his indifference. 'And what of Dal Verme?'

'My concern is for the troops of the Crown,' he snapped. 'I'll not appear before de Leiva with a half-wit adventurer and a pair of goatherds. Enough dignity has been lost as it is.'

With that he stepped towards a slight gap in the trees to the right, leaving me speechless at both his ruthlessness and his disloyalty. None of the other Spaniards shared any of my concern and swiftly hurried after him as I turned towards the water in shock. Our ferries were by now smaller specks alongside the crannog, and with a low curse I turned and hurried after de Cuéllar and his band, fearful that I might be left alone to the mercy of wolves and heretics. In the growing daylight our path seemed eerily familiar, and an ill omen greeted us before our journey was underway. We all averted our eyes from the two cairns where the hung Spaniards lay buried, a terrible reminder of what fate awaited us if we fell into enemy hands.

To make matters worse, the captain's old injury hampered our journey. He was still in severe discomfort, often pausing to take the weight off his legs and to rub his knee with tears in his eyes. Never once did he whimper or groan, yet the frequent halts on our march meant that by midday we could not have been more than three miles through the heavy cover of trees which lay ahead of us. By this time the weather had assumed a grey cast, with clouds gathered overhead and the odd drizzle of rainfall rendering us a band of hooded, solemn figures twisting and turning through the trees.

Valdo led the pack with Koldo at his shoulder. The elderly Catalan and the Basque made for a general westerly direction based on the lake we had left at our backs, which had long vanished from view. I followed closely upon their heels, wondering if they even knew what they were doing, and despairing

- XXXIII -

over my decision to partake of the wretched venture. The land of Dartry seemed reluctant to allow us to leave its clutches, for whenever we appeared to be putting some real distance between us and Lough Melvin, fat Juande and Enano would call to us from the rear, asking us to pause so that de Cuéllar could keep up with us.

Upon receiving their last summons, Valdo decided that we should pause for a half hour, for by this time de Cuéllar's countenance had gone from a discoloured hue to a deathly pale one. The captain crumpled to the ground as soon as the halt was called, and his companions instantly fell to their knees at his side, putting some water to his mouth and fanning his face wildly with the end of a mantle. Our chosen resting spot was an awkward one, being the incline of a hill littered with autumn leaves and trees, which had become more thinly scattered. My skirmisher's instincts protested against the exposed location, which left us vulnerable to an attack from above, yet I chose to keep my silence, knowing the derision which would follow if I dared to air my thoughts.

'Let us get our breath back and lie close to the ground,' said Valdo as he held his cassock closely about him and dropped to one knee. 'We should not yet risk a fire.'

As we huddled closely together, it seemed to me that the old Catalan was the wiliest and most sensible of the fellowship, and that he might provide a small glimmer of hope in the perilous days which lay ahead. I slept as soon as my wide-brimmed hat was pulled over the bridge of my nose, since my previous night had been troubled by emotions which had flooded through me and left me feeling drained. Although my passage into slumber was sweet, my awakening was bitter, coupled with the taste of a sticky hand reaching down my mouth and to the back of my throat. I gagged as my eyes shot open, taking in the cruel sneer of Enano whose fingers tickled the back of my throat.

In a fit of outrage I sought to push him away, only to find that my arms had been pinned back by Juande and Valdo. My jaws were savagely pried open by Juande's dagger as de Cuéllar sat upon my knees, stroking my crotch with the tip of his knife.

'Do not stir, whoreson,' he whispered, 'if you do not wish your purse to be cut open. Its valuables will do no one any good then, for there is no needle and thread for miles around.'

His warning instantly quelled any resistance, tempted as I was to kick at him in the nose and bite his dwarf's hand off. Enano had all but seized my throat when his hand was quickly drawn back and Juande's clutches released, causing me to retch my last oatmeal dinner all over my doublet. My temples throbbed in anger, and never in all my life had I seen my vomit so keenly inspected by others.

'No,' said Enano at last in disappointment, after he had picked through my spew with his dagger blade, 'nothing of value here. We will just have to try again -'

'Wait!' I shouted, as my assailants drew closer again. 'Wait! What is it you want from me?'

The prick of de Cuéllar's dagger point against my crotch had me start in shock, and my arms were held down firmly once more.

'Now, now, Santiago, don't play the fool,' he whispered. 'You know very well that a true fellowship shares both troubles and gains like brothers.'

His emphasis on the word 'gains' left me cursing beneath my breath, as I realised that he had overheard my conversation with

Treasach Bourke during the siege. The captain and his band must have long suspected that I concealed a worthy prize, one which had led the viceroy's army to besiege a meaningless fort upon the water and one which had encouraged the renegade Burke to risk his life so needlessly. It was obvious to me then that my inclusion in the captain's hunting party had been nothing more than a ruse to seize the trinket from me, and I did not dare think what would befall me if I surrendered my prize.

'I know not of what you speak,' I said at last, then groaned as Enano's fingers slipped into my mouth once more. His attempts to make me spew were repeated at least another half dozen times, so that at last my voice was hoarse when I spoke up again.

'Stop, I beg you,' I said, as Juande seized my jaw once more. 'I shall give you what I have.'

Enano stared at de Cuéllar with a broad grin, although the captain's weary expression hardly changed at all.

'Where is it?'

'I need my hands back first,' I said.

'We have hands of our own, if you hadn't yet realised,' was de Cuéllar's curt reply, 'but mention the place and Enano here shall gladly search it.'

'It is a place only I can access.'

De Cuéllar rolled his eyes.

'Believe me Santiago, there are no places in the human body that Enano has not explored. Very well lads; turn him over.'

'No not there!' I howled, as they proceeded to tug at my breeches. 'I meant the gun!'

'Valdo!' exclaimed de Cuéllar, but the Catalan had already seized the Marquardt rifle, shaking it wildly and looking down its bore.

This exercise lasted a few minutes longer until he finally flung the rifle onto the forest floor in frustration.

'I cannot see it!' he fumed.

'It is an old marksman's trick,' I explained from the ground, 'but release me a few instants and pass me the ramrod.'

The captain grunted as he got off my legs and slowly pushed himself onto his feet.

'Any tricks, whoreson,' he said, holding his dagger out before him, 'and you're food for the wolves.'

With this threat he stepped away, and his fellowship formed a close ring about me with their daggers also drawn. I coughed hard as I rolled onto my knees, and Valdo flung both the rifle and the ramrod at my feet.

'Be quick, Abel,' he rasped, 'for we have tarried longer than we first planned.'

With a silent nod, I took up the ramrod and jerked it down the bore of the Marquardt. I quietly thanked the saints that my ruse had worked, and that the fools had not attempted to inspect the bandolier slung about my shoulders. I jerked the ramrod about for close to a minute, during which I paused often for dramatic effect, pursing my lips and peering down it to inspire false hope. When I had also tired of the exercise, I turned the rifle around, placing my hand over the end of its bore and putting on a wide smile as I feigned to grab something from within it.

'Ah, here we are at last,' I said, then walked over towards Enano with an outstretched fist.

'Give it here!' he cried. 'What is it?'

- XXXIII -

'A blow of the hardest leather,' I replied, and he looked at me in puzzlement as I kicked him so hard in the crotch that his feet left the ground.

A roar had hardly left his lips when he fell over, and I shoved my rifle stock into the face of Koldo. The cracking of bone was heard as he staggered into the path of the onrushing Juande, leaving him to collapse in a heap.

'Seize him!' roared de Cuéllar, but I was already crashing through the trees downhill.

The captain's injury made him no threat to me, and I hoped that Valdo's age would help me outrun him. Yet the Catalan proved a hardier specimen than I had first hoped, and often did I look over my shoulder to see him but a few feet away from me, his face red with exertion. For how long he followed me I did not know, but a flurry of brown gold leaves was kicked up as I made for a gully-like cleft at the base of the incline. I was hardly a few feet from it when my fortune abandoned me. My foot was caught in the roots of an oak, which sent me flying headfirst into the trunk of a tree. The blow to the head left me feeling dazed for a few crucial moments.

The fleet-footed Catalan hurled himself upon me, and I soon discovered that he was as strong as he was fast. It was all I could do to fend off his blade. Both my hands were wrapped around the wrist of his dagger hand as he pushed me back against the bark of the tree.

'If you kill me now,' I gasped, 'you'll never have what you seek.'

'Damn you and your treasure,' was his gruff response, as he redoubled his efforts. 'I only want to go home.'

I tried to reply that my secret did not consist of mere gold and silver, yet my throat was crushed by his efforts and I could barely breathe, let alone talk. Dots appeared in the air before me as we remained locked in our fierce struggle for interminable minutes. His dagger point was all but kissing my right eye when a crash of branches was heard behind him.

'What is this?' came a soft voice in Latin, followed by a low growling that caused Valdo's assault to instantly slacken and my hands to fall to my side.

As my sight returned, I saw the glistening fangs of a wolfhound. Roe bared its teeth at us as it bristled before its mistress. Muireann beheld us from atop her dapple hobby, an arrow fitted to her raised bow. About the ollave a guard of kerns shared her look of profound astonishment, holding their spears above their heads as the Catalan rose to his feet, brushing the leaves off his breeches. His dagger was returned to its sheath as he attempted to smile disarmingly at the Dartrymen.

'Only we pretend fight, lady,' he said in his broken Latin, 'for when we find wolf we be strong.'

In feigning friendship, he reached his hand out to me, and I grudgingly snatched it before he hauled me back onto my feet. As I regained my breath, Valdo proceeded to punch me lightly on the shoulder and slap me heavily on the back as a chuckle left his lips.

'There, see? He not hurt, just weakling.'

As she studied our faces, Muireann appeared to doubt his explanation. My stoic gaze left her in no doubt that any suspicions she harboured were valid.

'Ye have tarried far north from your quarry, friends,' she said at last, 'for the tracks of *An Faolchù* were last seen leading

- XXXIII -

westwards from Rossfriar. The prints are less than a day old, and a mere child brought them to our notice.'

'Ah,' said Valdo as his face reddened, for he was the least shameless of de Cuéllar's band. 'Then we go tell Captain.'

He bowed slightly before the ollave's party before walking back up the hill. He was barely ten paces from me when he turned to face me, his stare darkening as he gestured for me to follow him. The ensuing silence lingered uncomfortably before the ollave spoke up again.

'Thou art reluctant to rejoin thy hunting party, friend Juan?'

'My powder has turned damp from our sparring,' I replied in respectable Gaelic, gesturing to some of the ampoules which had fallen from my belt during my struggle with the Catalan. 'This has rendered my part in the hunt worthless.'

'Yet it is unsafe to travel alone,' she replied at once. 'Wilt thou join my party until we return to the town?'

I engaged in a flourishing bow before picking up the ampoules and walking towards her men. Valdo bristled as he watched me approach her.

'You'll hang, deserter,' he hissed, then turned on his heel and made back towards the general direction of de Cuéllar.

'Remind thy master of our challenge upon the morrow, good Spaniard,' called out the ollave, yet the Catalan never acknowledged her.

The narrow escape left me feeling relieved, and I still struggled for breath. I fell among the kerns who marched alongside Lady Mac an Bhaird after she kicked her spotted mount forward into a slow canter. Muireann struck an eastward track as she kept along the gorge, and when she could finally no longer contain her curiosity, she turned to look at me over her shoulder.

'Was that truly sparring?' she asked in Gaelic.

'In truth 'twas but a small misunderstanding, my lady,' I replied, also using the vernacular.

'So small that it warranted the drawing of a knife?'

'We Spaniards are swift to draw steel, my lady,' I said with a shrug, 'and 'twas but a temporary heat of blood. It would not have gone any further.'

She did not seem convinced by my assurances, nodding slowly as I trudged alongside her.

'He seems a ruthless man, just like his master.'

'Hardly so, madam. I have served some devils who would make them seem docile by comparison.'

She fell silent at my response, to the point that she seemed ignorant of my presence as we progressed through the wood. Over her horse's neck swung the hares which she had coursed that morning, and I wondered if we were still on the hunt.

'Are you seeking fresh game, my lady?'

'No, for I have other duties that await me in the town. Yet before we return there, I have one last errand to attend to in the wood.'

After another half hour she strayed from the natural path and made back towards the tree-cloaked hill to our right. The way she took was a difficult one, what with the number of branches which had to be avoided and the tree roots in our path. Despite these obstacles we covered ground with confidence, and never once did the ollave pause to recover her bearings or examine her surrounds. After we had wended our way up and down two small summits, we came at last to the top of another incline, where the foliage was so dense that Muireann had to dismount and lead us on in single file.

- XXXIII -

As we kept to this path, the trees spaced out once more, leaving us to be soaked by a thin drizzle which had persisted over the last hour. At our appearance two wood kerns stepped away from the dell, their faces the picture of unmasked hostility. Horns hung from their belts, and each held a javelin over their shoulder, ready to be hurled at us. When they made out Muireann, the ends of these spears were rested upon the ground, and the ollave called out to them with a raised hand. In the bat of an eye, they disappeared like spirits in the wood, and for a moment I wondered whether I had seen them at all.

'Well watched, this place,' I muttered to our guide.

'We have been watched all the way uphill,' she replied, as casually as if she were discussing the weather.

After her horse was tethered, we made past two hazels, following a winding path through branches and trunks which had at first seemed impassable. The canopy overhead protected us from the rain as we made our way through the dense undergrowth. Just as I was about to query our end, we found ourselves in a glade of significant width, lined with rows of plants and domed structures. As we drew closer, I could see that they were skeps, whose wooded frames were closed tightly together.

'An apiary surrounded by weeds!' I exclaimed.

Low growls were heard from the wolfhounds as I neared them, their teeth bared beneath flickering, black lips that were peeled back to the snout. A great unease seized me. My hand had fallen to my sword when a sharp order was heard from the ollave, which left them cowering on the ground.

'Yes, Spaniard, it is an apiary,' replied Muireann, 'and the weeds which you refer to are in truth dye-plants, consisting mainly of woad and madder. This place was created by my late husband, and I have maintained it since his passing with the help of our retainers. Apart from my son, Lochlain, it is the sole earthly memory that I have left of him. You must not mention it to anyone.'

I stared about me once more in wonder, feeling more astonished than I had when entering Dervila's hidden apothecary.

'The number of hives here are beyond count! You must produce enough honey to feed the whole of Dublin!'

The ollave smiled.

'No, Spaniard, hardly that much. Yet significant profit is indeed made from this place, for our honeys and dyes find many buyers both on and off our shores. They pay for the upkeep of this place during the months of winter, and for its protection. The honey alone is worth its weight in gold, for it was cheap before the monasteries were torn down, yet it is now a luxury which few can afford, adding bitterness to people's lives. Aengus made a wondrous mead from it, to the great delight of his old friend Redmond.'

A deep tranquility filled me as I observed the beauty and orderliness of the hidden glen. It had qualities which I had not previously associated with the land I had so nearly fled like a thief in the night. The ingenuity of its concealment left me staring at the hives and plants again in silent wonder, as a question formed in my mind.

'Where are the bees?'

Muireann walked up to one of the skeps, and laid her hand down gently upon the wooden structure.

'They do not emerge during the colder months, but I assure you that there are hundreds inside these structures, all bunched together tightly for warmth. They will only sally forth if they are disturbed.'

So saying, she turned back towards the plants and knelt beside them, stroking at a single leaf.

'God willing, my lady Dervila should soon have the tunic she wants to wear on blessed Beltaine.'

The sight of her gesture reminded me of life's blessings in a land torn apart by the misery of perpetual war. The clearing had given me insight into the nature of her late husband Aengus, and I felt like I better understood the aura of respect that his name still commanded. I felt dwarfed by his life's vision and enterprise, given that I had spent mine spreading death and misery to enemies of the Spanish Crown and countless innocents. It was then that the memory of my previous advances on the ollave returned to haunt me, and I could barely meet her stare when she rose to her feet and addressed me.

'Will you join me for a light repast?'

The kind offer was accepted with a grudging nod, and after I sat down, we helped ourselves to a meal consisting of strips of chicken and pieces of bread. Muireann also had a flask filled with sweet-tasting cider, which she freely shared with me. We ate in silence with her guard of wood kerns keeping their own company near the skeps. While she ate, I secretly marvelled at how a woman who was possessed of such knowledge and refinement could in an instant turn into a fearless, deadly fighter.

Her beauty was also striking, so that my heart quickened whenever dimples formed in her cheeks or when she beheld me with her ochre eyes. When my food was wolfed down, I sat back and fiddled nervously with a twig whilst Muireann finished the rest of her meal. I looked about me again in disbelief, feeling both content and serene by the idyllic nature of our surroundings.

'It is the first time that I have seen you smile, Spaniard.'

I grinned broadly upon realising that she was right, and gratefully accepted the offer of her flask after she helped herself to it once more.

'Who else has seen this place?' I asked, wiping my lips upon my sleeve.

'Apart from the guards who are assigned to it?'

'Yes.'

'Only Lady Bourke and Father O'Ronayne.'

'Not even the chieftain?' I asked.

'He has never ventured here.'

'Then why bring me?'

'And why not?' she said quickly, averting her eyes from my stare. 'Who else could I trust if not an alien wanted dead by the enemy? One who owes us his life, no less.'

'Would you bring de Cuéllar?' I asked.

She returned a fleeting look of disdain, as if to imply that the subject was not even worthy of discussion.

'Why not bring the chieftain?'

'Because he has never asked to visit,' she replied.

'Does he even know of it?'

'I would be surprised if he did not, since he often enquires about its upkeep.'

'Then why not come see it for himself?'

Muireann cast me a look of impatience as she chewed the last piece of her meat.

'You are nothing if not curious, grey wolf. I consider my lord MacGlannagh a second father, indeed a father I know better than my own natural father, who taught me much during childhood. I would never speak ill of my lord MacGlannagh, for he is a man both honourable and reasonable in his own fashion, and I have seen him make huge sacrifices for the good of his tribe.'

'And yet?' I ventured, sticking my neck out a little further than I perhaps should have, and earning a hard stare from the ollave.

'And yet...' she said tentatively. 'And yet Aengus was something else. And much as his father dearly loved him, it could not but rankle with the chieftain at times. Lady Bourke drove this fact home often and mercilessly, as if she were plunging a dagger into her husband's pride. For his ways are forged from the ancient customs of this land, of petty alliances and seeking to preserve the old order of things at all costs.'

Her voice lowered to a whisper as she fixed me with a keen stare.

'So where Tadhg *Óg* could just about manage Latin, Dervila saw to it that Aengus also knew French and Spanish fluently. Where my lord recounted a famous cattle raid witnessed in his youth, his son could recite tales of Scipio and Hannibal. My foster father could at times be seen leafing through a Bible with the aid of a priest, but my husband was not yet half his age when he had already amassed a small library.'

I gently nodded at the implication of her words, but the ollave persisted with her explanation, seeming both heartened and relieved by the fact that she had someone with whom she could share her most private thoughts and knowledge.

'Bards across Connacht still sing praises of Tadhg *Óg* Mac-Glannagh, the Sheriff-Slayer of Dartry, yet all men still refer to Aengus as *'Cliste'*, which means the Salmon of Wisdom. So you understand that much as my lord chieftain admired both the mind and the counsel of his own son, seeing the works of my husband also served him with a pang of realisation that he would never match his own son for greatness, in spite of the power that he himself wielded. And once more do I repeat to you, that this state of affairs was not aided by his wife.'

'Quite the opposite, it does appear.'

She nodded back at me and I smiled. Then a look of sadness overcame the ollave, and her lip was curled bitterly as she fixed her stare on the ground between us.

'Your husband was indeed a rare man,' I said by way of comfort, 'possessed of great insight and a love of learning. He certainly sought to make the most of his gifts and position.'

Her lip trembled and her eyelids glistened, before she wiped her face on her sleeve and looked about the glen with a wry smile.

'This was our first secret meeting place. He would hold me close to him as we breathed words of love in each other's ears. He always took great delight in my thoughts on all matters, and his laugh was from the heart: great peals of laughter that caused creatures to rustle and scurry away in the grass. His shaggy mane of red hair appeared to sum up life itself, and his green Norman eyes danced merrily in his face as he exuded the warmth of our people. I was a young woman when I was sent to this land, Spaniard, both young and scared. And remember that Dartry was not a happy place then, for his uncle still held it in his iron grasp, slaying folk as he pleased. Yet I was fortunate to be drawn to a young man whose hand could be put to any task, a fearless warrior with a great appetite for all learning.'

- XXXIII -

She grimaced from the pain of his memory as a tear slid down her nose.

'And now he's gone,' she managed at last, quickly wiping her face with her hand, 'a man both wise and great. And a boon in all difficult times. I still miss his great embrace.'

Then she quivered as her tears flowed freely, and her reddening face was concealed in the palms of her hands.

'My pardon, Spaniard,' she stuttered. 'His loss still cuts deep!'

Although I was tired of hearing stories about her former husband, I could not but feel for Muireann. I reached out for her shoulder and patted it gently, expecting her to flinch or shrug it away. Yet Muireann did neither as she leant closer to me. The whole of my arm was next wrapped around the back of her shoulders, and I flicked my eyes at her kerns, who never stirred from their posts. We retained this pose for a few minutes more. Then the ollave's forehead slid against the side of my neck so that I could feel the warmth of her breath against my chest. Finally, she moved away from me as my arm fell back to my side, and she wiped her eyes one last time.

'Do not think less of me...' she said.

Her eyes briefly widened as she made out the dampness on my own cheeks. Her display of sorrow had rekindled the memories of my own loss. Our being in the glen had reminded me of happier and more carefree times, times which I had spent with Elsien in Willebroek.

'Grey wolf!' exclaimed the ollave, as her face reddened. 'Has my lapse moved you to tears? I ask that you forgive me, for I shall never again subject you to such a display of emotion.'

'Do not apologise, my lady,' I sniffed, swiftly wiping both my cheeks with my thumb and forefinger. 'There is no shame in sharing a great loss, with one who has known it too.'

'Did you also lose love?' she asked in surprise.

Her hand was rested gently upon my arm, then quickly looked away.

'Please ignore my question,' she said, 'I did not mean to open old wounds.'

'No, hardly so, my lady,' I finally managed, 'for I do not mind you knowing the truth of it.'

I had never shared the episode which led to Elsien's demise with another soul, for it had always been too painful a topic of conversation to raise with my Flemish brother-in-law as we rode, grim-faced and intent on revenge, on those long, rain-soaked nights in pursuit of Ramos. I frowned as I recalled poor Maerten, who had willingly turned from a fresh-faced young lad into a killer's aide overnight and who had perished beneath the waves. I could not tell for how long I had ceased to think of him, with all my energies devoted to saving my own life and hiding the ring, so I felt released as I recounted the fate of the van der Molens, which I had kept to myself for well over three years.

'Our paths crossed in Flanders in 1584, while the Imperial Army lay siege to Antwerp, where the heretics had held out for over a year. My fortunes in the army had dipped significantly back then, ever since the Iron Duke of Alba had been withdrawn from the conflict. I was in fact fortunate to still be alive, and I formed part of a fellowship of scoundrels who were barracked in Willebroek. It was a little village of some

- XXXIII -

strategic importance, since it lay along a canal which flowed into the Scheldt.'

I looked back at her, wondering if I had already said too much of little interest. Yet Muireann listened to me keenly, so I persisted with my account.

'One night we were returning to our cabin for sentry duty, having spent the best part of the day idling in the local tavern. It was then that we saw a band of men beating an elderly man who lay on the ground. My comrades laughed aloud at the sight of this hiding, since few Spaniards distinguished between believers and heretics, considering all Flemings to be subdued rebels. Yet despite all that we had already endured, I could not bear to see the man suffer any longer. I ran over towards him with my gun trained on his assailants, who scattered and ran at the sight of me. My companions mocked and jeered me from a distance as I helped the old man to his feet, helping him to return to his house as my fellows vanished off to their barracks.'

'Was he a heretic?' snapped Muireann.

'No!' I protested, shaking my head. 'He was a widowed Catholic and a self-taught humanist, devoted to his children. He had amassed a tidy fortune during times of peace, although the chaos of war had only just started to spell his ruin. When we reached his house, the door was opened by a woman of such beauty that I could not speak at the sight of her...'

Muireann's eyes narrowed at my description of Elsien, so that I ended it abruptly and carried on with my tale.

'The door was swiftly shut in my face without a word of gratitude, and I thought that would be the end of that. If only it had been. A week later a young boy found me seated outside my cabin, bearing me a message from his father who wished to meet and thank me in person. I had all but forgotten about the incident by then, and almost sent him away with a clip round the ear.'

I frowned at the memory of Pieter's face, as the ollave listened on intently.

'Thus began my friendship with the miller of Willebroek, Reynier van der Molen. He instantly offered me employment: to work the mill with his elder son, Maerten, until he had fully recovered from his blows. Like most men of his trade, Reynier was also a money-lender, which made him hugely unpopular with debtors whose struggles were heightened during a time of war, so after he recovered from his beating, he also employed my ragged comrades as his personal bodyguard. My companions soon took him up on his offer and no longer laughed as they had when I had rescued him. We were always to be found at his side, when we were not inspecting sailing vessels or skirmishing with enemy irregulars. It did not take Reynier long to deduce that I knew my letters, unlike the handful of scoundrels I had fallen in with, so although he opened his door to me freely, the other four members of my fellowship were always kept as far away as possible from his children.'

'Your companions sound like dishonourable men,' said the ollave, and I nodded at her quickly as I went on.

'They were. I have said that Reynier was self-taught, and his library, in all truth, did exceed that of your husband. Instead of wallowing around the cabins with the countless ruffians who plague the Imperial Army, I spent many hours reading his books in his library, often in the company of his own children. My year in Willebroek was one of great learning, yet it was also a year full of a love which I had thought was behind me, for Elsien and I were drawn to each other from the first.'

'What bliss,' said Muireann almost longingly. 'How could so happy a time have ended?'

'Nothing is certain in times of war,' was my immediate reply, 'but for a time things were indeed better than anything I can ever recall. My relations with Reynier became closer, but as the siege of Antwerp wore on, the surrounding countryside became further ravaged by mercenaries and regulars. The worthy miller's cunning could not spare him further impoverishment, and he was soon unable to make good for the services of my fellowship. This did not go down well with the other members of my band, and Reynier soon found himself fearing the very wolves he had run with. It was then that I began to hatch secret plans to abandon not only the Netherlands but the whole of Europe. I intended to set sail for the Indies.'

'You deserted?' exclaimed Muireann in genuine surprise.

'Not before I made an error of judgement which shall weigh upon my soul beyond the grave. Before Antwerp finally fell, a group of mercenaries were said to be riding past Willebroek. My fellowship volunteered to form part of a force sent to intercept them, yet in the ensuing ambush I fell from a tree. I knocked my head on a rock and lost all reckoning until I was found two days later by Maerten.'

A deep sigh left me then, at the recollection of what followed. Muireann appeared concerned at my distress and was about to speak, but I raised my hand towards her, urging her to allow me to finish.

'My worthy fellows had of course abandoned their search for me, but I was found by Maerten who rode out from the village at Elsien's bidding, with orders to find what had become of me. I instantly fell ill with worry since the four Spaniards who had abandoned me had long threatened to burn Reynier's house down if he did not honour his outstanding payment to them.'

The colour slowly left Muireann's face as she heard of the final tragedy.

'When we rode back to Willebroek I did not at first realise where all the smoke was coming from, but Maerten spurred his horse into a gallop, and as I made after him, I was shocked to see him fly off his mount and run into his smouldering house. We soon learned that in her efforts to rescue her sick father, Elsien had breathed too much of the deathly fumes. Her last breath was taken long before we found them both dead upon the ground.'

A muffled gasp was heard from the ollave, but I found myself strangely unburdened as I met her horrified stare.

'She was as beautiful in death as she had been in life. At first Maerten and I could not leave her side. We wept openly on our knees, with many villagers also sharing in our grief.'

'What happened next?' asked the ollave in wonder.

I cleared my throat awkwardly, deciding against telling her about my desertion from the army and my subsequent enslavement aboard one of the Armada's galleys.

'I left the village, intent on finding my company which had been recalled to Spain, to find my comrades who had caused my wife's death.'

'Did you find them?'

'I tracked them down to Seville,' I replied, 'yet the Armada robbed me of fully achieving my vengeance, for I was pressed into service aboard one of its galleys, which was shipwrecked on the Irish coast. Yet you may recall that two comrades did perish at my hand.'

'The men at Keeloges? Who hid in the church?'

'Yes.'

'One of them called you Abelito...'

'Yes, Abelito. In reference to Abelardo de Santiago, my name in the army.'

'And is it your true name?'

'It was my name in the army,' I said, 'and the man who uttered it was my sergeant, Curro Ramos.'

Muireann rested her hand upon my shoulder, and I was overcome by the look of compassion upon her face.

'You are an honourable man, Spaniard, and you have suffered much.'

I pulled my face away from her hand.

'I spent most of my life fighting for the Spanish Crown, and yet I could not even protect her.'

'Do not say that, Spaniard,' she said, 'for I have heard the MacFelim tell of your valour during the siege. There is much that is good that we must still fight for, while we still have life. We must make the most of our gifts, to the greater honour of those we loved that are now departed!'

I glared back at her, feeling annoyed that she had so readily surmised the meaning of my existence. I thought to tell her that perhaps I was not so different from men like Curro and that I held a treasure which had wrought much pain and misery among her people during the siege of Rosclogher. Instead I sighed and averted my stare from her, ashamed of what I still did and saying nothing. We sat for a few minutes in silence, until at last she returned to her feet.

'You are possessed of rare qualities, although you refuse to see them. Yet for as long as you remain among the tribe, you must always count on me as your ally. Now we must away to the town, for I must attend to my students early tomorrow morning.'

Despite the events of the day, no mention was made of de Cuéllar as we rode back towards Lough Melvin. A rose-tinted skyline stretched across the dark mountains ahead of us, and I could not but reflect as we descended the bluff that the ring desired by the Sassanas was hidden away in the eighth charge, which swung from my chest. Although I had secured an ally in the ollave Muireann, I wondered how she would have behaved towards me if she realised that she had returned Dartry's doom back to Rosclogher.

XXXIV

Rosclogher, Dartry, County Leitrim

3 January – 1 March 1589

'Where is the captain?' asked Saorla.

To my great distress, the day of the contest had dawned, and I was overcome with embarrassment. The effigy of an enemy trooper had been erected upon the green which had been whitened by snow. Tree branches had been slid through the armholes of a dented cuirass, which was in turn bound to an upright pole which ran through breastplate and backplate. A domed helmet had been perched upon this staff's topmost end, and a large rock had been placed sixty yards away from this figure.

Dervila's party were already gathered behind the stone. The queen of Dartry looked breathtaking in the morning cold, wearing a blue tunic as well as a silver necklace and earrings. The chieftain's wife had the appearance of one who was ready to court another, not to witness a shooting contest. The lady

Bourke was in high spirits as she giggled with her ladies, producing small clouds of mist. The rosewater which she wore reached my nostrils, which only added to my growing shame.

The whole of the ringfort had also emptied upon the green, with kerns standing along the grass as the gallowglass approached in small groups from the village. The townsfolk stood as far away as they could from these mercenaries, having long tired of the Scots' demands and brutal behaviour. This meant that Manglana met with a frosty reception when he arrived from across the water. I could make out his bard and steward in his retinue, along with scores of bluejackets that formed a protective ring around the chieftain and his red-headed grandson.

In their coterie I could also make out the raven-haired Cathal *Dubh*. The tanist's serene demeanour betrayed no knowledge of the captain's absence, as he conferred with the other nobles who had emerged from the tower-house. My trepidation grew with the number of onlookers, and the profane and the holy were soon also present as mad Orla and other whores from the village were seen on the left side of the green, O'Ronayne and his retainers staring on expectantly on the right.

Almost an hour passed before Saorla queried after de Cuéllar's whereabouts. Pages were sent to the huts on the periphery of the village, where even the empty lodgings of mad Orla and her daughters were searched. Yet one boy after another returned with the same reply; the captain and his fellows were nowhere to be seen. Murmurs of concern soon spread among the waiting throng. Dal Verme and the Canarians muttered amongst themselves, and behind the effigy I could see Donal MacCabe smirking from ear to ear.

- XXXIV -

I coughed uncomfortably and was doing my best to look astonished, when I caught Muireann staring straight at me with a severe expression. With a shake of her head she trudged off towards the lake. Lady Bourke turned her head towards her in astonishment.

'Muireann!' cried Dervila. 'Where are you going?'

'Back to the tower-house.'

'But what of the contest? And the prize?'

The ollave stopped abruptly and turned towards her mistress, and many drew a loud intake of breath as Muireann hurled her musket upon the ground before her.

'My lord's prize is already ours, my lady, for I fear that the contest is already over.'

With that she continued walking towards the keep with a band of kerns running after her. Further exclamations of woe were heard as the tanist was seen frantically gesturing to some boys, who ran to the town to fetch horses from the bawn. Upon their return, Cathal and his closest horsemen made for the trees with their steeds in tow, and I could see from their grim cast that they feared that the worst had befallen de Cuéllar and his band.

The whole town was soon also possessed of a great desire to find the missing Spaniards. Women searched for them in their houses, and men called their names along the banks of Lough Melvin. Large groups of children ran into the surrounding trees with their dogs, with the great search replacing the shooting contest as the town's diversion. As I trudged off silently towards the outhouse, I tore my eyes away from the distressed face of the lady Bourke.

Looks of shock and anger still abounded three days later, when search after search had proved fruitless. The erected effigy was soon removed from sight, as passions cooled and the townsfolk were overcome by a cold, stark truth. All throughout I had witnessed this transition with a growing dread, seeking the solace of solitude in the outhouse and helping myself to all of the bondsman's brandy. On the two previous evenings, Nial had appeared in the doorway with a flushed face and his brow streaked with sweat, worn out from yet another day spent travelling through the land to seek out the Spanish heroes of the tribe.

As he drifted off to sleep, he whispered to me of countless sightings reported by children that the captain had been seen along the borders with Breifne or in the company of a creaght near *Slieve Aradh*. It is doubtful that the ancient Greeks had had as many sightings of their pagan god Bacchus in their own forests, but the poor bondsman had to verify the truth of some of these rumours, which had of course proved to be nothing more than idle gossip and hearsay.

All of the tribesmen took part in various searches, save of course for the gallowglass, the ollave Muireann and the remaining Spaniards. When the heavens burst at noon on the fourth day, Nial appeared to summon me to the best hearth of Rosclogher. As I donned my cassock and slipped on my brogues, I tried to surmise the bondsman's mood from the corner of my eye, yet his face betrayed no sentiments as his hands rested upon his two sword pommels.

Our journey to the tower-house was a most miserable one, as we were barely protected from the rainwater by our hoods and the ends of our mantles. After the crannog was reached, we stepped through the door and climbed the ladder and stairs to the great hall. It was a sombre reception that greeted me as I stepped towards the gathered assembly. The wind howled outside while looks of bitterness and confusion could be seen upon the faces of the highborn.

Manglana himself looked bored, although his queen and tanist appeared worn and pale, since they had held much misplaced affection for the jovial de Cuéllar. Fearghal the bard appeared frustrated, since he could not glean any emotions from his master, who sat upon his exalted seat with his bearded chin resting on one hand and his legs crossed before him. O'Ronayne looked distraught, and the ollave was nowhere to be seen. Lochlain's expectant looks still irritated me and Constable MacCabe smirked openly along with two of his men. At last the chieftain spoke up without either greeting or salutation.

'Was it ever the captain's intention to seek to rid us of the wolf?'

The question caught me unawares as I fumbled for a reply.

'That is the intention he declared to me, my lord.'

'And when didst thou learn,' replied the chieftain, keeping to Latin despite my use of Gaelic, 'of his plans to flee?'

'Almost a month to the day,' I replied, keeping my knees from wobbling as a great fear grew within me.

'Then why didst thou not make these plans known to us?'

'I did not take them seriously, for often have men expressed the desire to return home when finding themselves in a foreign land. During my time spent in Flanders -'

'Why didst thou not also flee?' asked Manglana, leaving me to fear the worst, by the way in which he interrupted me.

'I believed the hunt to be a separate venture. I had not understood his true motives for seeking out *An Faolchù* -'

'And yet,' declared the chieftain loudly, with a great annoyance in his voice, 'I would have expected thee to know that the date chosen by the captain for the hunt was the false Nativity, celebrated by the heretics ten days after ours.'

Although his words stopped short of an open condemnation, it was clear that he was not convinced of my innocence. My eyes were fixed on the ground as I held my tongue, hoping that the ollave had not spoken of my fight with Valdo.

'If thou subsequently knew of the captain's flight,' asked Manglana, 'why didst thou not speak of it before the day of contest?'

It felt like an immense effort to raise my head and face him.

'I hoped that he would see the hopelessness of his venture,' I said, having prepared the response long in advance. 'I hoped that he would return.'

The chieftain was silent a few moments as he mulled over my words, then spoke again.

'Thou might exceed thy captain for glibness, but then again thou mayest not. If thy fellows or thee desire to leave Dartry, ye may do so whenever ye wish. Yet none of ye shall scurry off again like thieves with our arms and belongings, which we so desperately need in our struggle. The tanist acted towards ye with good faith, and he has been repaid with petty theft and a deathly wolf which still wanders our lands. Thy fellows' debt shall therefore be paid by thy services, as from this day forth thou art assigned to the command of Cathal *Dubh*, to do with thee what he will.'

No sooner did he say this than Manglana cast a stare towards his judge Echna, who quietly nodded her assent. He then rose to his feet with a grunt; his nobles drew back in surprise at his sudden movement and bowed deeply towards his throne. After the chieftain left the hall, Nial's hand fell to my shoulder and he whispered to me to follow him. As I turned towards the doors, a roar of mocking laughter was heard across the hall, and Constable MacCabe's voice boomed against the walls.

'Did not even wait until mid-winter, let alone first spring!'

My heart sank when I heard his words, and I could not help feeling wretched for the tanist Cathal, who had always staunchly defended Spanish castaways in the assembly as if we were his own men. My only solace as we proceeded down the steps was that in fleeing de Cuéllar's men I had spared the tanist a head from his herd. However, my disappointment grew when I later heard stories of Donal and his gallowglass escorting the ashen-faced tanist to his byre, where they had branded five of his best heads of cattle for each of the flown Spaniards.

'Such a waste of good cowflesh' said Nial, who seemed to have instantly picked up on the cause of my silence, 'to think that de Cuéllar and his men are as good as dead.'

'How can you be so sure?' I exclaimed, fearful that the captain might yet reveal himself again, together with my secret.

The bondsman smiled gently as we boarded the ferry alongside the lake, perhaps mistaking my outburst for concern for the welfare of my fellow Spaniards. By his reply I could tell that despite his master's harsh words, Nial harboured no ill will towards me.

'If word of the last sighting is to be believed,' he said, 'de Cuéllar and his band were seen passing into O'Donnell's lands not three days ago. The lord of Tirconnell is perhaps only second in power to O'Neill, yet he has been subdued by the Sassanas ever since a viceroy seized his son and held him kept captive in Dublin. The enemy now travels freely through his lands, and O'Donnell will not risk the life of his son for a handful of Spaniards. Which is not to mention that Lord MacGlannagh shall risk none of his men to recapture them'.

'But what if he reached de Leiva?' I asked, as we reached the first storey, where Nial and I fetched the ladder to slide it through the murder hole.

'He is still as good as dead,' said the bondsman, shaking his head, 'for surely de Leiva knows not to set off during the sailing season, when enemy ships keep a heavy watch upon our coasts.'

As we travelled back to the village, I fell silent, wondering what lay in store for me after I was assigned to the tanist. Nial was quick to pick up on the cause of my silence, placing a reassuring hand upon my shoulder.

'Do not fear, Spaniard, for the ollave has spoken of your tussle with one of de Cuéllar's band. Your being assigned to Cathal is only due to the tribe's disappointment with all things Spanish, but it shall pass as has happened so many times before. The tanist will not hold his loss against you, although the captain's dishonesty has wounded him deeply.'

The bondsman sighed as he dipped his fingers into the icecold water alongside our ferry.

'Cathal has not slept during the past two days, he searched long and hard for the captain around the lake. Many have told me how they heard him crying out de Cuéllar's name.'

As he spoke, the image of a lonely horseman came to mind, frantically charging up and down the water's edge in search of a friendship which had never truly existed. We did not exchange any more words even after the outhouse was reached.

- XXXIV -

I collapsed onto my litter and felt crushed by disappointment, worry and self-loathing. When the bondsman left the hut, I felt so angry at myself that it was all I could do to resist plucking the ring from my bandolier and flinging it outside the outhouse.

Then second thoughts prevailed as they always did. I breathed deeply and tried to calm down, until the weariness I had felt at the day's events permitted me to fall into a deep slumber. I was shaken awake after nightfall, and in the faint candlelight I could recognise Nial and the tanist standing behind him. Cathal had his hair tied above his head, and his eyes were as bloodshot as his voice was grim.

'Lady Mac an Bhaird has told me of your fight with one of the captain's men. I know that you would never abandon us, grey wolf. For too long have I been blind to your qualities, for many warned me of de Cuéllar's behaviour during the siege, but I paid them no heed. It was honourable of you not to betray your fellow Spaniards to us, even though it almost cost you your life to dissuade them from flight.'

I stared back at the tanist in awe, feeling relieved that he had somewhat misinterpreted events, and that I could still count on him as an ally. As he silently left the hut, I sat up on my bed and called out after him.

'I tried to tell them to stay behind, but the captain would not listen!'

The tanist turned back towards me.

'Your declaration of loyalty is needless, friend Juan. The only Spaniards who matter are the ones who would stay with us. From the very first you were always true to our cause, ever since you risked your life to rescue Muireann. For as long as you are with us, I shall believe that Spain is our ally, even though her armies are filled with some dishonourable men. Your privileges shall not be withdrawn by my hand, and I know that you will soon regain my lord MacGlannagh's favour.'

His words permitted me to breathe easier, and as he retired to bed, Nial grinned at me once before he blew out the candlelight. Yet in the days that followed, it was clear to me how much the Spaniards were missed by the tribe. There was no more laughter heard at Enano's latest antics, and the tall tales of de Cuéllar were also gone, together with his hearty laughter. At mealtimes men could not but recall the great appetite displayed by Juande, and the women missed the fortune telling of Koldo the Basque, and the little wooden statuettes which Valdo had carved for their children.

The Canarians and I had never taken to palm reading or colourful proclamations of gallantry, and Dal Verme did not know how to play any instruments. We were unable to fill the void that was left behind, and the natives' bitterness only grew in the following months when three Irish damsels of good repute were found to be with child. The Dartrymen's passion for all things alien had cooled, aided in part by Donal MacCabe's rumours that the Spaniards did not care for Dartry's struggle.

Of greater concern to me was the ollave's attitude towards me, for I had not spoken to her ever since the day she had walked away from the green. This cooling of her friendship towards me was troubling, since I felt that I had lost a good ally who understood me best of all. Her stance was as concerning as it was confusing, since both the tanist and bondsman told me that she had spoken of my tussle with Valdo, which she could only have mentioned in order to cool the tribesmen's resentment towards me.

- XXXIV -

One morning I saw her upon her steed, riding out of the village at a canter with a score of wood kern running alongside her. After pulling on my tunic I ran towards her horse, calling out her name as I waved at her with both hands. A slight gasp behind me revealed that Nial made after me, yet I ignored him as I ran towards the ollave's party.

'Lady *Mac an Bhaird*!'

Muireann frowned as she brought her mount to a halt, then fixed me with a cold stare. Her guards parted as I held her mount by its reins, and a mist rose from my mouth when I spoke.

'Where are you going?'

'To pay a visit to my kin in Banagh,' was her terse reply, 'on the feast of Brigid the Light Bringer.'

'But you did not bid us farewell.'

'Is that not the way of your people?' she snapped.

Her reply hit me like a kick to the stomach as she leaned over her hobby's neck.

'I know not what your argument was with de Cuéllar, but you also wanted to flee, did you not? Just as you did when Aengus was slain.'

'You...you would compare me to the captain?' I managed.

Her angry expression turned solemn once more, and her guardsmen glared at me as they closed in around her.

'I know not what to believe anymore,' she whispered, then kicked her horse forward at a canter, leaving the kerns to shove me out of the way as they hurried after her.

'Godspeed, ollave Muireann,' I said to myself, staring after her in surprise as I felt the hand of the bondsman upon my shoulder.

'Do not fret, friend Juan,' he said. 'Our women are as quick to friendship as they are to anger. She is only gone to *Banagh* and will return soon.'

My stare was still fixed on her party as they vanished into the trees.

'Ever since that damned captain escaped, no one is their true self with me anymore.'

'It is not that,' said Nial. 'The ollave is troubled, for she must soon choose a suitor. She has until her return to decide.'

'Already!' I snarled and shook his hand off as I marched back to the outhouse. 'Could they not have given her a year to mourn?'

'Matters of power do not wait, friend Juan. Her decision may well decide the kingship of Dartry.'

'But is Cathal *Dubh* not already the heir elect?'

The bondsman's voice was lowered as we returned to our room.

'Dartry is a land that has always been slow to change, yet ours is a time of great upheaval. Do not forget that the last chieftainship of *An Faolchù* lasted only four years.'

I slumped onto the ground and rested my hands on my face.

'Some days I feel like I have had my fill of everyone, tanist, lord and bard! Jesuit, ollave, queen and constable…to hell with them all! Perhaps I should have fled with de Cuéllar after all!'

Nial laughed as he leant over to pick up a skin from among his belongings.

'Let us share some wine, friend Juan,' he said gently. 'It may help to calm you down.'

We spoke for a while thereafter, long after the skin had been drained and discarded. Nial told me of gossip he had heard in

- XXXIV -

the keep, and how Muireann had long been confined to the women's quarters after de Cuéllar's disappearance, attending to Dervila who had been left heartbroken by his escape.

'It seems the captain was more than a friend to her,' I said. 'He was a window to a world she cannot be part of. It is the same with many in the village, since I have heard many speak of their memory of de Cuéllar's band. To me they were but a band of miscreants, but the pain of their escape still runs deep.'

'Dartry has survived both pestilence and invasion,' Nial shrugged. 'Life shall go on as it always has.'

'But Lady Bourke's pain must be the cause of the ollave's frostiness,' I replied. 'She must be afraid to become too close to me for fear that she might suffer the same disappointment.'

The bondsman shook his head slowly.

'Would you readily flee this land?'

'In truth, I have little reason to do so, save to avoid the threat of the heretics. Yet if I have survived a whole army of them behind the walls of your keep, there appears little else to fear from them.'

The bondsman smiled wryly at my remarks.

'It is just as well that you have not yet witnessed the fighting season.'

'Yet which land is spared its fighting seasons? Wherever there is man, then battle must follow.'

'Yes,' said Nial, 'yet the battles in this land are without mercy.'

'Where are they not? War is always bloody and brutal, and sick and disgusting. Nothing but misery. Were I not a sharpshooter assigned to hide and await my target, I would have been killed long ago.'

My idle chatter with the bondsman provided me with some solace, although I still tossed and turned late into the night. Sleep never came, for the slivers of distress at the ollave's words sank deeper into my chest than any piece of shrapnel had ever done. Dawn found me crushed with exhaustion, my blankets wrapped tightly about me as I stared at the ceiling.

'You know it is for the best,' I whispered to myself, 'for if we become too close, it will only end in sorrow for her.'

At Candlemas tribesmen thronged through the bare sycamores that grew outside Saint Mel, as the chancel and nave of the church swelled with people gathered to hear Mass. O'Ronayne read of Simeon who recognised the Virgin in the temple at Jerusalem and also spoke of divine light in the darkness of human sin. At the Lord's Prayer, all present shot to their feet to recite it fervently. When Mass was over, a candlelit procession was led around the church, with the luminous file eventually making back towards the dun.

I saw some of the chieftain's men making their way through the village to share food among the needy, while some of the townsfolk smoothened the ashes on their hearths with birch wands. They also placed offerings of cake and bread outside their huts for Brigid, who was said to walk through the town at night. The odd sheaf of corn could also be seen, which had been left for the white cow, which was said to travel with the revered saint. Scores of candles had been lit to ward away evil, as well as to remind everyone that the sun's return was forthcoming. For most of the day, cock fights and horse races were held upon the green, while some of the tribesmen spilt cockerel blood on the ground to honour the ancient pagan rites of Imbolc.

The days wore on, cold and drear, until signs of new life began to appear. Lambs were born after the snow had melted, and soft rain brought new grass. Spring was ushered in by the milking of ewes in the byre, and around the lake children began their search for duck eggs on reedbeds while their fathers readied their pastures. On my walks beyond Manglana's town, I saw primrose and dandelion sprouting from the snow. Ravens returned to build their nests in the trees whilst larks were heard singing again. Happier times seemed to have returned to the inhabitants of Rosclogher, who all yearned to see the back of winter.

Following the setbacks he had endured in recent months, the chieftain looked forward to the warmer weather which lay ahead, to restore his herd and defend his lands from the enemy. As salmon returned to the lake, I was surprised to receive an invitation to join Manglana on a boating expedition. Although this was declined by Dal Verme, the Canarian brothers were swift to join the chieftain's party, and they provided great amusement for the nobles with their islander tongue of shrill whistles, whilst also exhibiting great skill when snaring both fish and otters.

Yet O'Ronayne had hardly veiled his crosses and proclaimed our Lenten fast begun, before the attentions of the assembly strayed from the travelling jesters and carrows to the newsboys. They brought dark tidings to Rosclogher, telling of troubles that brewed beyond the mountains. There soon followed a trickle of fugitives who appeared with the first leaves of spring, having fled Mayo, Sligo and the Roscommon, which had each been laid to waste by the Sassanas. These wretches begged for Manglana's protection, while also telling of a rebellion against the heretics south-west of Dartry. It was led by a pretender called the Blind Abbot, who had united many tribes behind him.

Dervila was swift to provide shelter to the fugitives, for some of them even hailed from the land of her fathers. O'Ronayne also threw himself into providing shelter and succour to the foreigners, so that our outhouse was soon shared with a family of five. I was left with no choice but to sleep with my bandolier and rifle, due to the number of times I had to retrieve them from the hands of children. Yet the impositions of war had not yet come to fully rest upon the shoulders of Dartry, and these exiles were but the start of the storm which was to follow. On an early night in March, the air was thick with the sound of bugles. I emerged from the hut with Nial, and we stood in silence together as the family gathered behind us, watching trains of torches appearing beyond the bog. The bondsman scowled at the sight.

'Men from Breifne. As if we had not enough troubles already.'

'Have they come to fight?' I asked, nervously reaching for my rifle.

'No, they would only appear to gather tribute, although it is far too early in the year for that. This can mean one thing only.'

Scores of kerns made their way through the marsh, and in the torchlight I could see the crest of two lions splayed on a banner above them, with a mailed arm arising out of an Irish crown, holding a sword by its golden hilt. Beneath it were seen letters of victory, as the men gathered about it yelled with their weapons raised in the air.

'The O'Rourke is returned!'

- XXXIV -

There were at least a hundred foot soldiers and two score on horseback. The army instantly took over the green, filling the surrounds with muffled thuds as mallets struck tent pegs.

'I have not seen so many men since the viceroy passed through,' I whispered.

Nial nodded.

'Yes, and that is only his bodyguard.'

'For truth?'

'Yes, for truth. Our overlord has been known to rally over a thousand men to his banner. *Na Múrtha* is master of all lands from the banks of Lough Gill to the borders of *Angaile*. For he is the fourth most powerful lord in the whole of *Erin*.'

Townsfolk stirred from their beds to obtain a glimpse of their overlord, and from our slight promontory I could see him riding through the town flanked by his bard and bishop, with a ring of kerns and gallowglasses shielding him from the gathering admirers. When O'Rourke reached the banks of Lough Melvin, I could see that Manglana had appeared to greet him from across the water, with Dervila and at least a dozen other high born Dartrymen. Amid the great fanfare and bustling crowd, I glimpsed the O'Rourke being ferried across the water to the tower-house, where he was said to have kept secret counsel with Manglana late into the night. Meanwhile back in the town, the song of his soldiers about their fires kept us up nearly until sunrise.

The Spaniards at Rosclogher received a curious invitation the following morning, and I was left baffled as to why we were being summoned to the keep at midday. Pedro guessed that it was due to the intervention of the tanist Cathal the Black, while Nial said that the O'Rourke had asked to meet the

Spanish defenders of Rosclogher. We were soon stepping into our protector's hall, being regarded suspiciously by the retainers of the lord of West Breifne. Among them I recognised the wily face of the MacFelim, who greeted me with a sly smile and bowed his head once in my direction. It was a small miracle that I had noticed him at all, for the hall was twice as full as I had ever seen it before. Before us two new thrones had appeared in preparation for the overlord's visit, and as I knelt before them I saw that Manglana and his wife sat below the seats they usually occupied, upon which *na Múrtha* sat alongside his wife.

O'Rourke's spouse was rumoured to be a great beauty, and a quick glimpse revealed that her looks almost eclipsed those of Lady Bourke. It was therefore with effort that I next turned my stare onto her husband. O'Rourke appeared a sombre man garbed entirely in black, with a silver beard almost reaching his knees. His hands were clasped tightly together upon his lap, and his face was lean and haggard, with eyes like a hawk's which darted swiftly from left to right. As we rose to our feet, *na Múrtha* addressed us in a timbre which was both low and strong.

'Which of ye is the marksman?'

'I am,' I replied in a thin voice, then engaged in another low bow.

O'Rourke nodded slightly as he took in the sight of me.

'Geraldine hath spoken to me of thy part in the siege, as has my cousin MacFelim.'

Unsure what to say, I stood waiting for his next words until he gestured to Manglana's steward, who urged us to retire to the back of the hall. Meat already broiled upon the raging hearth, and when the salutations were over drink was brought out in plenty as men ate their fill. Muireann stepped forward to honour the overlord, by reciting his lineage from memory. When she was finished, Miler laid his fingers upon his harp, and Fearghal the bard stepped forward to recite a poem which was over twenty years old, and had been composed in O'Rourke's honour upon him becoming the lord of Breifne.

> *"O'er heaven favoured Breifne a chieftain commands*
> *In whom all endowments of excellence join:*
> *There is not a hero in Erin's green lands*
> *Equals Brian who dwells on the science-loved Boyne.*
> *Sincere are our praises of Breifne's great lord*
> *Like the father of Oisin in story renown'd:*
> *Since the hour when a stripling he first drew the sword*
> *Where the foe dar'd to meet him he never gave ground.*
> *But what were the sword, if the harper should be mute*
> *Or the deeds of the hero if silent the Bard:*
> *Be mind the proud strains that his dignity suit,*
> *And I'll offer to Brian a minstrel's reward.*
> *Well is the rapture of eulogy due*
> *To him in whom treachery never could lurk:*
> *Whose promise is sacred, whose friendship is true,*
> *The glory of Feargna, the gallant O Rourke.*
> *O Breifne, dear land of the mountain and vale,*
> *Where the heifers stray cheerily all the long year:*
> *How fragrant thy moorlands in summer's fresh gale,*
> *How green in its showers thy meadows appear."*

When the feasting was ended, the men sat back and patted their bellies amid the odd cackle of midafternoon laughter. All mirth was swiftly put aside however, when the O'Rourke was seen rising to his feet. He cast an ominous figure as the shadow of the fire flickered against the walls about him like the black wriggling fingers of a deity. The overlord glared at the hall from left to right, causing an acute silence to fall like a curtain as all those in attendance hung on his every word.

'But a few months ago, the enemy tried to ambush me upon the banks of Lough Gill. My crime was that of harbouring our shipwrecked allies. Dublin now offers me an olive branch, and Bingham has invited me to a peace commission. But my mind is already made up, and I am of a mind to tell our enemies where they can put their olive branch. I have decided to show them the peace they have shown our people!'

His brow darkened.

'I have borne tidings of woe with me, which many of you have already heard. Countless villages have been pillaged and burned by the enemy in Mayo. This trespass shall not go ignored, for we have suffered endless atrocities at the hands of the heretics. The Blind Abbot has declared rebellion, and I am resolved to back his rightful claim to the MacWilliam, and to aid the Burkes in their plight. A great stirring up has already commenced throughout the land, backed by honourable lords. These are men of the true faith, unlike others who have long betrayed the cause - chiefly that fawning hound of O'Reilly!'

He pulled a face when he mentioned the lord of East Breifne, as if a foul odour had just entered the hall, and his listeners loudly cursed the name of the Gaelic lord who sought favour with the Sassanas. O'Rourke was a seasoned orator who knew how to move his listeners, and he roared the names of his fellow rebels with the force of a drum roll.

'O'Malley! O'Flaherty! MacDonal! MacNally! MacConroy! Clandonnel! All great fighting tribes! Yet when our need is greatest, I instantly know to call upon my most faithful allies, the men of the Sheriff-Slayer, the MacGlannaghs of Dartry! We stood together long before we rejected the Composition, and I call on you now to unite with me once more. We must hasten to battle with all sails set! Together we freed the land of one sheriff; I say let us be rid of one more! Fight and you shall be freed from your tribute, and for each man you lose, I shall pay you blood-money! The enemy has driven your beasts from your lawns. I say let us now drive their milk cows from theirs!'

The hall erupted into loud cheers of approval and a great banging of tables, for the anger of the rebels towards the heretics still smouldered like embers on a hearth that would burst into flame at the slightest prodding. The assembly of freemen instantly voted in favour of accepting their overlord's invitation to take up arms. Meanwhile I looked about nervously, asking myself if I would play any part in the upcoming fight. It appeared that the ancient enmities among the Gaelic tribes had been put aside to unite against their common enemy, and Fearghal the bard also delivered an impassioned ode to war.

The O'Rourke conversed with Manglana as the usual revelry and singing ensued, then lasted late into the night. I wandered about the hall after Nial, attempting to keep out of sight and averting my eyes from the MacFelim and the Croat Ohmunevic for fear that they might ask me to join them in an upcoming venture against the heretic. After an hour of this pointless exercise, I noticed one of the men in O'Rourke's company serving me with a cheerful grin.

At first I made nothing of it, though upon giving him the odd sidelong glance I noticed the hair on his ears that sprouted from the sides of his helmet. He was indeed a hairy specimen, with dark tufts also covering his only hand. The man appeared a poor wretch, with a bandage wrapped over his left eye. A tin arm was also strapped to his right elbow, with a hook at its end instead of a hand. The red spots on the man's cheeks suddenly left me wondering if I had seen him before, and when he spoke, a cold fright pierced the pit of my stomach.

'Abelardo de Santiago. Now that's a sight for sore eyes.'

Curro Ramos grinned as my knees shook, and my temples throbbed with rage. With a howl I pushed tribesmen away and made towards him, then grabbed him by the scruff of his mantle.

'You...you...' I barely managed.

'In the flesh, Abelito!' he laughed. 'By the black Madonna, this is an unlikelier meeting than that between Ulysses and his son!'

'You...' I choked, my teeth bared. I released his clothing and seized him by the throat instead.

'Easy does it!' he growled angrily while seizing my wrist. 'I am an officer of your master's overlord!'

'I don't care!' I cried. 'Have you no shame calling me by my name here? You are as good as dead now!'

'Your womanly self-pity!' he scoffed. 'Still upset about being a galley slave? It made you stronger, brother!'

He shoved my hand away from his throat.

'I myself rowed the galleys!' he snorted. 'It made a man of me!'

'Truly?' I cried, then punched him in the face.

- XXXIV -

When he landed upon the ground, I flung myself upon him, blinded by rage. I landed three more blows in his mouth until a swing of his metal arm sent me rolling across the straw. Men sprang to their feet as I crashed into their table, plates and cups falling upon me before the hounds did. I beat the dogs away and pushed myself to my feet, then ran at Ramos once more. We grappled for a few moments longer, during which I punched him in the nose again as he tried to hold me off with his remaining arm. I was finally dragged away from him kicking and yelling, not yet realising that the forest Croat had slung me over his shoulder and walked off as if he were bearing a young lad to school on his first day.

It was many long minutes before I stopped howling threats and insults. Dario thrust me upon a stool and held me down until the worst of my rage had passed. My chest heaved with sharp breaths when Nial himself appeared behind the Croat, seizing me by the collar and snarling at me in profound annoyance.

'Whatever your previous disputes, we are all on the same side in here! Try that again, and the chieftain's bodyguard shall lead you away!'

While I regained my breath, I glowered at Ramos, who stood holding his chin and chuckling with another tribesman. Many men from Breifne were gathered around him, regarding me with suspicion. For although the Irish usually laughed off the odd scuffle, they had been amazed by the ferocity of my altercation with the whoreson. When the tension had simmered down a little, I twitched nervously as Ohmunevic left my side and spoke to Ramos. When Dario left his side, my former sergeant advanced swiftly upon me with a stare that was at once mocking and mirthful.

I was so stunned by his sudden approach that I did not stir until he had seated himself on the bench opposite me. I issued a screech of fury as I shot to my feet with clenched fists once more. Yet as I readied to strike him again, he further astonished me by sticking his chin out and patting his left cheek with his hand.

'What are you doing?' I snapped, surprised by his gesture.

'Why, helping you to get your revenge!' he replied, 'for one-eyed cripples need all the punishment that they can get!'

His gall left me hesitant once more as I observed his pitiful eyepatch and metal arm. I felt some pity for the wretched, portly sergeant, whom I had always remembered as a formidable figure. Yet a great rage soon smouldered again within me at the memory of his past wickedness. He smiled at my hesitation, and my right hand formed a fist again as I made towards him, leaving him to raise his arm in front of his face.

'Listen to me, *friend Juan!*' he said sternly, mocking the pronunciation used by the Dartrymen. 'It will do you no good to take another step in my direction.'

'I disagree,' I snarled, as I stepped before him. 'I think giving you another thrashing is worth the hanging.'

'It is not,' he said. 'For I know you enjoy a new life in this land. A life which may vanish if your hosts learn the truth of your background.'

His threat somehow reminded me of the ring, and to my amazement my hands dropped to my sides. I decided to hate him and wait for the right moment to strike, if it ever presented itself, rather than compromise my ownership of the trinket. Ramos knew he had me then, and grinned broadly as I returned to my seat. Behind him I noticed a number of Irishmen returning to their discussions, after having been briefly distracted by our last exchange.

'Santi!' Ramos exclaimed suddenly. 'It is good to see your face again. I feared we'd lost you to the heretics!'

I cringed as he affectionately patted me upon the cheek. With the rage that seized me, I could barely breathe, let alone move. My face must also have reddened, for when Ramos noticed it, he put on a great show of astonishment.

'You are still angry at me, Santi,' he said, 'but it was only to teach you manners! I would have picked you up in England, for good skirmishers don't grow on trees! You must not be so cross. Lighten up a little! Here, have some usquebaugh. It's not wine from Cyprus, I'll grant you that, but still-'

'What are you doing here?' I asked as my voice trembled in outrage. 'You should be dead.'

'You almost got your wish,' he replied. 'It cost me an eye and an arm to keep this life.'

'The riders!' I gasped. 'How did you survive?'

'Three riders,' he said, 'who attacked me after you shot me in the back. I hauled the first one off his horse and broke his neck. Was quite the fumble to find his pistol, and the second took my eye with his sword point, for I saw him a moment too late. Yet he swiftly earned a shot through the face in exchange for his blinding thrust.'

'And the third?' I asked, stunned by the man's fortitude.

'Broke my arm with a pistol shot, so that it dangled all over the place. Bastard even tugged on it a few times before I finally choked him to death. I have never known such agony, but I suppose one does not disable three men and live to tell the tale unscathed.'

'And you then just sauntered into rebel territory?'

'No. I was found by rebel tribesmen who bore me away to their village. I was lying in a rain-soaked ditch and dying, with each breath harder than the last. Halfway through their journey I passed out, and I awoke in the castle at Carha to find the arm gone. My sight was awkward at first. I was treated by O'Rourke's own physician, and he also visited me when I was recovered. I owe him my life.'

'Shame about the arm and hand,' I said scornfully, 'although you look sightlier for the rag which hides half your face.'

Ramos grinned as he raised his mead horn to his lips.

'Life at the oar made you bitter, Abelito. But pray, what are your thoughts on this rabble? And the quandary we find ourselves in?'

'Why do you care about my thoughts? If it were up to you my bones would be chained at the bottom of the sea!'

'Is that true, Abelito?' he retorted. 'So was I the only Spaniard to know that the Armada would meet such an end?'

He slammed the table before him in outrage.

'How did I know the horrors we were to endure at Calais? Everyone spoke of certain victory, Santi, yet I am not a man of the sea! You should count yourself fortunate to have avoided the misery on deck. Dead men everywhere, no gunpowder left! All I wanted was for you to do a bit of work until you reached England. To get you to change your mind, to rejoin me.'

'You mean your offer still stands?' I replied, in a tone which was full of sarcasm.

'It is,' he replied, with the utmost seriousness.

- XXXIV -

'Do not talk idly,' I growled. 'What is it you want?'

Ramos feigned a look of incredulity and nudged Ohmunevic a couple of times with his elbow, then issued a bark of laughter. He next spread his hands out innocently as if to imply that he had no hidden motives for seeking me out.

'What do I want? Abelito, we meet again after over a year and you ask me what I want? I am only glad to meet an old friend again!'

I looked away from his mirthful expression and sighed, holding my face in my hands. There followed an awkward silence in which Ramos still did not leave my side. Suddenly he spoke again.

'Very well, Abelito. You may not share my joy at our meeting again, yet I know that like me, you are also a veteran of the Army of Flanders. And I know that you will be keen to hear what I have to say.'

He leant over towards me, his breath reeking of stale mead, flecks of spittle hitting my nose when he hissed a word in my face.

'Plunder!'

The man was simply incredible, for in the blink of an eye he had turned into the same avaricious Curro Ramos of old. I found his gall impressive as he casually sat in front of me as if he had never condemned me to the rower's oar. It evidently mattered little to him whether or not I liked him, due to the trust he had in my aim. I could not but help feeling somewhat flattered at this. Although my wellbeing was of no importance to him, he demonstrated the highest seriousness when discussing his plans with me.

'I am here to talk of plunder,' Ramos said again, whispering the last word in awe and with a glint in his one eye, as if it were the most important word on earth.

'How much?' I asked, resigning myself to having to bear his vile presence, though also finding myself a little curious.

The big Croat reached over the table to snatch up a hunk of beef, and its juices dribbled down his chin when he sank his teeth into it. Meanwhile Curro prattled on, seemingly ignorant to the food on offer as I drummed the table impatiently with my fingertips.

'Plenty. We are thinking of training troops here.'

I laughed him off.

'They have no experience of real battle.'

Ramos leaned over towards me as his eye widened.

'Yet they do not come much braver, or keener. After all, their motivation is not hard to understand, for their plight is not an enviable one, what with their being caught between enemies both east and west. At some point they must learn how to take to the field.'

'And is the O'Rourke open to your ideas?'

Curro coughed awkwardly as he drew away slightly.

'He has said as much, and I have fourteen Spaniards training his wood kerns. Yet there has been some resistance from the men of Breifne to adapt their fighting ways. Namely from the old tanist and bard, not to mention the cursed Scots with their big axes last seen in the time of Caesar.'

I could not resist a chuckle at his reference to the weapons and armour of the gallowglass. Ramos grinned at me, which made me swiftly resume my severe expression.

- XXXIV -

'Have you encountered the same resistance yourself in Dartry?' he asked.

'None from our tanist,' I replied, 'since Cathal the Black is a worthy man. And although he is celebrated for fighting in the ancient ways, he has himself admitted to me that the customs of the tribe must change. At least upon the battlefield.'

'Not just a pretty face, our lord Cathal,' joked Ramos, nodding his approval.

'Indeed. He is an honourable man, unlike yourself.'

Of a sudden Ramos squinted at me and stopped himself from saying something. It was a few moments until he spoke again.

'You seem most committed to the cause of the Irish. Why have you not yet escaped?'

'I could ask the same of you.'

Ramos chuckled, and the big Croat smiled alongside him.

'The English want me dead, and I hate my Spanish masters,' said my old sergeant at last. 'What better choice than to fight for the Irish?'

I frowned when he carried on.

'Better to fight than scurry off to Scotland. At least here I have the authority to lead dozens of men instead of having to serve fools like de Cuéllar.'

He gave me a knowing glance when he mentioned the captain, yet I ignored it as he reached out for a chicken wing.

'Listen, Santiago, you know what I think of your ability. I am good friends with the Anglo-Norman Thomas Geraldine. He tells me that you fought valiantly during the siege of Rosclogher.'

I laughed.

'And you think that flattery will commit me to your farce?'

Pieces of chicken flew from his mouth when he leant towards me again.

'Hear me well, Abelito! I tell you that I am military advisor to the O'Rourke. I have seen how desperate the rebels are to raise an army which can stand the field. They cannot run like wolves forever, at the first sight of an English force. In this land O'Rourke has an arm which is almost as long as a Habsburg jawline! You and I could make a serious fortune here. This place will soon blow up like a powder keg, for a fratricidal war will soon commence. Many Irishmen will also fight for the heretics, since they know that it will save their hide. But if we muster a few victories on the field, the tide will turn. The old rivalries will be forgotten as the rebels unite behind aliens of the same faith. They will gather behind us like moths to a flame, for it will sit easier on their conscience. For much as they value their cows, do not forget that all Irishmen are papist whoresons at heart. Just like us, Santiago!'

After this last exclamation he sat back again and finished off his chicken, and I noticed O'Ronayne staring at us curiously. I glared back at my old sergeant and leant towards him.

'Do not use that name again!' I hissed. 'I thought that you were supposed to keep it a secret.'

Ramos shrugged as he drew his skene dagger and used it to pick at his teeth.

'Forgive me, Abelito,' he said, staring absently at the space above my head. 'I sometimes think you have more names than the devil himself. It is easy to forget them.'

'Well then,' I replied, as I tapped the table with my finger, 'you can at least remember this: I will not abandon my plans to return to Spain, so as to partake in your harebrained scheme.'

- XXXIV -

Ramos grimaced at me.

'You may not have long to wait before Spain returns to claim us so that we can then spend our time between gaol and trench all over again. But until then we can give ourselves orders, to aid these tribesmen who give us respect!'

'And food,' added Dario the Croat drily, as he reached out for more beef.

'And women!' exclaimed Ramos, and a reverential gaze overcame him while his one eyelid fluttered dreamily.

'Magical,' agreed Dario, lifting a jug of usquebaugh which ran as freely down his gullet as it did onto his collar, 'for they are wild vixens who lack hesitation.'

'They are sirens,' breathed Ramos, 'not of this earth.'

I spluttered on my wine, for I still found the vulgarity of Spanish troopers amusing despite my profound dislike for Ramos. My old sergeant instantly turned towards me and clapped me on the shoulder, which shoved my nose into my beaker and caused me to splutter some more.

'Easy! Easy, Abelito! So you can still laugh at old Curro when the fancy takes you? So you have elected not to share a severe face with these miserable heretics?'

His unjust reference to heretics reminded me of both Flanders and Maerten, who had drowned with the Santa Maria de Visión. I also remembered Elsien and Reynier, both choked to death by the actions of the devil who still slapped my back. I shot to my feet and grabbed his wrist, pushing it away and raising my forefinger before his nose with a low growl.

'Do not get too friendly, you scum. Don't forget that you and I still have a score to settle.'

'Plenty of time left for that, Abelito!' he exclaimed. 'I mean Juan! As much time as there will be to fight with your fellows over a cutting of tainted meat in a trench! Our bankrupt king will gladly treat us like sheep led to the slaughter once more, in exchange for nothing! Last I recall, even sharpshooters were charged for their own munitions!'

I bristled at these words, recalling the outrageous decision which had further impoverished riflemen who selflessly served king and country.

'I can see that you are still angry about it,' said Ramos with a wry smile.

'That would never have happened under Alba,' I snarled, 'yet he was replaced by fools and profiteers like yourself, bringing disrepute to an honourable profession.'

'Alba is underground!' he snapped. 'Buried! Dead! You are the fool for not accepting it. For how long shall you cling to the triumphs of the past?! Do you really want to return to an army where positions are sold, where you cannot even swear or blaspheme in anger without some useless officer around to fine you?'

When he said this he instantly howled an obscenity about the nether regions of some poor saint which did not bear repeating. This profanity confirmed that O'Ronayne overheard us, for his face turned the crimson colour of dulse as he choked on his drink.

'And if the memory of Alba is still so dear to you,' proceeded my old sergeant hotly, 'you can help me to enforce his old rules here. We can command our own militia, for this field is ready and ripe for the harvesting, Santi – I mean Juan! Youths are fleeing the coveted training of the gallowglasses to enlist

- XXXIV -

with me. With me! I train them every single day, just like the Romans did, yet you alone can teach them how to split a tarot card with a musket shot! Once they are trained there will be no force like them in this land, and as their numbers grow, we can contract their services to king or pope or whichever whoreson offers us the highest pension!'

'Your dedication to the rebel cause is deeply moving.'

Ramos burst out laughing at my thinly veiled sarcasm, knowing that I could see his true motives.

'Everyone wins, Abel - I mean Juan! Our troops will need to be battle-hardened before we can contract them. We shall profit from a fight that is truly just, not fought just to fill a king's coffers. If we seize the moment, who knows where this might all end? England might be next for the taking! Listen to me and forget Spain and the Indies, for this is the Indies for us! After a few battles we need never fight again. We'll feast on meat off the bone and have the pick of their wenches in bed! We shall live free from the imperial yoke and spend the rest of our days feted by these wealthy cattle lords, whose riches shall only grow once we hurl all the Sassanas into the sea! Spain itself will release more bonds to recruit our Irish troops to serve it on the Continent. We shall become richer than Adolph of Holstein himself!'

I nodded at his mention of the notorious double-dealing contractor, then sat back and helped myself to a horn of wine as the feasting still raged about us. Deep down I knew that what Ramos said might well be true, yet the lure of a venture to the Indies was still strong and all but guaranteed by the priceless trinket borne in my bandolier.

'We can have everything we want here, and more,' said Curro as his one eye bore into me. 'Let us begin the fightback together, without waiting upon the king of Spain's pleasure. Why return to living as side-street cutthroats or embark on an uncertain voyage to an unknown world?'

We sat in silence, as I struggled to ignore the temptation of Ramos' offer. Then at last I spoke up as a brawl among a few wood-kerns broke out near the hearth.

'These men had best become accustomed to pike and shot,' I said, 'for both the viceroy and the Binghams have it in for them.'

'That they do,' agreed Ramos. 'Yet much as they hate the rebels, they dislike each other even more.'

'Yes, I have heard men tell of that,' I replied, 'and yet they raided Connacht together.'

Dario nodded while Ramos beheld me slyly.

'That is true. And since the siege their relations have worsened significantly.'

'Truly?'

My former sergeant nodded furiously.

'Of a certainty! The Sassanas have excellent spies, but we also have ours. The ones in Dublin tell us that the English viceroy is furious, that he complains of the Binghams being a law unto themselves in Connacht. By all accounts, he has also gone as far as to send a damning report about them to London.'

I felt taken aback as the sergeant continued.

'Word has also leaked out of Athlone that the viceroy was especially angered after he met an old Spanish don named Hurtado.'

Ramos watched me closely as he uttered the name, and I did my best to wear my most impassive expression, which I usually

- XXXIV -

saved for card games. I suddenly remembered the old prado deep in the dungeons of Sligo, holding the emerald ring which I had forcibly taken from him.

'The Binghams had him moved there from Sligo,' continued Ramos, 'since he was one of only fifty Spaniards whose lives were spared for ransoming. Before you ask, the viceroy ordered that they be put to death, but before he issued that order, FitzWilliam spoke at length with this old prado, who bade him swear an oath to honour the wish of a doomed man. It sparked an argument between the viceroy and the Binghams which, to our fortune, keeps getting worse.'

'That is indeed fortunate.'

Ramos edged closer towards me.

'They tell me that you were imprisoned in Sligo. Did you hear anything about a ring?'

I creased my brow in feigned concentration.

'If I did I would have remembered it. There was surely much talk of jewels and coins. Do you have a description of it?'

'No. But whatever type of ring it was, the viceroy has accused the Binghams of hiding it from the Crown treasury. It is said to be a bauble of huge value.'

'What value?' I asked, doing my best to fix my stare on the space between his eyes.

Ramos looked over both his shoulders, then shoved his forehead against mine and rasped a whisper in my face.

'It is a ring said to belong to the prince of Ascoli. Do you remember that highborn whoreson on your hospital ship, whining that he lost a ring given to him by his mother?'

'Yes,' I said, knowing that to deny it would be an obvious lie.

'Well, that is the one!' exclaimed Ramos. 'A ring given to him by his mother Eufrasia! We thought Gabri had taken it, yet somehow it ended up with Hurtado, who claimed it was taken by a fellow Spanish captive.'

'That is ever more curious,' I observed, delighting in the irony that the ring Ramos spoke of was hidden on my person, barely a handspan away from Ramos' breast.

'It is,' agreed Ramos, pulling away from me, 'yet I discovered something more curious still.'

'Oh?' I said, attempting to feign a passing interest, although I yearned to learn more about the trinket I carried.

'It seems the Binghams also learned from the viceroy, that the ring was a gift to the Prince of Ascoli's mother from the king himself!'

No sooner did he say this than my jaw hung open, as I recalled the inscription along the inside of the ring.

F.R... I thought to myself, *F.R...could it be...Felipe Rey?*

As I regained my composure I noticed that Ramos was staring straight at me, his face severe.

'What is it Santi? You know something? Speak it.'

For a few moments I was unsure what to say, but the sergeant was on the scent and I knew that he would not go unanswered. Then I suddenly thought of a way to shake him off, and I smacked my hand on the table, feigning upset.

'Little wonder then that de Cuéllar was in such haste to flee!'

Ramos' eye widened at my exclamation, and Dario instantly rose to his feet and strode towards the MacFelim. My old sergeant was silent for a few moments until he spoke again.

'The captain shall have a hard time of getting away with it. The Binghams are desperate to find this ring. It is said that

- XXXIV -

the English viceroy in Dublin has vowed to bring them down unless they surrender it to him.'

XXXV

Rosclogher, Dartry, County Leitrim to Boyle, County Roscommon to Rosclogher, Dartry, County Leitrim

1 – 4 March 1589

O'Rourke was hardly two days at Rosclogher, and no sooner had his force departed than the Dartrymen readied for battle. For two weeks the whole town busied itself in preparation for the ensuing conflict, although none save the chieftain knew of its whereabouts. Manglana did not disclose this to anyone, since our reports of the treachery experienced during the siege had not fallen upon deaf ears. Meanwhile hammers rang upon the anvils near the forge, and bowyers set about feathering scores of arrows to the scrape of blades upon the whetstone. The training in arms ensued with greater vigour, and I was asked to teach marksmanship for longer hours upon the green, where the snow of winter had all but melted away.

This endeavour helped me to forget the reappearance of Ramos which had left me shaken, though in the coming days I could not forget his final words. In our last meeting the sergeant had assured me that he could bring me under his command again, and was enraged when I refused his offer time and again. He had finally risen from his stool with a look of outrage.

'I know you, Santiago,' he said. 'You will squander your new-found status. You are no longer able to fit into civilized society, for you are a lone wolf.'

My rebuttal had incurred a great anger on his behalf.

'You feel that you have risen to lofty heights among this small tribe,' he had sneered, 'yet I know you, Santiago, and you will mess this one up too. You have no place remaining to you in society, for killing is your only true calling.'

His words left me incensed as they rang true, and they plagued my thoughts for many days thereafter as the battle preparations persisted. Much as I hated the direction in which my life had taken me, there was no denying that I was now no more than a seasoned marksman, trained to shoot defenceless men from far off. So I was irked for long after Ramos' departure, and the training of the chieftain's musketeers was a tiresome and a stinking business which left me drained of all life.

There were few moments of solitude available to me, which I often spent walking along the banks of the lake with two of the tanist's kerns shadowing my footsteps. The assignment of these bodyguards had commenced after the O'Rourke's visit, since his praise for me had restored my favour with the chieftain. Manglana had once even acknowledged my presence, after his overlord had passed into the south-west to raid those lands held by the enemy. This protection proved to be a great hindrance to me, since it deprived me of the solitude I craved in which I could keep to my own thoughts and also examine the prize I still kept hidden away.

Such an opportunity was eventually granted to me in the outhouse shared with Nial, after I posted the two apes assigned to the door of the hut, with orders to warn me of anyone's approach. This meant that I could pull out the emerald ring in great comfort as I sat with my back to the abode's entrance, then hold it up before my eyes as I turned it between my fingers.

'You bloody beauty,' I whispered smugly, as it glinted back at me wordlessly. 'Bloody Hurtado just would not stop worrying about you, would he?'

When I rubbed the emerald with my thumb it seemed to shine ever more brightly, and I enjoyed looking upon its flawless perfection in such a conflicted and impoverished part of the world. As it gleamed at me, the thought could not help passing through my head time and again, that it was the cause of severe divisions between our enemies that could yet lead to a revival in the rebels' fortunes. Not that the rebels were waiting on any turn of luck to attempt to banish their enemies from their own lands. Once again, I looked at the inscription upon its band.

'to my Eufrasia, with all my love for you and our child - F.R.'

'Our child...' I whispered to myself, burning with curiosity. 'Our child...but who?'

The following day the chieftain girded himself for battle, and orders were issued for his militia to be ready to depart the town at any moment. Manglana cut a figure of finery from head to foot, and his cloak was tied with a gold brooch after his boots had been tanned by oak bark. Dartry's king was ferried across the water in a jerkin trimmed with marten fur, as his knaves brought him his best sword and stallion. Midafternoon found his party gathered outside the Abbey of Saint Mel, where O'Ronayne recited prayers in Latin to us before he showered us with phials of holy water. Ahead of us a herald held up the *Catach*, which was the tribe's talisman. It consisted of a copy of psalms said to have been written over a thousand years before by the saint *Colum Cille*.

As he rode at a canter out of the town, Manglana was shadowed by his bard, who did not bear weapons. Cathal the Black rode at his shoulder, with a tail of cavalrymen behind him. Scores of kerns encircled them, armed with their spears and long skene daggers. The constable Donal MacCabe and his troop of gallowglass rode in the rear. Upon reaching the green, we saw the lady Bourke surrounded by a small group of her retainers, watching us ride out of the village. Her grandson stood before her, red curls fluttering in the wind. Young Lochlain's face was flushed as he stared up at us in awe.

I recognised Muireann making towards us with her bow over her shoulder, and her step never faltered until she had taken the reins of the palfrey brought to her by a horseboy. She silently led the mount towards the ring of bog, and the horsemen in our party instantly followed her as she proceeded to lead us through the mire. Upon leaving the town Muireann still led us on towards the mountains, and men whispered that she wore a leather jerkin to battle which had belonged to her late husband. Our band numbered fifty horse and over a hundred foot, and except for the Scots the rest of us travelled light, bearing only our arms and a few provisions.

As we skirted the bog we soon entered the forest, then proceeded through valleys and the craggy slopes of the mountains. As we marched with our steeds held behind us, Nial cast a long face at the rifle over my shoulder.

'Tools of the devil,' he muttered.

I frowned in protest.

'Gunpowder is the way of the future.'

Cathal gestured at us to lower our voices when our route became encircled by wooded hills.

'What is the game like in these parts?' I asked.

Ahead of us Manglana looked at me over his shoulder with a grin.

'If you are lucky, you might see a Sassenach. Bandits also infest these woods.'

His words left me on edge, although the mounted freemen were readily armed, with their scabbards bouncing upon their thighs and their javelins strapped onto their backs. They also bore short lances, which consisted of broad-headed blades on thick handles of ash. For my first raid I had sought added protection, and beneath my cassock was a steel cuirass of armour taken during the siege of Rosclogher. At my side rode a horseboy named Pirib, who had also been assigned to me by the tanist, Cathal. I had sworn to keep him in my employ until instructed otherwise, although this request had left me baffled. After all, the lad was ill at ease on horseback and of poor health, besides being the first horseboy I had met who seemed to have no idea about horses. I once caught him feeding my stallion unthreshed oats.

The land was often impassable due to thick woods and bog, and those riders among us were often forced to dismount and march for long stretches. My hosts proved tireless on the march. I had learned from Nial that they could cover forty of their own miles on a winter day, with the Irish mile being longer than the English one by a quart, which meant that four Irish miles were equal to five of the heretics'.

After crossing Bocóid we pressed through forests of oak and hazel, before cutting through the heights of Dartry. The ollave led us over less used passes which were not even marked out by goats' hooves. All was quiet in the glen as we persisted through Breifne under cover of night, taking our rest at dawn when we were within sight of Clooneen, which was one of the keeps held by the O'Rourke. After I had fallen to the grass and regained my breath, I retired to the tent which had been pitched by Nial and my useless horseboy, where I once more tumbled to the ground and fell into a dreamless sleep. We were roused at dusk and handed strips of red cloth, which were passed onto us by the chieftain's bodyguards with strict instructions to tie one about our arms.

"'Tis the sign of our alliance' said Nial before I could ask why we had been issued with this order.

It occurred to me that the O'Rourkes and their allies would not hinder our journey to our secret destination, and that news of our passage had already been communicated to the lords of those lands through which we were venturing. Although this did little to protect us from the prying eyes of enemy spies, it at least ensured that our passage through the foreign lands outside Dartry would not be dogged by the pursuit of other tribesmen, who might send word to their fellows to meet us in ambush. A path was beaten beneath Mount Benbo, which was shrouded with dark cloud, before we proceeded to ford the river Bonet. My teeth were gritted as I trudged through the dark water, for if there was something I hated more than walking through cold water, it was walking through cold water during the dark of night.

A chill gale froze our faces and rippled the grass about us after the crossing, and we caught sight of the friary at Creevela when Lough Gill vanished and Lough Bo glimmered before us. Our journey had largely been without incident, save for the midges which attacked us upon the banks of the lakes we passed. They only stopped harassing us when we reached the river Unshin, where I gritted my teeth with displeasure as I readied to wade through the dark water once more.

We were hardly halfway through when one of the Manglanas in front of me tripped and collapsed into the river, causing my blood to surge as the splash from his fall soaked me to my bristling skin. As he re-emerged, coughing and spluttering, I issued a spate of blasphemy of the darkest pitch, since I had been drenched from head to foot, with water dripping off my nose and the ends of my powder charges.

'By the holy host of the Madonna!' I swore aloud. 'These charges are useless to me now!'

'Keep your voice down,' hissed Nial at my back, 'for we are out of Breifne now and must not alert any spies to our presence.'

'We may as well issue a blast on a bugle,' I snapped back at him, 'for my part in our errand – whatever it is – has been rendered useless.'

- XXXV -

'Hardly so,' said the bondsman as we ventured on, 'for we have stocks of fresh powder with us, and you can dry the ampoules when we retire for the day.'

As always the exchange with my companion served to relieve my distress. However the prospect of having to empty the powder charges was not one that appealed to me, since the ring was still held in the last charge. I berated myself for having consigned it to the ampoule, although in truth there was no safer place in which to hide it, other than within my stomach. Yet I had tired of retrieving the ring each time after it was swallowed, and I hesitated to hide it in my clothing or brogues after de Cuéllar had picked them apart during the siege of Rosclogher.

My mind was filled with thoughts of other hiding places, until dawn was announced by a rim of sunlight, which appeared behind a lofty hillside to our left. As the ollave led us up it I cursed and groaned with effort, for it was very steep and even caused the horses behind us to whinny with strain. Muireann skillfully led us over a sideways track which wended its way gently towards the summit, and as we drew closer to it I saw that its promontory was dotted by a ring of caves. Upon catching sight of them I jerked my mount to a standstill, my jaw left hanging open by weariness and bewilderment. Nial grinned at my amazement as he fell in beside me.

'Those are the caves of Ceis Churainn, friend Juan. One of the high kings of yore, Donal Mac Airt, was raised there by a she-wolf.'

Ahead of us Fearghal the bard spoke up in a haughty voice, having evidently overheard the bondsman.

'That he was! And his daughter Gráinne hid there when she spurned the vengeful Fionn Mac Cumhail! She ran off with one of his warriors, Diarmuid son of Donn!'

Manglana called a halt as the ollave proceeded ahead of us with a handful of her kerns to inspect the caves. His act of caution was soon justified, for no sooner had they disappeared into a black cave mouth than a loud growl was heard, which was shortly followed by a beast's spitting and snarling amid the cries of men. The loud patter of footsteps was heard as Muireann's hounds growled at the distant shadows, but it was a din that lasted only a few instants, with silence soon returning. One of the ollave's men summoned us towards the caverns. Our approach was greeted by the scent of yellow flowers on the rock face outside, and then I saw the ollave's retainers dragging a slain wolf into the cave which they were to reside in for the day.

The force split up to occupy another three caverns, with the chieftain's men occupying the largest and the tanist and the gallowglass constable leading their men into the remaining two. As the sun commenced its slow but steady ascent, I could see that the floor of our new quarters was very muddy, and there came the constant sound of water dripping off the ceiling. A small wander about the back of the cave did not reveal anything else, save for the lichens and spiders' webs in its corners. Although the bones of different beasts could be seen on the cavern floor, to my relief our natural quarters were not possessed of a foul smell, and as the kerns wrapped themselves in blankets and slept in the corners of cave, I stepped back to its face and marvelled at the view of the countryside below, rubbing my hands closely together and taking in the distant sight of yet another great lake in the distance.

- XXXV -

The riders among the tanist's men had hitched their horses to rocks at the back of the cave. Meanwhile the kerns used spears and rocks to erect a pole on both sides of the cavern before tying the ends of a hempen cord to both spearheads. The tribesmen then gathered about this makeshift line to sling all wet clothing, scabbards and other belongings over it, leaving them to dry as they retired for the day. No fire was hazarded since our mission clearly depended on moving secretly at night, and the men huddled together closely for warmth in the vicinity of the horses, as they wrapped their blankets tightly about themselves. Many were already snoring after our long march, as I busied myself with inspecting the bandolier, discovering to my great relief that the ampoules were not as wet as I had first feared.

I decided to sling the bandolier over the rope for the remainder of the day, since it would adequately remove all moisture until I could change the powder as a precaution. When this was done I cast myself upon the ground alongside the bondsman, who had already fallen into a deep slumber. No sooner was my mantle wrapped tightly about me and my eyes closed than I knew nothing more. An hour before dusk, Nial shook me awake by the shoulder.

'Ready yourself for the march, Juan,' he whispered. 'The chieftain's fleet-footed scouts have examined our surrounds and there have been no enemy sightings.'

We heard the clink of weaponry around us as men fastened their sword belts and picked up their spears and axes. The ring occupied my first thoughts whenever I stirred from sleep, and with a low gasp I hurried towards the line from which the bandolier still hung. I had sighed in relief and reached out for it when behind me I heard someone's voice.

'Santiago?'

I turned to find the Jesuit O'Ronayne peering at me suspiciously, and was about to return my attentions to the pile of weapons when he spoke again.

'Is that your true name?'

'My pardon,' I replied, 'but I do not understand...'

'O'Rourke's Spaniard mentioned that word to you many times. I wondered if and why you conceal your true name from us.'

I ignored the discomfort he caused me while forcing a smile upon my face.

'"Twas but a name of affection assigned to me by close comrades due to my great veneration for the patron of Spain, for I am devoted to James the apostle, who I believe has protected me for all these years.'

Manglana's confessor squinted at me with a bemused frown as he mulled over my explanation.

'My lord is right, that you are indeed a glib specimen. But be warned that great woe may yet befall you if you are not telling the truth of it.'

'Do you threaten me?' I asked, as my stare turned into a glare.

'"Tis but the truth', he replied, as he turned away.

I issued a curse beneath my breath as I turned away from the suspicious prelate, then fell to my knees when I saw that the bandolier had vanished from the pile of weapons. In great distress I rummaged through all the weapons that were still hanging from the line, desperately seeking to understand what had become of it as I found two other belts of powder charges. One of them belonged to a highborn horseman who proceeded

- XXXV -

to snatch it from my hands, and the last one belonged to the tanist.

With a gasp I hurried towards the cave mouth, where tribesmen and mercenaries had gathered to make their way back down the incline. Ahead of them Cathal the Black could be seen in the last light of day, walking alongside Manglana and engaged in a deep debate, with my belt of charges fastened around his breast

'Holy host,' I snarled inwardly.

I would have smacked my forehead in rage were it not for the Irishmen gathered about me. With a curse I pulled Cathal's own bandoleer over my head, then rushed out of the cave with a low growl, resolved to somehow recover the ring before it was either discovered or lost. As nightfall set in, the ollave proved a worthy guide once more. In the light of the moon we passed through the mensal lands around Ballymote, where parts of the forest had been cleared. I had by this time managed to get within eavesdropping distance of both Manglana and Cathal the Black, and overheard the chieftain's grumbling at the ease with which we covered ground.

'The royalists bear axes against our trees uninvited. I should like to know where all of the timber goes.'

'To build their fleets, sire,' was his tanist's dry reply.

A small wood was next reached on the knolls near Lough Arrow's inlets, and after a hard climb through the speckled mountains we plunged again into the dark gloom of forest, following the ollave through defiles that curved between pine and oak as the path became steeper again. When we approached another range of heights flanked by two lakes, I heard Pirib speak for the first time that night.

'At last we have reached the rugged mountains.'

From above their summits, the faint moonlight revealed nothing but woodland, which ran north in the direction of Breifne, over which the heights of Ben Bulben and Truskmore kept a timeless watch. Towards midnight we undertook yet another difficult uphill climb into thick, dark forest, though our passage eased by the thinning of the trees closer to the summit. As we drew nearer, the lights of the town of Boyle were revealed beneath us.

As we kept to our ascent we saw many stumps of the whitethorn and hawthorn in the first light of dawn. Their trunks had fallen to the axes of the colonists, although they were the trees most venerated by the Gaels. At least a half-dozen of them were sighted before Manglana called a halt, and tears streaked his reddened face as he beheld yet another stump in stunned silence.

'The ruin of the thorn stirs my sorrow,' he said, 'as well as my rage. May those that committed these foul deeds find themselves in our path when we swoop.'

His words left me wondering as to the nature of our errand, as my eyes fell upon the distant settlement of Boyle to our right. From our vantage point it appeared that the walled garrison town was not too dissimilar to Sligo, and the chieftain's kerns sneered at the fields and farmsteads maintained about it. In muffled voices they said that the Irish living there were no more than *betaghs*, which in their tongue meant serfs.

A range of outbuildings beyond the garrison walls included the usual boulting and milk houses, together with barns which would have been loaded with carts and other stores. A few privies could be seen on the periphery of the fields, as well as

- XXXV -

large cattle pens, with mounted troopers patrolling the confines, ever ready to send a word of warning back to the fortified town. Boyle was afforded another shield of defence in the form of a shimmering river which ran before it, out of Lough Key.

When we reached a hillside with a large clearing, the chieftain called a halt. The horseboys busied themselves with hitching their masters' steeds while tents were pitched by the kerns. Strict orders were issued to subalterns not to allow the men to stray from the camp, although most had already retired to the tents and fallen asleep. My tent was shared with Nial and some of Cathal the Black's riders. Despite my concern for the ring I collapsed into a dreamless sleep for the rest of the day, until Pirib aroused me after nightfall.

'What is it?' I growled, furious that my hapless horseboy should dare to waken me without my having requested it.

'My lord MacGlannagh requests your presence, sire.'

To my surprise the horseboy did in fact lead me towards the tent of the chieftain. Manglana's bodyguards parted before the scrawny horseboy, who barely raised his hand towards them. As I entered after him I caught sight of a glowing brazier, which warmed Manglana and his tanist. The chieftain observed me with a distracted air as Cathal spoke.

'Greetings, friend Juan. We meet on an evening when our need for you is greatest.'

I was disappointed to see that he did not bear my bandolier, nor could I see it anywhere. For a few moments I wondered whether I should ask him as to its whereabouts, then decided to delay since the matter at hand appeared more serious than I had first thought.

'It would be an honour to serve you, my lords.'

Cathal's lips parted when he smiled back at me, revealing purple gums and yellowed teeth.

'We need you to reach the outskirts of the town tonight,' he said, 'for there is no one we can trust more with this mission, save perhaps for the ollave. Yet she is resting after a day spent scouting our surrounds and shall revisit the passes again before dawn.'

'It would be both lonely and hungry to be trapped in these mountains,' added the chieftain, then raised his cup and drained it in one gulp.

'That is why you must go, friend Juan' resumed the tanist, 'for you are a seasoned skirmisher.'

'But if captured I am as good as dead,' I protested, 'for the Sassanas have not spared a single Spaniard.'

'Which is why you are the only one we can trust. Yet do not fear, for we are convinced that your task will proceed without incident. The horseboy Pirib will travel with you, as will a handful of our fiercest kerns. They are hand-picked men who will die before your safety is threatened.'

'What would you have me do?' I asked, feeling no less relieved about the errand which had been assigned to me.

'That is not for others to hear,' said the tanist. 'Pirib here shall be your guide, and you will know what it is that you have to do. Travel light. You must not use your rifle or it will rouse the town.'

I left the exalted company of Manglana and Cathal with a deep bow and a promise to honour their trust, then gritted my teeth in frustration as I followed the horseboy out of the tent. I left most of my belongings in the tent alongside the slumbering Nial, and when I re-emerged from it I found Pirib

- XXXV -

awaiting me with the chieftain's promised kerns. Each of them brandished two spears and surrounded me as we started our march downhill.

The horseboy led us on a tricky descent for the better part of an hour. Upon reaching the foot of the mountains we crept towards the farmsteads about the town, and I wondered if we were to approach the gates of Boyle itself. Pirib only stopped where the trees had almost petered out altogether, then produced a faint sound resembling the cry of a thrush. A few moments later a similar noise was heard in the darkness, and Pirib frantically gestured to me to follow him. I barely made a sound as I hurried after him, the five other kerns like invisible wolves at my back. After covering twenty yards, we collapsed upon one another behind a privy that stood apart from the rest of the settlement.

'Wait here,' Pirib had the cheek to mumble, but before I could reply, he was already gone.

I was left behind in the cold, wondering what to do next when a scuffle was heard in the distance. I snatched the rifle off my shoulder and I poised the end of its muzzle in the direction of the growing sounds as the kerns in my company raised their spears and drew their daggers.

'Who goes there?'

'Well met, friend Juan.'

The voice was immediately familiar, as I made out Pirib in the company of two fellows. One of them was his spitting likeness; the other I already recognised as the Anglo-Norman.

'Old Tom? What are you doing here?'

'Spying,' he said disdainfully. 'What else?'

Much as I was happy to see Geraldine, he ignored me as he held his head and groaned.

'My head is spinning, for they are drunk as lords in the town. They have good beer and cider. You could probably take them all now.'

"Tis a merry banquet,' I remarked.

'These heretics lack for little,' he said. 'We've a pound of bread or biscuit daily; cheese, butter and beef each week. One fish a day and a quart of cleas once a week with pork on the Sunday.'

'It sounds like you have found your true calling.'

'Do not jest!' he snapped, outraged that I had even suggested that he join the enemy. 'For it is all I can do not to slip poison into their drink. To think how well victualled they are when the true natives of this land have thin air with which to feed their children. My blood seethes every day, and it is all I can do to play the puppet! Would that my lord had consigned me to the field of battle instead.'

Geraldine's voice became tighter as he whispered further information to us, for despite his inebriation he clearly feared for his life.

'Gilson has orders to head for the Roscommon tomorrow. Word has reached them of the raids of the O'Rourke, and he is leaving to subdue the troubles in the west.'

'So the cattle is to be left undefended?'

'But a token force shall be left behind to defend the town. You could almost call it a squadron. Other recruits are bound this way from Athlone but they are due late tomorrow.'

'How many heads are there in the pens?'

- XXXV -

'Over a hundred, easy pickings. Now begone before you get us both killed! We are concealed from the eyes of the sentinel, but there are two riders on patrol who shall soon reappear!'

His whisper was a shrill rasp as the twin horseboys undressed and exchanged their clothing before swiftly embracing.

'Take Pilip back with you!' hissed Geraldine. 'If all goes to plan, we shall switch horseboys a few more times this year!'

I was impressed by the ingenuity with which the rebels obtained information. We disappeared back into the shadows just as the clink of saddles was heard behind us and two domed riders appeared, riding at a slow trot towards the privy. I found myself excited at the cunning ploy which had been hatched while also realising that the rustle of so many heads would restore Manglana's fortunes and weaken the English suppression of the Blind Abbot.

Upon our return to the camp, we found the chieftain and tanist as we had left them. Both shot to their feet when we entered their tent and listened carefully to our report.

'Then it is all as we suspected,' said Cathal.

Manglana's face was the picture of defiance and a long-repressed joy.

'Let us make haste to rest,' he said, 'for we must not fail our overlord. On the morrow we shall sack both town and bawn, we shall rival the exploits of *Cú Chulainn*.'

As we returned to our tents we saw a party of the fearsome gallowglass warriors, bent over their dreaded two-handed longswords. The weapons reminded me of the blades used by German mercenaries in Spain's employ, who would reap death with the fearsome swords. The Scots ignored us as we walked past them, yet the hair rose upon the back of my neck when I heard a few of them murmuring a song which they sang before battle.

> *'Tonight we pray for death,*
> *For we've nothing from life.*
> *With each last newborn's breath*
> *Comes hunger, war and strife.*
> *Tonight we pray for death,*
> *For life is naught but war,*
> *To earn a seat in the beyond,*
> *To feast and whore, forevermore!'*

A bark from the constable MacCabe soon had them refrain from anymore of their ghastly verse. I had almost reached my tent when a group of kerns called out to me. Quarts of beer and usquebaugh were passed among them to raise their spirits, for all singing, clapping and lighting of fires had been strictly prohibited by Manglana. They laughed and slapped me upon the back when I had also had my fill. Despite my great distress about my bandolier, I was touched by the warmth extended to me by these soldiers, who were mostly fathers and sons, and whose company was a far cry from the bitter military camps that I was used to.

We were woken at dawn by the blare of bugles, when the gates of the town opened to let out two squadrons of enemy troopers. I silently joined the hidden tribesmen who had gathered like wolves to watch the Sassanas ride off, until Gilson's force vanished beyond the cornfields which were enlivened by sunlight. Some townsfolk were already stirring, and beneath us we could see men leading huge horses before their ploughs, with crossbars bound to the tails of hackneys and cobs. The local houses were square structures of timber and brick, having been built in the manner ordered by Dublin. Hundreds of cattle could already be heard lowing, and their noise grew when bales of hay were hurled into their pens. The chieftain scowled at the land below us which had been cleared for fields.

'This plain once echoed with the bellow of bulls that ran freely,' he growled. 'It is now drained of the spirit of the old kings and queens. Let us hasten to fill it with the clatter of shield and spear. Today we shall make good on our losses.'

So saying, he led us down the mountainside. We struggled to keep our footing as the decline became sharper, yet in less than an hour the whole of the chieftain's force was gathered once more on low land, behind the cover of trees which skirted the settlements outside the town. The raiders of Cathal the Black, already champing at the bit were keen to lead the first charge. They prodded their mounts in a feverish frenzy as they followed the tanist towards the plain before them. Joy lit up their faces as they made towards the settlement like an evil gust of wind, their war cry filling the air as they burst through the trees.

'MacGlannagh Abuuuuuù!'

The moment they saw us, most settlers ran away or towards the town, with some even tearing towards their houses. One of the settlers collapsed to the ground when a spearpoint tore through the back of his leg just below his buttocks, leaving him to kick and scream upon the ground as he was trampled by the mounts of the onrushing Dartrymen. Cathal's men had hardly commenced their attack when the chieftain was next to commit his kerns to the fray. As we made after the tanist's forces, I could see that they had already set fire to a number of farmsteads and byres in their path, despatching many of the scattered townsfolk by sword and spear. The alarm was already raised in the town, and the ringing of bells was soon followed by mounted troopers who charged over the bridge of Boyle, the points of their lances twitching before them.

It was then that I witnessed Cathal's cunning first maneuver, as the tanist's force drew the troopers towards the edge of the lake. Upon reaching it, the muddied banks slowed the charge of their pursuers, reducing their approach to less than a canter. Manglana's force next trapped them from behind. The wood-kerns who had raced alongside us were already upon the struggling Sassanas, as they tore over the thick mud with their bare feet.

These barefoot kerns hauled the troopers off their mounts and set upon them with skene daggers, and the air was full of the hiss of slit throats as Sassana blood mingled with the muck underfoot. Ahead of me I spotted Nial fighting stoutly, and as both his swords flashed about him, two horsemen fell before his awesome skill. A third trooper sneaked up behind the bondsman with a raised pistol, yet I swiftly felled the coward with a shot of my own.

Close on two score of mounted troopers had emerged from the fort to attack us, yet less than a dozen managed to beat a retreat. Cathal felled the last fleeing rider with a splendid spear thrust, which burst through the trooper's backplate and sent him flying off his horse. The tanist then summoned his riders to him as he made for firmer ground, galloping towards the bridge to cut off the fleeing troopers' escape. I kept to the chieftain's side as Manglana led the kerns back to the settlements about the town. Manglana's sword strokes fell upon the fleeing colonists who had long followed the ways of the heretic.

- XXXV -

'Juan!'

The cry of a tribesman alerted me to an enemy, who ran towards my back with a raised pitchfork. As I turned and shot him down, some of the Dartrymen ahead of me whooped with delight. I stared at them with miscomprehension as they returned my stare with broad smiles. I suddenly realised the bond of kinship which they felt with me, as I returned to loading my rifle and shooting. Yet in the corner of my eye I realised that I was myself looking out for the Dartrymen, and calling their name whenever danger was close. A shudder of fear ran through me when a crossbow bolt missed Manglana by a hair's breadth.

Just as my affections for the tribe were laid bare to me, the memory of the ring stirred in my mind once again. I sought the tanist and my bandolier as I refilled my gun with powder and ball. The MacGlannaghs kicked pens open as they rounded up cattle droves with their huge hounds, while also hurling their torches onto the thatched roofs about us. The bark and low of beasts drowned out the cry of Cathal's chargers, whose spears felled many troopers before they reached the bridge to the town's gate.

Across the river countless tribesmen hung from the turrets on the walls of Boyle, and the rotted skulls of many others hung on spikes as a threat to all rebels. No sooner had I glimpsed them than I suddenly noticed a dozen archers gathering above the gate and raising their longbows. A gasp of amazement left me when I drew out my scouring stick, with my curse only heard by the horseboy Pilip.

'Archers!'

Their bolts filled the sky as the tanist called back his riders, and the flight of the hafts resembling the swoop of a flock of birds. All but two of Cathal's subalterns were felled as with his sword half raised, he was flung to the ground. The fleeing English troopers were suddenly heartened by the disarray which the archers' volley had caused, and they wheeled their mounts about on the bridge and thundered towards the fallen Irish horsemen. Their lances pricked the air before them as they readied to avenge their fellows by the lake, and it was only the tanist's remaining riders who delayed the Sassanas' advance, as they engaged in a desperate charge towards the advancing troopers.

Some of the Dartrymen's spears met their mark, but the ensuing collision was brutal as the stirrupless Irish were sent clattering to the ground by their heavier adversaries, so that they lay dead or dazed around their leader's limp form. As I stared on in horror, Cathal *Dubh* betrayed no movement from his position on the ground, with my bandolier still strapped about his shoulders.

My head swung both left and right in desperation. Manglana shouted at his men to round up the cattle while a few riders still struggled out of the mire about the lake. In the town, Muireann appeared between two burning huts, then reined in her horse as she observed the happenings outside the gate. Her face turned pale when she realised the danger that Cathal was in. Her lips parted as she screamed at her men to join her, but there was still no sign of the gallowglasses.

Dark blasphemy left my lips as I ran up to a kern who led a fallen trooper's horse behind him. The native stood back in fright as I snatched the reins from his hand and struggled to clamber atop the horse. With a curse I next wrapped my mount's reins about my forearm and galloped towards the bridge. A quarter of my rifle's spanner was wound as I kicked my steed forward, just as the second volley of arrows slammed into the earth ahead of us.

Cathal's bravest and most loyal retainers drew back at the sight of the falling hafts, and a fearful stir seized me as it always did in moments of acute danger. As a mounted Sassana bore towards the form of the tanist, I cursed the missing stirrups and gritted my teeth, then shot the trooper off his horse. The man struck the ground with blood spurting from his chest, dragged after his maddened mount with one of his feet still entwined in its stirrup. When the smoke cleared, I saw another rider bearing down upon the tanist. I released another ampoule from my bandolier, as I reined in my steed and hurled myself to the ground. The approaching trooper turned towards me instead, digging his heels in hard as his horse veered sideways.

The rifle was barely loaded when the heretic was almost upon me. The ground shook beneath me as his mount drew closer. He was barely the length of two spears away when I pulled the rifle stock to my shoulder and shot the trooper off his horse. The charger barely missed me as I rolled away across the ground. To my distress, I next made out another four riders galloping towards the tanist and my bandolier. I was overcome by fear as I howled the tribesmen's war cry and seized the lance of a fallen trooper. I held it out in front of me like a pike, then raced at the advancing horsemen.

'MacGlannagh Abuuuuuù! MacGlannagh Abuuuuuuuuuù!'

The foremost horse buckled and fell backwards as the end of my weapon caught it through the chest, causing the lance to snap in half and send me hurtling across the grass. When my senses were recovered, I picked up the remaining half of the spear and ran before the body of the tanist, lunging at the circling troopers who made their way past the kicking body of the wounded stallion.

Their lances were discarded as I parried their thrusts, but one of them drew a pistol and took aim at me. I hurled myself over the body of the tanist and seized his shield, which flew from my hands when the shot was fired. I rose to my feet and drew my sword to see one of the troopers laughing aloud as he rode at me, his own blade drawn. His first blow was parried, as was his second; then I blocked the thrust of another rider who galloped in behind me and tried to split my head open.

I was both winded and outnumbered, and would not have lasted much longer had Muireann and her retainers not engaged in a brave sally. For unknown to me, my desperate attempt to retrieve the ring had stirred the passions of Cathal's men. With a howl of their own they swiftly entered the fray and hurled their spears at the enemy. Three riderless horses were soon riding away from us.

I exchanged a look of disbelief with the ollave, then sank to one knee and proceeded to pull the bandolier off the tanist's torso. No sooner did I do this than another swooshing sound was heard overhead - another volley had been fired from the walls. Pain shot through my shoulder which was struck by a bolt, while another arrow tore through my cassock and hit my back. The force of its impact left me to collapse alongside the tanist, still clutching the bandolier as I lay upon the ground in a daze.

- XXXV -

Muireann's screams filled my ears as she rallied those kerns who had survived the deadly rain of darts. In moments they seized me and Cathal beneath our arms and sprinted off with us as the next volley was released. No sooner were we dragged beyond bowshot range than countless arrowheads sank into the earth behind us. I howled at my rescuers to help me undo my breastplate.

One of them drew his dagger and cut the clasps on the armour, allowing me to groan in relief. As the plate was removed and the tips of the wretched shafts left my flesh, the agony of the bruises beneath it grew quickly. When I tried to move my head, the pain in my chest was sheer torment. I fell back on all fours when I tried to stand. The bruise near my backbone felt like the repeated stabbing of a knife. Behind me Muireann held Cathal's head in her lap; blood trickled from his nose while his forehead was lined by a gash. Redmond ran up to us and put his ear to the tanist's mouth.

'He is still alive!' he gasped.

'The Lord be praised,' whispered the ollave, 'yet we must hasten him to safety.'

A screeching whinny had us turn our attention to the chieftain, who approached us with the gritted teeth of a cornered wolf.

'We must away!' he cried. 'Our scouts have sighted Gilson returning!'

He turned to shake his fist at the town, where a great pyre blazed upon its battlements.

'A trap?' howled the Jesuit. His face turned white, yet the chieftain had no time to reply.

He charged back towards his kerns who led away as many heads of cattle as they could bind with thin lengths of sheep gut, which was stronger than the stoutest rope. The wounded were hurled upon cloaks bound to spear-truncheons, then borne away by small bands of wood kerns. I wobbled from side to side on the makeshift stretcher like a ship in a storm, amid the cries of distress and the dreaded sound of hoofbeats resounding across the plain. I lifted my head but once to see the men of John Gilson charging back towards the town. Their bugles pealed as the Dartrymen fled their deadly advance; mounted troopers ran them down across the field and outside the bawns.

Meanwhile Manglana had already ordered a retreat. His trumpeter was red in the face as kerns and horsemen made for the trees at the foot of the mountain, with many of our wounded howling for help on the field we abandoned. After cutting off all stragglers and ensuring the safety of the town, Gilson rallied his riders to him before the bridge. A curse left my lips as he next led them at a charge in our direction. The heretics primed their petronels and waved their swords in the air as they covered the few yards that lay between us.

The ensuing rout was inevitable, and as our enemy broke into a gallop I shut my eyes and commended my soul to the Lord. The usual cries and jingle of reins reached my ears, and the sounds were soon so loud that I could not hear the kerns' cries of alarm. Unknown to me, the chieftain was not a novice when it came to fleeing ambushes, so that Manglana next played his last hand.

Our closest assailants were met by a shower of spears, with most of them being true to their mark. They were hurled by a score of Scottish harness bearers who had burst forth from the bush. A great peal of thunder was then heard overhead as the other Sassanas tugged at the reins and wheeled away from their fallen comrades. Two riders were tossed off the backs of their mounts in the ensuing melee, for the gallowglasses were already there, racing up towards the horsemen and waving their axes and doublehanded swords. Amid a flurry of swings they injured both enemy riders and horses, and Gilson's face turned violet as he roared at his horsemen to stand their ground.

Yet it was too stern a test of his men's mettle, and the forefront of his attack soon wilted before the battle-hardened Scots. The heavens opened, and the ensuing rainfall drowned the clink of mail and clash of steel, as the gallowglasses still hacked at anything that lived. One of their number brained horse after horse with his axe, while another issued a battle cry as he hacked at a lance which had run through him. Their constable's face was spattered with gore as he urged them on amid great swings of his axe, and the shriek of their pipes mingled with that of their victims as the troopers were scattered by the ferocity of the Scots' attack.

The sudden downpour had also rendered the English firearms useless, which further delayed Gilson's attempts to regroup his men. It was all the time we needed to make our escape, with at least two score heads of cattle spurred up the mountain by the surviving Dartrymen. Sighs of relief were heard all round as the Scots covered our flight, the banner of Donal's force still held aloft.

After escaping up the mountain, Manglana's men veered towards deep forest through hidden paths known to the ollave. I drifted in and out of consciousness because of my wounds, and when I stirred again the kerns who bore me said that we had reached Breifne. The bondsman next found me trying to rise to my feet. I saw the sun setting behind him, and the tribesmen gathered about a fire. The odd groan of the wounded could be heard alongside me, mingled with the nicker of the hitched horses.

'Rest, Juan,' whispered Nial, 'and do not stir until our return to Rosclogher.'

'Have they followed us?' I asked fearfully.

'The enemy? No, they never follow us into the woods, for they know that we will fall back and slay them unawares.'

'If the Scots had not intervened...'

'Yes,' he said, placing his hand on my shoulder, 'yet do not worry about it now, for it is over. All speak of your great bravery, and the tanist still lives because of you.'

For the rest of the following day I stared at the grey sky overhead and shielded my eyes from the rain, until we finally returned to Rosclogher. During the last part of the journey, the surviving riders rested their beards upon their shoulders and held their bridles loose, their hands gripping their weapons while they listened for any cry from our scouts. Half the wounded died along the way, to be served their last rites by O'Ronayne, so I considered myself fortunate when I found myself once more in the infirmary along the banks of Lough Melvin.

Nial and O'Ronayne visited me often, as did Muireann's son, Lochlain. He beheld me wide-eyed as he repeated the account of my bravery which he had heard from other tribesmen. I shook my head in disbelief when Muireann's son told me that the bard Fearghal had composed an ode to my stand at Boyle.

- XXXV -

The boy frowned at my laughter, after he told me how the bard had compared Manglana's attack on Boyle to the exploits of the great Carthaginian general Hannibal and the Roman hero Scipio.

'Why are you laughing?' asked the boy, with a look of annoyance.

Despite his irritation, the boy quickly agreed to help me retrieve my bandolier, when I asked that he fetch it back for me together with my rifle. From him I learned that both items had been retrieved from the field of battle, and later that night I breathed a sigh of relief upon discovering that the ring was still in its ampoule.

The attack on Boyle had been nothing short of a disaster, for the chieftain had returned with a third of the cows he had set off to claim and lost more than a third of his force. I had been left shocked by the lack of tactics used to assault the town, and it was clear that the Irish could not withstand the enemy upon the field. Two days after our return I was able to return to my feet, and as I stepped out of the building that evening, I saw dim figures approaching the town as if they were arising from the bog itself. A lump formed in my throat when I saw that it was the blood-spattered gallowglass, who kicked a severed head before them as they returned to Rosclogher.

Upon learning of my recovery, the chieftain summoned me to his hall. After crossing the lake, it was in high spirits that I walked towards Manglana's throne. The freemen within it regarded me almost reverentially while the chieftain rose to address me before his assembly.

'You showed great courage upon the battlefield, Juan,' he said, 'and the Jesuit O'Ronayne has advised me that the tanist shall mend. Our own kin would do well to aspire to the great gallantry you showed on the field, risking your life to save one of our own. You are a true son and hero of Rosclogher, so that I shall therefore press for your adoption among the freemen. And if it is approved by the *derbfine*, you will be my son in the eyes of the law by the next gathering of this assembly.'

Here ends
HERO OF ROSCLOGHER,
being the third part of
THE SASSANA STONE PENTALOGY.

The fourth part is called
TRIALS IN TUMULT,
which tells of the growing upheaval across Connacht,
and of Abel de Santiago's forbidden pursuit
of the ollave Muireann Mac an Bhaird.

Historical Note

It is not easy to obtain a glimpse into the way of life of the Gaelic peoples who ruled Ireland up until the end of the sixteenth century. Which is what makes the letter by Captain Francisco de Cuéllar so fascinating to so many. De Cuéllar has in recent years been glorified by those who strive to highlight the fate of the Gran Armada shipwreck survivors in Ireland. His account of his challenges in his letter, if entirely true, is remarkable and makes for fascinating reading. Readers who find Santiago's adventures to be of interest would definitely enjoy reading de Cuéllar's letter. It is easily available on the internet and can be found with minimal online surfing.

As a fellow European, albeit one who dislikes imperialism and supports the self-determination of peoples, I found his letter contemptuous and haughty. It is to be expected from a Spaniard of his day, and its tone easily reveals why the Spaniards were hated by many, much like the nationals from leading powers today also irritate other peoples. De Cuéllar's view of the Irish was that they were uncivilised, lawless savages. He fled their protection without seeking their blessing, even though their protection would cost them their lives.

Yet this is hardly surprising behaviour from one who endured so much during the Armada's disastrous journey, and who has self-confessed problems with respecting authority. He also

- Historical Note -

makes no qualms about his womanising, which was a common trait among the men of his day.

I do not seek to judge de Cuéllar, yet I decided to have fun with him in much the same way that other authors have had fun with holy cows, such as Bernard Cornwell did with Lancelot, or Hilary Mantel did with Thomas More. I wanted to dig at a side of him which is less often explored and discussed; to provoke some while entertaining others, something I'll always find delicious.

Yet I owe him a debt of gratitude. It was probably his story that most stirred me when reading T.P. Kilfeather's great account of the Armada landings in Ireland: *'Ireland Graveyard Of The Spanish Armada'*, the pocket-size book which led me to dedicate thirteen years of my life to writing this series. For all its arguable 'shortcomings', de Cuéllar's letter casts light on the fate that was met by many Armada castaways in Ireland, an account which has been confirmed by the letters of other Spaniards such as the survivor of the Gran Grifon, Don Alonso de Luzon, as well as Francisco de Borja. The seventeen-day siege of the Rosclogher tower-house described in this story is also included in de Cuéllar's letter, though I have added fictional anecdotes of my own.

I'll proceed to say a word about the goings-on in Connacht during the period this book is set in. 'The MacGlannagh' was a name used by the Binghams when writing about the Mac-Clancies that ruled and inhabited Dartry. Their overlord was indeed the valiant Sir Brian O'Rourke, who ruled over Breifne O'Rourke (as opposed to Breifne O'Reilly, home to Sir Brian's bitter, Crown-serving enemies, the O'Reillys). O'Rourke is said to have been the fourth most powerful chieftain in Ireland after the two great Ulster lords of O'Neill and O'Donnell, as well as O'Brien of Thomond in Munster.

Although I play around with the unknown characters who are figments of my imagination, the movements of MacGlannagh and O'Rourke are based on fact. Following the revolt of the Blind Abbot, O'Rourke did raid lands held by the English and their allies beyond his borders. There can be little doubt that the MacGlannagh, described in various sources as the O'Rourke's first lieutenant, would have been involved in these raids.

Although I do not recall it being stated anywhere, I have read sources which indicate that Queen Elizabeth I in London was concerned about the upheaval in Connacht. It is also confirmed that a deep enmity ran between the English viceroy, William FitzWilliam, in Dublin, and the Bingham family in Connacht, who were often accused of acting as if they were a law unto themselves and unsettling the local populace. Whether or not this is fair is up to academics and history buffs to decide, but there can be little doubt that in rocking the boat, the O'Rourke and the MacGlannagh were further unsettling the country and lending weight to the viceroy's accusations.

Acknowledgements

Heartfelt thanks to all those who supported my stories during 2022:

Anton Tagliaferro, Donna Madden, Frank Vella Bardon, Josanne Vella Bardon, Joseph Calleja, Brett & Bec Kelly, Dery Sultana, Jorge Perez y Asenjo, Colin Azzopardi, Anton Caruana Galizia, Ramon Mizzi, Nicol Kindness, Teresa Quinn, Mark McKendry, Robert Tagliaferro, Malcolm Miller, Michael Vella de Fremeaux, Christian at Abbey's Bookshop, Nicky Valenzia and Timothy Vella Bardon.

And, of course: anyone else that I've forgotten to mention.

About the Author

James was heralded as 'the new king of historical fiction' by respected British newspaper The Scotsman in July 2022, in the publication's review of James' acclaimed novella *Mad King Robin*, a thrilling story about the famous Scottish king Robert the Bruce.

He was born and raised in Malta, an island nation influenced by thousands of years of imperial history, from the Romans to the British. His burning passion for exciting and dramatic historical events was forged in this environment.

After reading law and history at the Universities of both Malta and Sydney, James qualified as a lawyer and also completed a doctoral thesis on the rights and freedoms of peoples at international law. He subsequently worked for years on editing and publishing content for various multinational government bodies like the European Union as well as US and Australian corporations.

Upon emigrating to Sydney in 2007, James turned his hand to novel writing, crafting dramatic and well-researched stories about various peoples' struggle for freedom.

His debut novel *The Sheriff's Catch* is a highly acclaimed thriller, which recounts the adventures of a Spanish Armada castaway in Tudor Ireland, who joins in the great struggle to liberate western Ireland from brutal suppression. Following its

- About the Author -

release in 2018, the novel made bestseller lists in Europe and was also named an 'Outstanding Historical' by the IAN Book Awards in 2019, while receiving various other international awards and nominations.

The Sheriff's Catch was recommended as a 'must-read of the week' by leading British newspaper The Yorkshire Evening Post, with global institution Reader's Digest also reviewing it and stating 'while Vella-Bardon's writing displays its own signature, readers will see favourable comparisons with historical fiction greats such as Conn Iggulden, Wilbur Smith and Bernard Cornwell.'

Also by James Vella-Bardon

The Bruce Books

The Cream Of Chivalry
Mad King Robin

The Sassana Stone Pentalogy

The Sheriff's Catch
A Rebel North

Coming soon:
Trials In Tumult
Ring Of Ruse

www.ingramcontent.com/pod-product-compliance
Lightning Source LLC
Chambersburg PA
CBHW022040290426
44109CB00014B/924